LEGENDS OF THE EGYPTIAN GODS

Hieroglyphic Texts and Translations

E. A. WALLIS BUDGE

DOVER PUBLICATIONS, INC.
NEW YORK

Bibliographical Note

This Dover edition, first published in 1994, is an unabridged republication of the work first published by Kegan Paul, Trench, Trübner & Co. Ltd., London, in 1912 under the title *Legends of the Gods: The Egyptian Texts, Edited with Translations*, as Volume XXXII in the Series "Books on Egypt and Chaldea" (Volume I in the subseries "Egyptian Literature"). The placement of the plates has been altered in the Dover edition.

Library of Congress Cataloging in Publication Data

Budge, E. A. Wallis (Ernest Alfred Wallis), Sir, 1857–1934.
[Legends of the gods]
Legends of the Egyptian gods : hieroglyphic texts and translations / E. A. Wallis Budge.
p. cm.
Originally published: Legends of the gods. London : Kegan Paul, Trench, Trübner, 1912.
ISBN-13: 978-0-486-28022-6 (pbk.)
ISBN-10: 978-0-486-28022-5 (pbk.)
1. Mythology, Egyptian. 2. Egyptian language—Texts. 3. Egyptian language—Writing, Hieroglyphic. I. Title.
BL2450.G6B83 1994
299'.31—dc20 93-49097
CIP

Manufactured in the United States by LSC Communications
28022510 2018
www.doverpublications.com

PREFACE

THE welcome which has been accorded to the volumes of this Series, and the fact that some of them have passed into second and third editions, suggest that these little books have been found useful by beginners in Egyptology and others. Hitherto the object of them has been to supply information about the Religion, Magic, Language, and History of the ancient Egyptians, and to provide editions of the original texts from which such information was derived. There are, however, many branches of Egyptology which need treatment in a similar manner in this Series, and it has been suggested in many quarters that the time has now arrived when the publication of a series of groups of texts illustrating EGYPTIAN LITERATURE in general might well be begun. Seeing that nothing is known about the authors of Egyptian works, not even their names, it is impossible to write a History of Egyptian Literature in the ordinary sense of the word. The only thing to be done is to print the actual works in the best and most complete form possible, with translations, and then to put them in the hands of the reader and leave them to his judgment.

With this object in view, it has been decided to publish in the Series several volumes which shall be devoted to the reproduction in hieroglyphic type of the best and most typical examples of the various kinds of EGYPTIAN LITERATURE, with English translations, on a much larger scale than was possible in my "First Steps in Egyptian" or in my "Egyptian Reading Book." These volumes are intended to serve a double purpose, i.e., to supply the beginner in Egyptian with new material and a series of reading books, and to provide the general reader with translations of Egyptian works in a handy form.

The Egyptian texts, whether the originals be written in hieroglyphic or hieratic characters, are here printed in hieroglyphic type, and are arranged with English translations, page for page. They are printed as they are written in the original documents, i.e., the words are not divided. The beginner will find the practice of dividing the words for himself most useful in acquiring facility of reading and understanding the language. The translations are as literal as can reasonably be expected, and, as a whole, I believe that they mean what the original writers intended to say. In the case of passages where the text is corrupt, and readings are mixed, or where very rare words occur, or where words are omitted, the renderings given claim to be nothing more than suggestions as to their meanings. It must be remembered that the exact meanings of many Egyptian words have still to be ascertained, and that the ancient Egyptian scribes were as much puzzled as we are by some of the texts which they copied, and that owing to carelessness, ignorance, or weariness, or all three, they made blunders which the modern student is unable to correct. In the Introduction will be found brief descriptions of the contents of the Egyptian texts, in which their general bearing and importance are indicated, and references given to authoritative editions of texts and translations.

E. A. WALLIS BUDGE.

BRITISH MUSEUM,
November 17, 1911.

CONTENTS

LIST OF PLATES AND ILLUSTRATIONS

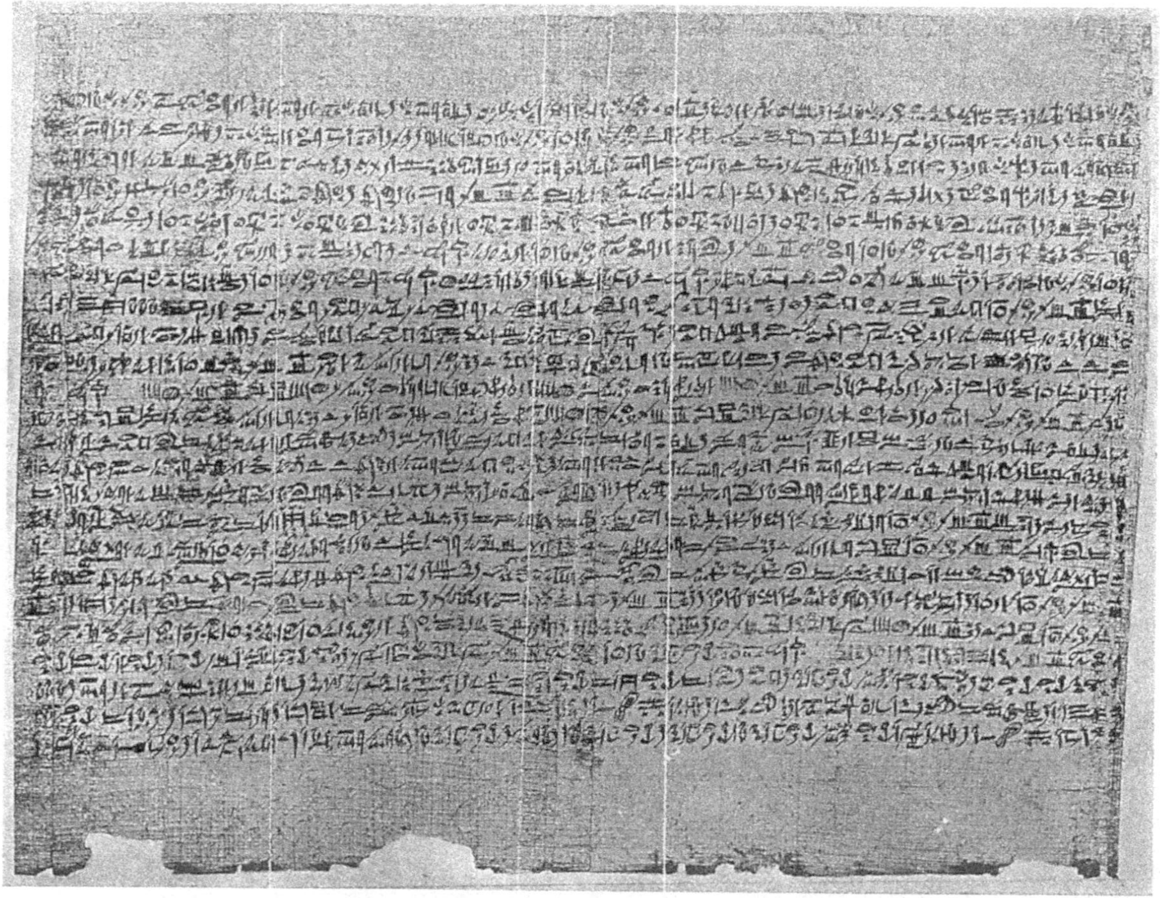

THE HISTORY OF CREATION. (Brit. Mus. Papyrus, No 10,188.)

INTRODUCTION

I.

The Legend of the God Neb-er-tcher, and the History of Creation.

The text of the remarkable Legend of the Creation which forms the first section of this volume is preserved in a well-written papyrus in the British Museum, where it bears the number 10,188. This papyrus was acquired by the late Mr. A. H. Rhind in 1861 or 1862, when he was excavating some tombs on the west bank of the Nile at Thebes. He did not himself find it in a tomb, but he received it from the British Consul at Luxor, Mustafa Âgha, during an interchange of gifts when Mr. Rhind was leaving the country. Mustafa Âgha obtained the papyrus from the famous hiding-place of the Royal Mummies at Dêr-al-Baḥari, with the situation of which he was well acquainted for many years before it became known to the Egyptian Service of Antiquities. When Mr. Rhind came to England, the results of his excavations were examined by Dr. Birch, who, recognising the great value of the papyrus, arranged to publish it in a companion volume to *Facsimiles of Two Papyri*, but the death of Mr. Rhind in 1865 caused the project to fall through. Mr. Rhind's collection passed into the hands of Mr. David Bremner, and the papyrus, together with many other antiquities, was purchased by the Trustees of the British Museum. In 1880 Dr. Birch suggested the publication of the papyrus to Dr. Pleyte, the Director of the Egyptian Museum at Leyden. This *savant* transcribed and translated some passages from the *Festival Songs of Isis and Nephthys*, which is the first text in it, and these he published in *Recueil de Travaux*, Paris, tom. iii., pp. 57–64. In 1886 by Dr. Birch's kindness I was allowed to work at the papyrus, and I published transcripts of some important passages and the account of the Creation in the *Proceedings of the Society of Biblical Archaeology*, 1886–7, pp. 11–26. The Legend of the Creation was considered by Dr. H. Brugsch to be of considerable value for the study of the Egyptian Religion, and encouraged by him[1] I made a full transcript of the papyrus, which was published in *Archaeologia* (vol. lii., London, 1891), with translitera-

[1] Ein in möglichst wortgetreuer Uebersetzung vorglegter Papyrustext soll den Schlussstein meines Werkes bilden. Er wird den Beweis für die Richtigkeit meiner eigenen Untersuchungen vollenden, indem er das wichtigste Zeugniss altägyptischen Ursprungs den zahlreichen, von mir angezogenen Stellen aus den Inschriften hinzufügt. Trotz mancher Schwierigkeit im Einzelnen ist der Gesammtinhalt des Textes, den zuerst ein englischer Gelehrter der Wissenschaft zugänglich gemacht hat, auch nicht im geringsten misszuverstehen (Brugsch, *Religion*, p. 740). He gives a German translation of the Creation Legend on pp. 740, 741, and a transliteration on p. 756.

tions and translations. In 1910 I edited for the Trustees of the British Museum the complete hieratic text with a revised translation.[1]

The papyrus is about 16 ft. 8 in. in length, and is 9¼ in. in width. It contains 21 columns of hieratic text which are written in short lines and are poetical in character, and 12 columns or pages of text written in long lines; the total number of lines is between 930 and 940. The text is written in a small, very black, but neat hand, and may be assigned to a time between the XXVIth Dynasty and the Ptolemaïc Period. The titles, catch-words, rubrics, names of Āpep and his fiends, and a few other words, are written in red ink. There are two colophons; in the one we have a date, namely, the "first day of the fourth month "of the twelfth year of Pharaoh Alexander, the son of "Alexander," i e., B.C. 311, and in the other the name of the priest who either had the papyrus written, or appropriated it, namely, Nes-Menu, or Nes-Ȧmsu, 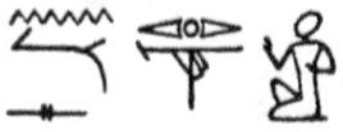.

The Legend of the Creation is found in the third work which is given in the papyrus, and which is called the "Book of overthrowing Āpep, the Enemy "of Rā, the Enemy of Un-Nefer" (i.e., Osiris). This work contained a series of spells which were recited during the performance of certain prescribed ceremonies,

[1] *Egyptian Hieratic Papyri in the British Museum*, London, 1910, folio.

with the object of preventing storms, and dispersing rain-clouds, and removing any obstacle, animate or inanimate, which could prevent the rising of the sun in the morning, or obscure his light during the day. The Leader-in-chief of the hosts of darkness was a fiend called Āpep, , who appeared in the sky in the form of a monster serpent, and, marshalling all the fiends of the Ṭuat, attempted to keep the Sun-god imprisoned in the kingdom of darkness. Right in the midst of the spells which were directed against Āpep we find inserted the legend of the Creation, which occurs in no other known Egyptian document (Col. XXVI., l. 21, to Col. XXVII., l. 6). Curiously enough a longer version of the legend is given a little farther on (Col. XXVIII., l. 20, to Col. XXIX., l. 6). Whether the scribe had two copies to work from, and simply inserted both, or whether he copied the short version and added to it as he went along, cannot be said. The legend is entitled:

Book of knowing the evolutions of Rā [and of]

overthrowing Āpep.

This curious "Book" describes the origin not only of heaven, and earth, and all therein, but also of God Himself. In it the name of Āpep is not even mentioned, and it is impossible to explain its appearance in the Āpep Ritual unless we assume that the whole "Book" was regarded as a spell of the most potent character, the mere recital of which was fraught with deadly effect for Āpep and his friends.

The story of the Creation is supposed to be told by the god Neb-er-tcher, . This name means the "Lord to the uttermost limit," and the character of the god suggests that the word "limit" refers to time and space, and that he was, in fact, the Everlasting God of the Universe. This god's name occurs in Coptic texts, and then he appears as one who possesses all the attributes which are associated by modern nations with God Almighty. Where and how Neb-er-tcher existed is not said, but it seems as if he was believed to have been an almighty and invisible power which filled all space. It seems also that a desire arose in him to create the world, and in order to do this he took upon himself the form of the god Kheperȧ, , who from first to last was regarded as the Creator, *par excellence*, among all the gods known to the Egyptians. When this transformation of Neb-er-tcher into Kheperȧ took place the heavens and the earth had not been created, but there seems to have existed a vast mass of water, or world-ocean, called Nu, 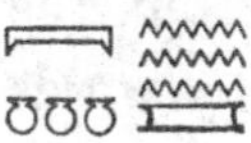, and it must have been in this that the transformation took place. In this celestial ocean were the germs of all the living things which afterwards took form in heaven and on earth, but they existed in a state of inertness and helplessness. Out of this ocean Kheperȧ raised himself, and so passed from a state of passiveness and inertness into one of activity. When Kheperȧ raised himself out of the ocean Nu, he found himself in vast empty space, wherein was nothing on which he could stand. The second version of the legend says that Kheperȧ gave being to himself by uttering his own name, and the first version states that he made use of words in providing himself with a place on which to stand. In other words, when Kheperȧ was still a portion of the being of Neb-er-tcher, he spake the word "Kheperȧ," and Kheperȧ came into being. Similarly, when he needed a place whereon to stand, he uttered the name of the thing, or place, on which he wanted to stand, and that thing, or place, came into being. This spell he seems to have addressed to his heart, or as we should say, will, so that Kheperȧ willed this standing-place to appear, and it did so forthwith. The first version only mentions a heart, but the second also speaks of a heart-soul as assisting Kheperȧ in his first creative acts; and we may assume that he thought out in his heart what manner of thing he wished to create, and then by uttering its name caused his thought to take concrete form. This process of thinking out the existence of things is expressed in Egyptian by words which mean "laying the foundation in the heart."

In arranging his thoughts and their visible forms Kheperȧ was assisted by the goddess Maāt, who is usually regarded as the goddess of law, order, and truth, and in late times was held to be the female counterpart of Thoth, "the heart of the god Rā." In this legend, however, she seems to play the part of Wisdom, as described in the Book of Proverbs,[1] for it was by Maāt that he "laid the foundation."

Having described the coming into being of Kheperȧ and the place on which he stood, the legend goes on to tell of the means by which the first Egyptian triad, or trinity, came into existence. Kheperȧ had, in some form, union with his own shadow, and so begot offspring, who proceeded from his body under the forms of the gods Shu and Tefnut. According to a tradition preserved in the Pyramid Texts[2] this event took place at On (Heliopolis), and the old form of the legend ascribes the production of Shu and Tefnut to an act of

[1] "The Lord possessed me in the beginning of his way, before his "works of old. I was set up from everlasting, from the beginning, "or ever the earth was. When there were no depths I was brought "forth . . . . . . Before the mountains were settled, before the hills "was I brought forth: while as yet he had not made the earth, "nor the fields, nor the highest part of the dust of the world. "When he prepared the heavens I was there: when he set a "compass upon the face of the depth: when he established the "clouds above: when he strengthened the fountains of the deep: "when he gave to the sea his decree, ... when he appointed "the foundations of the earth: then I was by him, as one brought "up with him . . . . . ." Proverbs, viii. 22 ff.

[2] Pepi I., l. 466.

masturbation. Originally these gods were the personifications of air and dryness, and liquids respectively; thus with their creation the materials for the construction of the atmosphere and sky came into being. Shu and Tefnut were united, and their offspring were Ḳeb, the Earth-god, and Nut, the Sky-goddess. We have now five gods in existence; Kheperȧ, the creative principle, Shu, the atmosphere, Tefnut, the waters above the heavens, Nut, the Sky-goddess, and Ḳeb, the Earth-god. Presumably about this time the sun first rose out of the watery abyss of Nu, and shone upon the world and produced day. In early times the sun, or his light, was regarded as a form of Shu. The gods Ḳeb and Nut were united in an embrace, and the effect of the coming of light was to separate them. As long as the sun shone, i.e., as long as it was day, Nut, the Sky-goddess, remained in her place above the earth, being supported by Shu; but as soon as the sun set she left the sky and gradually descended until she rested on the body of the Earth-god, Ḳeb.

The embraces of Ḳeb caused Nut to bring forth five gods at a birth, namely, Osiris, Horus, Set, Isis, and Nephthys. Osiris and Isis married before their birth, and Isis brought forth a son called Horus; Set and Nephthys also married before their birth, and Nephthys brought forth a son named Ȧnpu (Anubis), though he is not mentioned in the legend. Of these gods Osiris is singled out for special mention in the legend, in which Kheperȧ, speaking as Neb-er-tcher, says that his name is ÅUSÅRES, 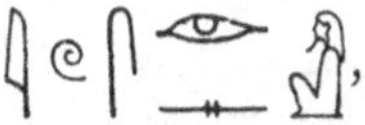, who is the essence of the primeval matter of which he himself is formed. Thus Osiris was of the same substance as the Great God who created the world according to the Egyptians, and was a reincarnation of his great-grandfather. This portion of the legend helps to explain the views held about Osiris as the great ancestral spirit, who when on earth was a benefactor of mankind, and who when in heaven was the saviour of souls.

The legend speaks of the sun as the Eye of Kheperå, or Neb-er-tcher, and refers to some calamity which befell it and extinguished its light. This calamity may have been simply the coming of night, or eclipses, or storms; but in any case the god made a second Eye, i.e., the Moon, to which he gave some of the splendour of the other Eye, i.e., the Sun, and he gave it a place in his Face, and henceforth it ruled throughout the earth, and had special powers in respect of the production of trees, plants, vegetables, herbs, etc. Thus from the earliest times the moon was associated with the fertility of the earth, especially in connection with the production of abundant crops and successful harvests.

According to the legend, men and women sprang not from the earth, but directly from the body of the god Kheperå, or Neb-er-tcher, who placed his members together and then wept tears upon them, and men and women, 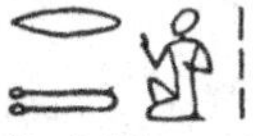, came into being from the tears which had fallen from his eyes. No special mention is made of the creation of beasts in the legend, but the god says that he created creeping things of all kinds, and among these are probably included the larger quadrupeds. The men and women, and all the other living creatures which were made at that time, reproduced their species, each in his own way, and so the earth became filled with their descendants which we see at the present time.

Such is the Legend of Creation as it is found in the Papyrus of Nes-Menu. The text of both versions is full of difficult passages, and some readings are corrupt; unfortunately variant versions by which they might be corrected are lacking. The general meaning of the legend in both versions is quite clear, and it throws considerable light on the Egyptian religion. The Egyptians believed in the existence of God, the Creator and Maintainer of all things, but they thought that the concerns of this world were committed by Him to the superintendence of a series of subordinate spirits or beings called "gods," over whom they believed magical spells and ceremonies to have the greatest influence. The Deity was a Being so remote, and of such an exalted nature, that it was idle to expect Him to interfere in the affairs of mortals, or to change any decree or command which He had once uttered. The spirits or "gods," on the other hand, possessing natures not far removed from those of men, were thought to be amenable to supplications and flattery, and to wheedling and cajolery, especially when accompanied by gifts. It is of great interest to find a legend in which the power of God as the Creator of the world and the sun and moon is so clearly set forth, embedded in a book of magical spells devoted to the destruction of the mythological monster who existed solely to prevent the sun from rising and shining.

II.

The Legend of the Destruction of Mankind.

The text containing the Legend of the Destruction of Mankind is written in hieroglyphs, and is found on the four walls of a small chamber which is entered from the "hall of columns" in the tomb of Seti I., which is situated on the west bank of the Nile at Thebes. On the wall facing the door of this chamber is painted in red the figure of the large "Cow of Heaven." The lower part of her belly is decorated with a series of thirteen stars, ★★★, and immediately beneath it are the two Boats of Rā, called Semketet and Māntchet, or Sektet and Māṭet. Each of her four legs is held in position by two gods, and the god Shu, with outstretched uplifted arms, supports her body. The Cow was published by Champollion,[1] without the

[1] *Monuments*, tom. iii., p. 245.

text. This most important mythological text was first published and translated by Professor E. Naville in 1874.[1] It was republished by Bergmann[2] and Brugsch,[3] who gave a transcription of the text, with a German translation. Other German versions by Lauth,[4] Brugsch,[5] and Wiedemann[6] have appeared, and a part of the text was translated into French by Lefébure.[7] The latest edition of the text was published by Lefébure,[8] and text of a second copy, very much mutilated, was published by Professor Naville, with a French translation in 1885.[9] The text printed in this volume is that of M. Lefébure.

The legend takes us back to the time when the gods of Egypt went about in the country, and mingled with men, and were thoroughly acquainted with their desires and needs. The king who reigned over Egypt was Rā, the Sun-god, who was not, however, the first of the Dynasty of Gods who ruled the land. His predecessor on the throne was Hephaistos, who, according to Manetho, reigned 9000 years, whilst Rā reigned only 992 years; Panodorus makes his reign to have lasted

[1] *Trans. Soc. Bibl. Arch.*, vol. iv., p. 1 ff.

[2] *Hieroglyphische Inschriften*, Bl. 85 ff.

[3] *Die neue Weltordnung nach Vernichtung des sündigen Menschengeschlechtes*, Berlin, 1881.

[4] *Aus Aegyptens Vorzeit*, p. 71.

[5] *Religion der alten Aegypter*, p. 436.

[6] *Die Religion*, p. 32.

[7] *Ä. Z.*, 1883, p. 32.

[8] *Tombeau de Seti I.*, Part IV., plates 15–18.

[9] *Trans. Soc. Bibl. Arch.*, vol. viii., p. 412 ff.

less than 100 years. Be this as it may, it seems that the "self-created and self-begotten" god Rā had been ruling over mankind for a very long time, for his subjects were murmuring against him, and they were complaining that he was old, that his bones were like silver, his body like gold, and his hair like lapis-lazuli. When Rā heard these murmurings he ordered his bodyguard to summon all the gods who had been with him in the primeval World-ocean, and to bid them privately to assemble in the Great House, which can be no other than the famous temple of Heliopolis. This statement is interesting, for it proves that the legend is of Heliopolitan origin, like the cult of Rā itself, and that it does not belong, at least in so far as it applies to Rā, to the Predynastic Period.

When Rā entered the Great Temple, the gods made obeisance to him, and took up their positions on each side of him, and informed him that they awaited his words. Addressing Nu, the personification of the World-ocean, Rā bade them to take notice of the fact that the men and women whom his Eye had created were murmuring against him. He then asked them to consider the matter and to devise a plan of action for him, for he was unwilling to slay the rebels without hearing what his gods had to say. In reply the gods advised Rā to send forth his Eye to destroy the blasphemers, for there was no eye on earth that could resist it, especially when it took the form of the goddess Hathor. Rā accepted their advice and sent forth his Eye in the form of

Hathor to destroy them, and, though the rebels had fled to the mountains in fear, the Eye pursued them and overtook them and destroyed them. Hathor rejoiced in her work of destruction, and on her return was praised by Rā for what she had done. The slaughter of men began at Suten-ḥenen (Herakleopolis), and during the night Hathor waded about in the blood of men. Rā asserted his intention of being master of the rebels, and this is probably referred to in the Book of the Dead, Chapter XVII., in which it is said that Rā rose as king for the first time in Suten-ḥenen. Osiris also was crowned at Suten-ḥenen, and in this city lived the great Bennu bird, or Phoenix, and the "Crusher of Bones" mentioned in the Negative Confession.

The legend now goes on to describe an act of Rā, the significance of which it is difficult to explain. The god ordered messengers to be brought to him, and when they arrived, he commanded them to run like the wind to Abu, or the city of Elephantine, and to bring him large quantities of the fruit called *ṭāṭāàt*, 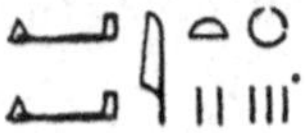. What kind of fruit this was is not clear, but Brugsch thought they were "mandrakes," the so-called "love-apples," and this translation of *ṭāṭāàt* may be used provisionally. The mandrakes were given to Sekti, a goddess of Heliopolis, to crush and grind up, and when this was done they were mixed with human blood, and put in a large brewing of beer which the women slaves had made from wheat. In all they made 7,000 vessels of beer. When Rā saw the beer he approved of it, and ordered it to be carried up the river to where the goddess Hathor was still, it seems, engaged in slaughtering men. During the night he caused this beer to be poured out into the meadows of the Four Heavens, and when Hathor came she saw the beer with human blood and mandrakes in it, and drank of it and became drunk, and paid no further attention to men and women. In welcoming the goddess, Rā called her "Åmit," , i.e., "beautiful one," and from this time onward "beautiful women were found in the city of Åmit," which was situated in the Western Delta, near Lake Mareotis.[1] Rā also ordered that in future at every one of his festivals vessels of "sleep-producing beer" should be made, and that their number should be the same as the number of the handmaidens of Rā. Those who took part in these festivals of Hathor and Rā drank beer in very large quantities, and under the influence of the "beautiful women," i.e., the priestesses, who were supposed to resemble Hathor in their physical attractions, the festal celebrations degenerated into drunken and licentious orgies.

Soon after this Rā complained that he was smitten

[1] It was also called the "City of Apis," 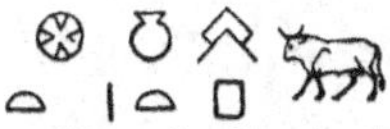 (Brugsch, *Dict. Geog.*, p. 491), and is the Apis city of classical writers. It is, perhaps, represented by the modern Kôm al-Hisn.

with pain, and that he was weary of the children of men. He thought them a worthless remnant, and wished that more of them had been slain. The gods about him begged him to endure, and reminded him that his power was in proportion to his will. Rā was, however, unconsoled, and he complained that his limbs were weak for the first time in his life. Thereupon the god Nu told Shu to help Rā, and he ordered Nut to take the great god Rā on her back. Nut changed herself into a cow, and with the help of Shu Rā got on her back. As soon as men saw that Rā was on the back of the Cow of Heaven, and was about to leave them, they became filled with fear and repentance, and cried out to Rā to remain with them and to slay all those who had blasphemed against him. But the Cow moved on her way, and carried Rā to Ḥet-Åḥet, 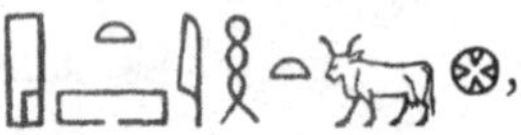, a town of the nome of Mareotis, , where in later days the right leg of Osiris was said to be preserved. Meanwhile darkness covered the land. When day broke the men who had repented of their blasphemies appeared with their bows, and slew the enemies of Rā. At this result Rā was pleased, and he forgave those who had repented because of their righteous slaughter of his enemies. From this time onwards human sacrifices were offered up at the festivals of Rā celebrated in this place, and at Heliopolis and in other parts of Egypt.

After these things Rā declared to Nut that he

intended to leave this world, and to ascend into heaven, and that all those who would see his face must follow him thither. Then he went up into heaven and prepared a place to which all might come. Then he said, "Ḥetep sekhet āa," i.e., "Let a great field be produced," and straightway "Sekhet-ḥetep," or the "Field of peace," came into being. He next said, "Let there be reeds (*åaru*) in it," and straightway "Sekhet Åaru," or the "Field of Reeds," came into being. Sekhet-ḥetep was the Elysian Fields of the Egyptians, and the Field of Reeds was a well-known section of it. Another command of the god Rā resulted in the creation of the stars, which the legend compares to flowers. Then the goddess Nut trembled in all her body, and Rā, fearing that she might fall, caused to come into being the Four Pillars on which the heavens are supported. Turning to Shu Rā entreated him to protect these supports, and to place himself under Nut, and to hold her up in position with his hands. Thus Shu became the new Sun-god in the place of Rā, and the heavens in which Rā lived were supported and placed beyond the risk of falling, and mankind would live and rejoice in the light of the new sun.

At this place in the legend a text is inserted called the "Chapter of the Cow." It describes how the Cow of Heaven and the two Boats of the Sun shall be painted, and gives the positions of the gods who stand by the legs of the Cow, and a number of short magical names, or formulae, which are inexplicable. The general meaning of the picture of the Cow is quite clear. The Cow represents the sky in which the Boats of Rā sail, and her four legs are the four cardinal points which cannot be changed. The region above her back is the heaven in which Rā reigns over the beings who pass thereto from this earth when they die, and here was situated the home of the gods and the celestial spirits who govern this world.

When Rā had made a heaven for himself, and had arranged for a continuance of life on the earth, and the welfare of human beings, he remembered that at one time when reigning on earth he had been bitten by a serpent, and had nearly lost his life through the bite. Fearing that the same calamity might befall his successor, he determined to take steps to destroy the power of all noxious reptiles that dwelt on the earth. With this object in view he told Thoth to summon Ḳeb, the Earth-god, to his presence, and this god having arrived, Rā told him that war must be made against the serpents that dwelt in his dominions. He further commanded him to go to the god Nu, and to tell him to set a watch over all the reptiles that were in the earth and in water, and to draw up a writing for every place in which serpents are known to be, containing strict orders that they are to bite no one. Though these serpents knew that Rā was retiring from the earth, they were never to forget that his rays would fall upon them. In his place their father Ḳeb was to keep watch over them, and he was their father for ever.

As a further protection against them Rā promised to impart to magicians and snake-charmers the particular word of power, *ḥekau* , with which he guarded himself against the attacks of serpents, and also to transmit it to his son Osiris. Thus those who are ready to listen to the formulae of the snake-charmers shall always be immune from the bites of serpents, and their children also. From this we may gather that the profession of the snake-charmer is very ancient, and that this class of magicians were supposed to owe the foundation of their craft to a decree of Rā himself.

Rā next sent for the god Thoth, and when he came into the presence of Rā, he invited him to go with him to a distance, to a place called "Ṭuat," i.e., hell, or the Other World, in which region he had determined to make his light to shine. When they arrived there he told Thoth, the Scribe of Truth, to write down on his tablets the names of all who were therein, and to punish those among them who had sinned against him, and he deputed to Thoth the power to deal absolutely as he pleased with all the beings in the Ṭuat. Rā loathed the wicked, and wished them to be kept at a distance from him. Thoth was to be his vicar, to fill his place, and "Place of Rā," 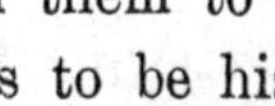, was to be his name. He gave him power to send out a messenger (*hab*), so the Ibis (*habi*) came into being. All that Thoth would do would be good (*khen*), therefore the

Tekni bird of Thoth came into being. He gave Thoth power to embrace (*ànḥ*) the heavens, therefore the Moon-god (*Àāḥ*) came into being. He gave Thoth power to turn back (*ānān*) the Northern peoples, therefore the dog-headed ape of Thoth came into being. Finally Rā told Thoth that he would take his place in the sight of all those who were wont to worship Rā, and that all should praise him as God. Thus the abdication of Rā was complete.

In the fragmentary texts which follow we are told how a man may benefit by the recital of this legend. He must proclaim that the soul which animated Rā was the soul of the Aged One, and that of Shu, Khnemu (?), Ḥeḥ, &c., and then he must proclaim that he is Rā himself, and his word of power Ḥeka. If he recites the Chapter correctly he shall have life in the Other World, and he will be held in greater fear there than here. A rubric adds that he must be dressed in new linen garments, and be well washed with Nile water; he must wear white sandals, and his body must be anointed with holy oil. He must burn incense in a censer, and a figure of Maāt (Truth) must be painted on his tongue with green paint. These regulations applied to the laity as well as to the clergy.

III.

The Legend of Rā and Isis.

The original text of this very interesting legend is written in the hieratic character on a papyrus preserved at Turin, and was published by Pleyte and Rossi in their *Corpus* of Turin Papyri.[1] French and German translations of it were published by Lefébure,[2] and Wiedemann[3] respectively, and summaries of its contents were given by Erman[4] and Maspero.[5] A transcript of the hieratic text into hieroglyphics, with transliteration and translation, was published by me in 1895.[6]

It has already been seen that the god Rā, when retiring from the government of this world, took steps through Thoth to supply mankind with words of power and spells with which to protect themselves against the bites of serpents and other noxious reptiles. The legend of the Destruction of Mankind affords no explanation of this remarkable fact, but when we read the following legend of Rā and Isis we understand why Rā, though king of the gods, was afraid of the reptiles which lived in the kingdom of Ḳeb. The legend, or "Chapter of the Divine God," begins by enumerating the mighty attributes of Rā as the creator of the

[1] *Papyrus de Turin*, pll. 31, 77, 131–138.

[2] *Ä. Z.*, 1883, p. 27 ff.

[3] *Die Religion*, p. 29.

[4] *Aegypten*, p. 359 ff.

[5] *Les Origines*, p. 162–4.

[6] *First Steps in Egyptian*, p. 241 ff.

universe, and describes the god of "many names" as unknowable, even by the gods. At this time Isis lived in the form of a woman who possessed the knowledge of spells and incantations, that is to say, she was regarded much in the same way as modern African peoples regard their "medicine-women," or "witch-women." She had used her spells on men, and was tired of exercising her powers on them, and she craved the opportunity of making herself mistress of gods and spirits as well as of men. She meditated how she could make herself mistress both of heaven and earth, and finally she decided that she could only obtain the power she wanted if she possessed the knowledge of the secret name of Rā, in which his very existence was bound up. Rā guarded this name most jealously, for he knew that if he revealed it to any being he would henceforth be at that being's mercy. Isis saw that it was impossible to make Rā declare his name to her by ordinary methods, and she therefore thought out the following plan. It was well known in Egypt and the Sûdân at a very early period that if a magician obtained some portion of a person's body, e.g., a hair, a paring of a nail, a fragment of skin, or a portion of some efflux from the body, spells could be used upon them which would have the effect of causing grievous harm to that person. Isis noted that Rā had become old and feeble, and that as he went about he dribbled at the mouth, and that his saliva fell upon the ground. Watching her opportunity she caught some of the saliva of the god, and mixing it with dust, she moulded it into the form of a large serpent, with poison-fangs, and having uttered her spells over it, she left the serpent lying on the path, by which Rā travelled day by day as he went about inspecting Egypt, so that it might strike at him as he passed along. We may note in passing that the Banyoro in the Sûdân employ serpents in killing buffaloes at the present day. They catch a puff-adder in a noose, and then nail it alive by the tip of its tail to the ground in the middle of a buffalo track, so that when an animal passes the reptile may strike at it. Presently a buffalo comes along, does what it is expected to do, and then the puff-adder strikes at it, injects its poison, and the animal dies soon after. As many as ten buffaloes have been killed in a day by one puff-adder. The body of the first buffalo is not eaten, for it is regarded as poisoned meat, but all the others are used as food.[1]

Soon after Isis had placed the serpent on the path, Rā passed by, and the reptile bit him, thus injecting poison into his body. Its effect was terrible, and Rā cried out in agony. His jaws chattered, his lips trembled, and he became speechless for a time; never before had he suffered such pain. The gods hearing his cry rushed to him, and when he could speak he told them that he had been bitten by a deadly serpent. In spite of all the words of power which were known to

[1] Johnston, *Uganda*, vol. ii., p. 584. The authority for this statement is Mr. George Wilson, formerly Collector in Unyoro.

him, and his secret name which had been hidden in his body at his birth, a serpent had bitten him, and he was being consumed with a fiery pain. He then commanded that all the gods who had any knowledge of magical spells should come to him, and when they came, Isis, the great lady of spells, the destroyer of diseases, and the revivifier of the dead, came with them. Turning to Rā she said, "What hath happened, O divine Father?" and in answer the god told her that a serpent had bitten him, that he was hotter than fire and colder than water, that his limbs quaked, and that he was losing the power of sight. Then Isis said to him with guile, "Divine Father, tell me thy name, for he who uttereth his own name shall live." Thereupon Rā proceeded to enumerate the various things that he had done, and to describe his creative acts, and ended his speech to Isis by saying that he was Kheperȧ in the morning, Rā at noon, and Temu in the evening. Apparently he thought that the naming of these three great names would satisfy Isis, and that she would immediately pronounce a word of power and stop the pain in his body, which, during his speech, had become more acute. Isis, however, was not deceived, and she knew well that Rā had not declared to her his hidden name; this she told him, and she begged him once again to tell her his name. For a time the god refused to utter the name, but as the pain in his body became more violent, and the poison passed through his veins like fire, he said, "Isis shall search in me, and my name shall pass from my body into hers." At that moment Rā removed himself from the sight of the gods in his Boat, and the Throne in the Boat of Millions of Years had no occupant. The great name of Rā was, it seems, hidden in his heart, and Isis, having some doubt as to whether Rā would keep his word or not, agreed with Horus that Rā must be made to take an oath to part with his two Eyes, that is, the Sun and the Moon. At length Rā allowed his heart to be taken from his body, and his great and secret name, whereby he lived, passed into the possession of Isis. Rā thus became to all intents and purposes a dead god. Then Isis, strong in the power of her spells, said: "Flow, poison, come out of Rā. Eye of Horus, come "out of Rā and shine outside his mouth. It is I, Isis, "who work, and I have made the poison to fall on the "ground. Verily the name of the great god is taken "from him, Rā shall live and the poison shall die; if "the poison live Rā shall die."

This was the infallible spell which was to be used in cases of poisoning, for it rendered the bite or sting of every venomous reptile harmless. It drove the poison out of Rā, and since it was composed by Isis after she obtained the knowledge of his secret name it was irresistible. If the words were written on papyrus or linen over a figure of Temu, or Ḥeru-ḥekenu, or Isis, or Horus, they became a mighty charm. If the papyrus or linen were steeped in water and the water drunk, the words were equally efficacious as a charm against snake-bites. To this day water in which the written words of a text from the Ḳur'ân have been dissolved, or water drunk from a bowl on the inside of which religious texts have been written, is still regarded as a never-failing charm in Egypt and the Sûdân. Thus we see that the modern custom of drinking magical water was derived from the ancient Egyptians, who believed that it conveyed into their bodies the actual power of their gods.

IV.

The Legend of Ḥeru-Beḥuṭet and the Winged Disk.

The text of this legend is cut in hieroglyphics on the walls of the temple of Edfû in Upper Egypt, and certain portions of it are illustrated by large bas-reliefs. Both text and reliefs were published by Professor Naville in his volume entitled *Mythe d'Horus*, fol., plates 12–19, Geneva, 1870. A German translation by Brugsch appeared in the *Abhandlungen der Göttinger Akademie*, Band xiv., pp. 173–236, and another by Wiedemann in his *Die Religion*, p. 38 ff. (see the English translation p. 69 ff.). The legend, in the form in which it is here given, dates from the Ptolemaïc Period, but the matter which it contains is far older,

Horus holding the Hippopotamus-fiend with chain and spear. Behind stand Isis and Ḥeru Khenti-Khaṭṭi.

Horus driving his spear into the Hippopotamus-fiend ; behind him stands one of his "Blacksmiths."

Horus driving his spear into the belly of the Hippopotamus-fiend as he lies on his back; behind stands one of his "Blacksmiths."

Horus and Isis capturing the Hippopotamus-fiend.

and it is probable that the facts recorded in it are fragments of actual history, which the Egyptians of the late period tried to piece together in chronological order. We shall see as we read that the writer of the legend as we have it was not well acquainted with Egyptian history, and that in his account of the conquest of Egypt he has confounded one god with another, and mixed up historical facts with mythological legends to such a degree that his meaning is frequently uncertain. The great fact which he wished to describe is the conquest of Egypt by an early king, who, having subdued the peoples in the South, advanced northwards, and made all the people whom he conquered submit to his yoke. Now the King of Egypt was always called Horus, and the priests of Edfû wishing to magnify their local god, Horus of Beḥuṭet, or Horus of Edfû, attributed to him the conquests of this human, and probably predynastic, king. We must remember that the legend assumes that Rā was still reigning on earth, though he was old and feeble, and had probably deputed his power to his successor, whom the legend regards as his son.

In the 363rd year of his reign Rā-Harmakhis[1] was in Nubia with his army with the intention of destroying those who had conspired against him; because of their conspiracy (*auu*) Nubia is called "Uaua" to this day. From Nubia Rā-Harmakhis sailed down the river to Edfû, where Ḥeru-Beḥuṭet entered his boat, and told

[1] I.e., Rā on the horizon.

him that his foes were conspiring against him. Rā-Harmakhis in answer addressed Ḥeru-Beḥuṭet as his son, and commanded him to set out without delay and slay the wicked rebels. Then Ḥeru-Beḥuṭet took the form of a great winged Disk, and at once flew up into the sky, where he took the place of Rā, the old Sun-god. Looking down from the height of heaven he was able to discover the whereabouts of the rebels, and he pursued them in the form of a winged disk. Then he attacked them with such violence that they became dazed, and could neither see where they were going, nor hear, the result of this being that they slew each other, and in a very short time they were all dead. Thoth, seeing this, told Rā that because Horus had appeared as a great winged disk he must be called "Ḥeru-Beḥuṭet," and by this name Horus was known ever after at Edfû. Rā embraced Horus, and referred with pleasure to the blood which he had shed, and Horus invited his father to come and look upon the slain. Rā set out with the goddess Āshtherṭet (Ashtoreth) to do this, and they saw the enemies lying fettered on the ground. The legend here introduces a number of curious derivations of the names of Edfû, &c., which are valueless, and which remind us of the derivations of place-names propounded by ancient Semitic scribes.

In gladness of heart Rā proposed a sail on the Nile, but as soon as his enemies heard that he was coming, they changed themselves into crocodiles and hippopotami,

Horus standing on the back of the Hippopotamus-fiend, and spearing him in the presence of Isis.

The " Butcher-priest " slicing open the Hippopotamus-fiend.

so that they might be able to wreck his boat and devour him. As the boat of the god approached them they opened their jaws to crush it, but Horus and his followers came quickly on the scene, and defeated their purpose. The followers of Horus here mentioned are called in the text "Mesniu," i.e., "blacksmiths," or "workers in metal," and they represent the primitive conquerors of the Egyptians, who were armed with metal weapons, and so were able to overcome with tolerable ease the indigenous Egyptians, whose weapons were made of flint and wood. Horus and his "blacksmiths" were provided with iron lances and chains, and, having cast the chains over the monsters in the river, they drove their lances into their snouts, and slew 651 of them. Because Horus gained his victory by means of metal weapons, Rā decreed that a metal statue of Horus should be placed at Edfû, and remain there for ever, and a name was given to the town to commemorate the great battle that had taken place there. Rā applauded Horus for the mighty deeds which he had been able to perform by means of the spells contained in the "Book of Slaying the Hippopotamus." Horus then associated with himself the goddesses Uatchet and Nekhebet, who were in the form of serpents, and, taking his place as the winged Disk on the front of the Boat of Rā, destroyed all the enemies of Rā wheresoever he found them. When the remnant of the enemies of Rā saw that they were likely to be slain, they doubled back to the South, but

Horus pursued them, and drove them down the river before him as far as Thebes. One battle took place at Tcheṭmet, and another at Denderah, and Horus was always victorious; the enemies were caught by chains thrown over them, and the deadly spears of the Blacksmiths drank their blood.

After this the enemy fled to the North, and took refuge in the swamps of the Delta, and in the shallows of the Mediterranean Sea, and Horus pursued them thither. After searching for them for four days and four nights he found them, and they were speedily slain. One hundred and forty-two of them and a male hippopotamus were dragged on to the Boat of Rā, and there Horus dug out their entrails, and hacked their carcases in pieces, which he gave to his Blacksmiths and the gods who formed the crew of the Boat of Rā. Before despatching the hippopotamus, Horus leaped on to the back of the monster as a mark of his triumph, and to commemorate this event the priest of Ḥeben, the town wherein these things happened, was called "He who standeth on the back" ever after.

The end of the great fight, however, was not yet. Another army of enemies appeared by the North Lake, and they were marching towards the sea; but terror of Horus smote their hearts, and they fled and took refuge in Mertet-Ȧment, where they allied themselves with the followers of Set, the Arch-fiend and great Enemy of Rā. Thither Horus and his well-armed Blacksmiths pursued them, and came up with them at the town

Horus of Beḥuṭet and Rā-Harmakhis in a shrine.

Horus of Beḥuṭet and Harmakhis in a shrine.

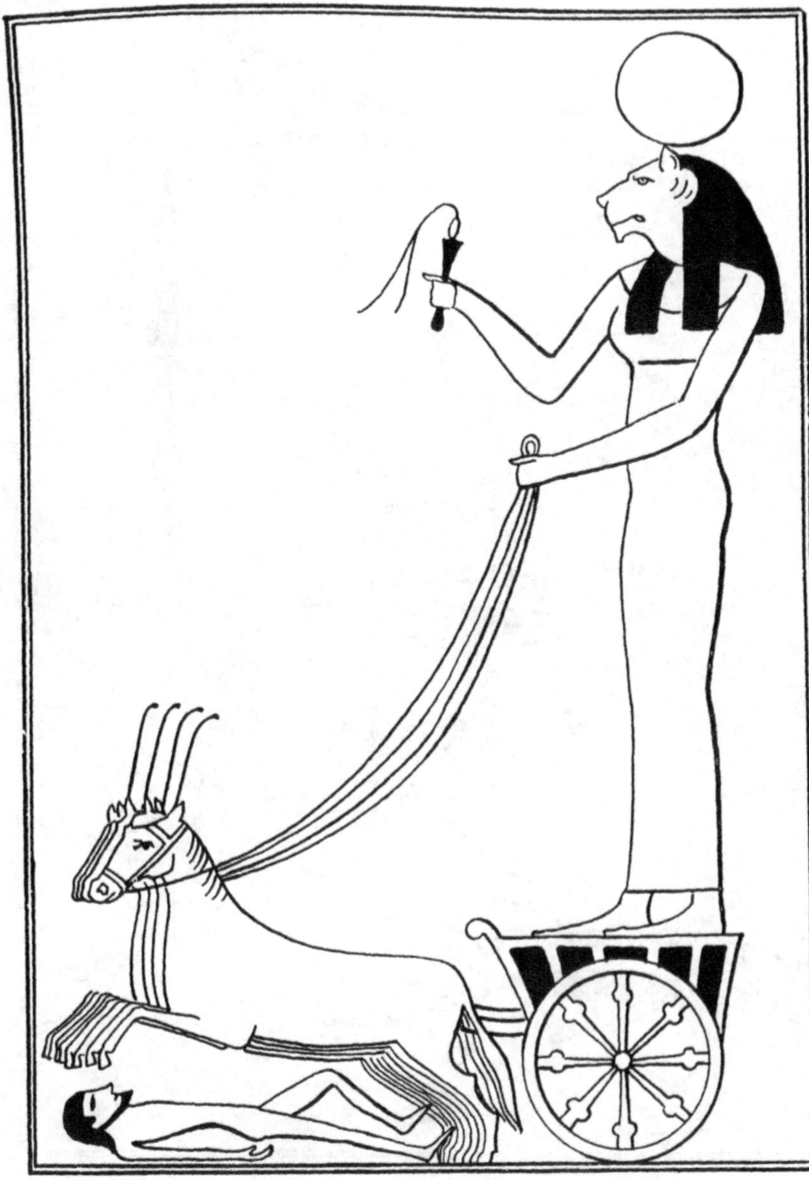

Āshthertet (ʿAshtoreth) driving her chariot over the prostrate foe.

Horus of Beḥuṭet spearing a Typhonic animal, and holding his prisoners with ropes.

Horus of Beḥuṭet, accompanied by Rā-Harmakhis and Menu, spearing the Hippopotamus-fiend.

called Per-Rereḥu, which derived its name from the "Two Combatants," or "Two Men," Horus and Set. A great fight took place, the enemies of Rā were defeated with great slaughter, and Horus dragged 381 prisoners on to the Boat of Rā, where he slew them, and gave their bodies to his followers.

Then Set rose up and cursed Horus because he had slain his allies, and he used such foul language that Thoth called him "Neḥaḥa-ḥer," i.e., "Stinking Face," and this name clung to him ever after. After this Horus and Set engaged in a fight which lasted a very long time, but at length Horus drove his spear into the neck of Set with such violence that the Fiend fell headlong to the ground. Then Horus smote with his club the mouth which had uttered such blasphemies, and fettered him with his chain. In this state Horus dragged Set into the presence of Rā, who ascribed great praise to Horus, and special names were given to the palace of Horus and the high priest of the temple in commemoration of the event. When the question of the disposal of Set was being discussed by the gods, Rā ordered that he and his fiends should be given over to Isis and her son Horus, who were to do what they pleased with them. Horus promptly cut off the heads of Set and his fiends in the presence of Rā and Isis, and he dragged Set by his feet through the country with his spear sticking in his head and neck. After this Isis appointed Horus of Beḥuṭet to be the protecting deity of her son Horus.

The fight between the Sun-god and Set was a very favourite subject with Egyptian writers, and there are many forms of it. Thus there is the fight between Ḥeru-ur and Set, the fight between Rā and Set, the fight between Ḥeru-Beḥuṭet and Set, the fight between Osiris and Set, and the fight between Horus, son of Isis, and Set. In the oldest times the combat was merely the natural opposition of light to darkness, but later the Sun-god became the symbol of right and truth as well as of light, and Set the symbol of sin and wickedness as well as of darkness, and ultimately the nature myth was forgotten, and the fight between the two gods became the type of the everlasting war which good men wage against sin. In Coptic literature we have the well-known legend of the slaughter of the dragon by St. George, and this is nothing but a Christian adaptation of the legend of Horus and Set.

After these things Horus, son of Rā, and Horus, son of Isis, each took the form of a mighty man, with the face and body of a hawk, and each wore the Red and White Crowns, and each carried a spear and chain. In these forms the two gods slew the remnant of the enemies. Now by some means or other Set came to life again, and he took the form of a mighty hissing or "roaring" serpent, and hid himself in the ground, in a place which was ever after called the "place of the roarer." In front of his hiding-place Horus, son of Isis, stationed himself in the form of a hawk-headed staff to prevent him from coming out. In spite of this,

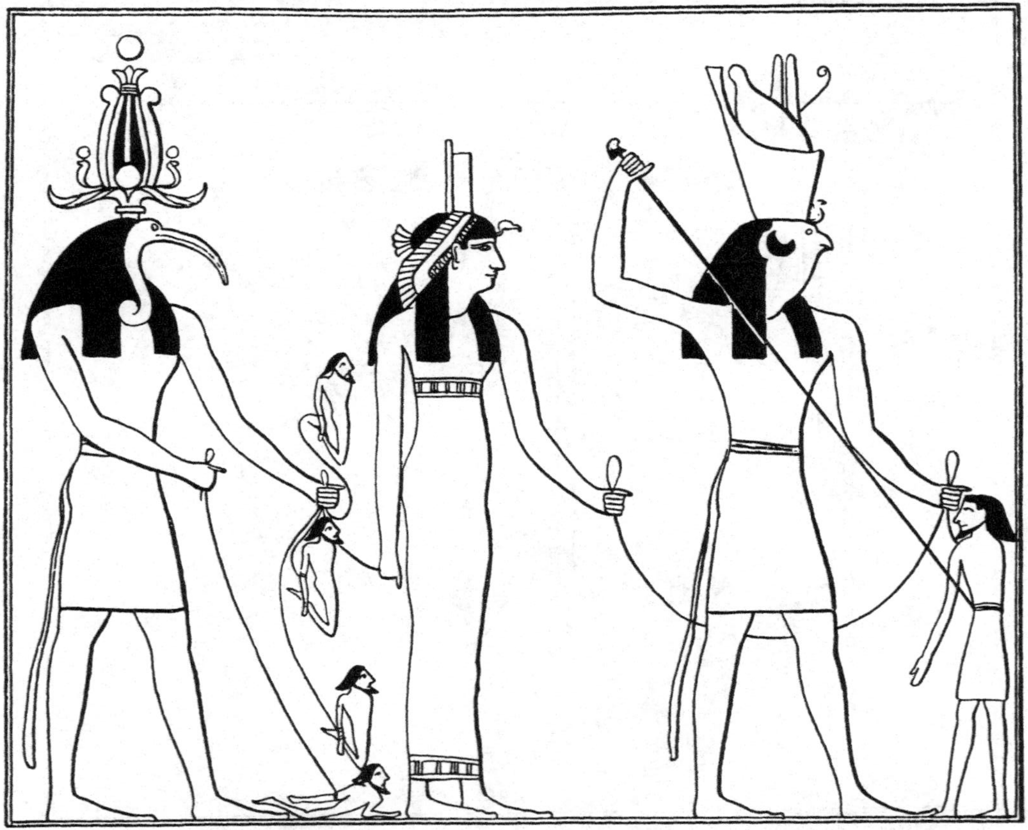

Horus of Beḥuṭet and Thoth spearing human victims with the assistance of Isis.

PLATE XII.

Horus of Beḥuṭet spearing Set in the form of a crocodile.

however, Set managed to escape, and he gathered about him the Smai and Sebȧ fiends at the Lake of Meḥ, and waged war once more against Horus; the enemies of Rā were again defeated, and Horus slew them in the presence of his father.

Horus, it seems, now ceased to fight for some time, and devoted himself to keeping guard over the "Great God" who was in Ȧn-rut-f, a district in or near Herakleopolis. This Great God was no other than Osiris, and the duty of Horus was to prevent the Smai fiends from coming by night to the place. In spite of the power of Horus, it was found necessary to summon the aid of Isis to keep away the fiends, and it was only by her words of power that the fiend Ba was kept out of the sanctuary. As a reward for what he had already done, Thoth decreed that Horus should be called the "Master-Fighter." Passing over the derivations of place-names which occur here in the text, we find that Horus and his Blacksmiths were again obliged to fight bodies of the enemy who had managed to escape, and that on one occasion they killed one hundred and six foes. In every fight the Blacksmiths performed mighty deeds of valour, and in reward for their services a special district was allotted to them to dwell in.

The last great fight in the North took place at Tanis, in the eastern part of the Delta. When the position of the enemy had been located, Horus took the form of a lion with the face of a man, and he put on his head the Triple Crown. His claws were like flints, and with them he dragged away one hundred and forty-two of the enemy, and tore them in pieces, and dug out their tongues, which he carried off as symbols of his victory.

Meanwhile rebellion had again broken out in Nubia, where about one-third of the enemy had taken refuge in the river in the forms of crocodiles and hippopotami. Rā counselled Horus to sail up the Nile with his Blacksmiths, and when Thoth had recited the "Chapters of protecting the Boat of Rā" over the boats, the expedition set sail for the South. The object of reciting these spells was to prevent the monsters which were in the river from making the waves to rise and from stirring up storms which might engulf the boats of Rā and Horus and the Blacksmiths. When the rebels and fiends who had been uttering treason against Horus saw the boat of Rā, with the winged Disk of Horus accompanied by the goddesses Uatchet and Nekhebet in the form of serpents, they were smitten with fear, and their hearts quaked, and all power of resistance left them, and they died of fright straightway. When Horus returned in triumph to Edfû, Rā ordered that an image of the winged Disk should be placed in each of his sanctuaries, and that in every place wherein a winged Disk was set, that sanctuary should be a sanctuary of Horus of Beḥuṭet. The winged disks which are seen above the doorways of the temples still standing in Egypt show that the command of Rā was faithfully carried out by the priests.

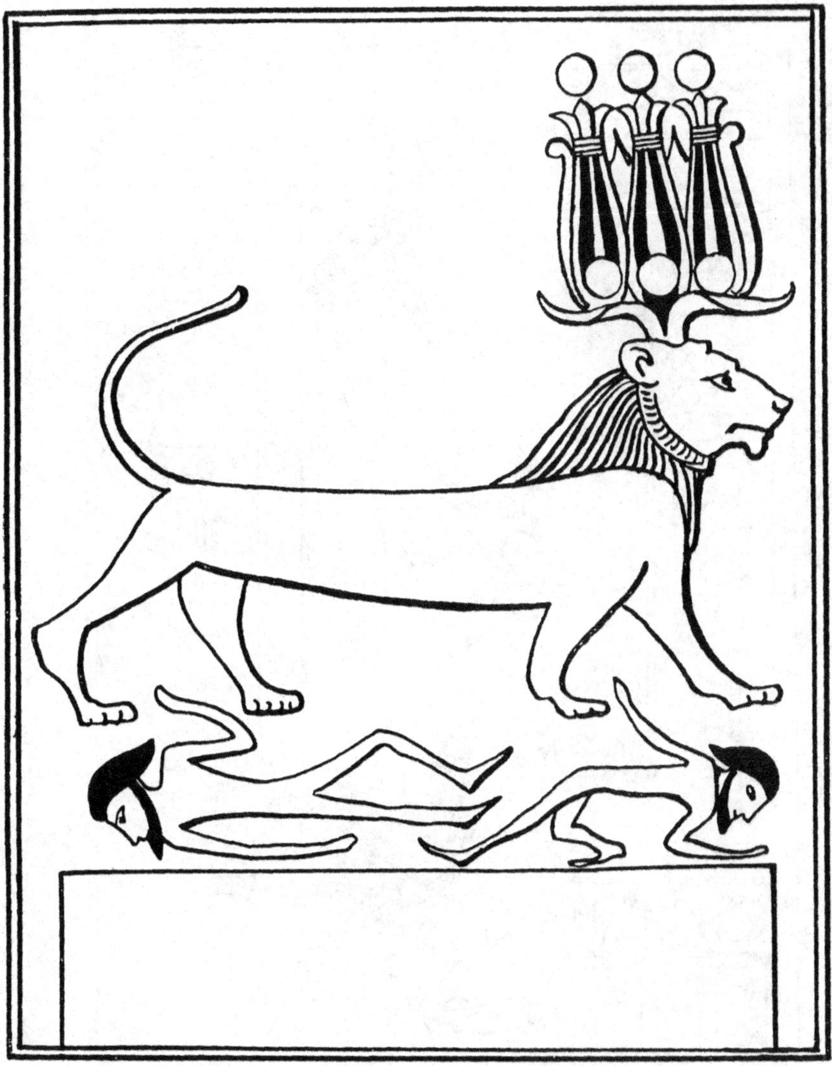

Horus of Beḥuṭet in the form of a lion slaying his foes.

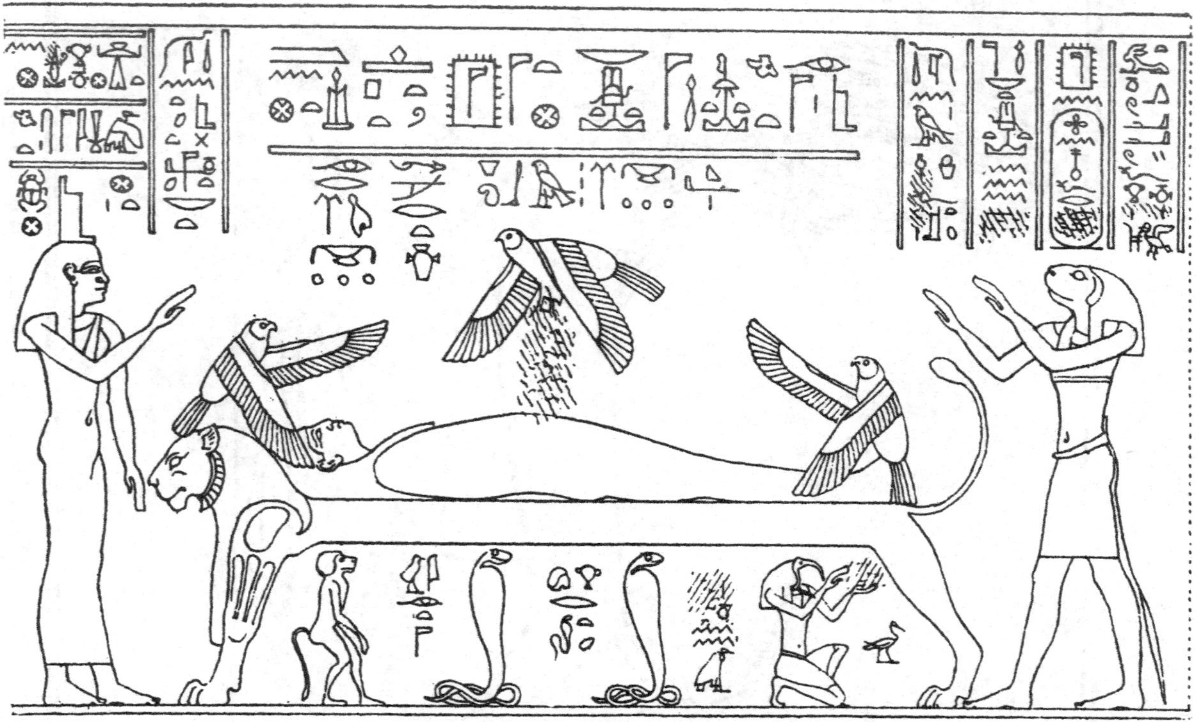

The Procreation of Horus, son of Isis.

V.

Legend of the Birth of Horus, son of Isis and Osiris.

The text which contains this legend is found cut in hieroglyphics upon a stele which is now preserved in Paris. Attention was first called to it by Chabas, who in 1857 gave a translation of it in the *Revue Archéologique*, p. 65 ff., and pointed out the importance of its contents with his characteristic ability. The hieroglyphic text was first published by Ledrain in his work on the monuments of the Bibliothèque Nationale in Paris,[1] and I gave a transcript of the text, with transliteration and translation, in 1895.[2]

The greater part of the text consists of a hymn to Osiris, which was probably composed under the XVIIIth Dynasty, when an extraordinary development of the cult of that god took place, and when he was placed by Egyptian theologians at the head of all the gods. Though unseen in the temples, his presence filled all Egypt, and his body formed the very substance of the country. He was the God of all gods and the Governor of the Two Companies of the gods, he formed the soul and body of Rā, he was the beneficent Spirit of all spirits, he was himself the celestial food on

[1] *Les Monuments Égyptiens* (*Cabinet des Médailles et Antiques*), In the *Bibliothèque de l'École des Hautes Études*, Paris, 1879-1882, plate xxii. ff.

[2] *First Steps in Egyptian*, pp. 179-188.

which the Doubles in the Other World lived. He was the greatest of the gods in On (Heliopolis), Memphis, Herakleopolis, Hermopolis, Abydos, and the region of the First Cataract, and so he embodied in his own person the might of Rā-Tem, Apis and Ptaḥ, the Horus-gods, Thoth and Khnemu, and his rule over Busiris and Abydos continued to be supreme, as it had been for many, many hundreds of years. He was the source of the Nile, the north wind sprang from him, his seats were the stars of heaven which never set, and the imperishable stars were his ministers. All heaven was his dominion, and the doors of the sky opened before him of their own accord when he appeared. He inherited the earth from his father Ḳeb, and the sovereignty of heaven from his mother Nut. In his person he united endless time in the past and endless time in the future. Like Rā he had fought Sebȧ, or Set, the monster of evil, and had defeated him, and his victory assured to him lasting authority over the gods and the dead. He exercised his creative power in making land and water, trees and herbs, cattle and other four-footed beasts, birds of all kinds, and fish and creeping things; even the waste spaces of the desert owed allegiance to him as the creator. And he rolled out the sky, and set the light above the darkness.

The last paragraph of the text contains an allusion to Isis, the sister and wife of Osiris, and mentions the legend of the birth of Horus, which even under the XVIIIth Dynasty was very ancient. Isis, we are told, was the constant protectress of her brother, she drove away the fiends that wanted to attack him, and kept them out of his shrine and tomb, and she guarded him from all accidents. All these things she did by means of spells and incantations, large numbers of which were known to her, and by her power as the "witch-goddess." Her "mouth was trained to per-"fection, and she made no mistake in pronouncing her "spells, and her tongue was skilled and halted not." At length came the unlucky day when Set succeeded in killing Osiris during the war which the "good god" was waging against him and his fiends. Details of the engagement are wanting, but the Pyramid Texts state that the body of Osiris was hurled to the ground by Set at a place called Neṭȧt, 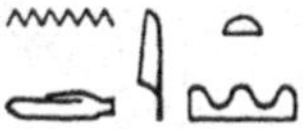, which seems to have been near Abydos.[1] The news of the death of Osiris was brought to Isis, and she at once set out to find his body. All legends agree in saying that she took the form of a bird, and that she flew about unceasingly, going hither and thither, and uttering wailing cries of grief. At length she found the body, and with a piercing cry she alighted on the ground. The Pyramid Texts say that Nephthys was with her that "Isis came, Nephthys came, the one on the right "side, the other on the left side, one in the form of a "*Ḥat* bird, the other in the form of a *Tchert* bird, and "they found Osiris thrown on the ground in Neṭȧt by

[1] Pepi I., line 475; Pepi II., line 1263.

"his brother Set."[1] The late form of the legend goes on to say that Isis fanned the body with her feathers, and produced air, and that at length she caused the inert members of Osiris to move, and drew from him his essence, wherefrom she produced her child Horus.

This bare statement of the dogma of the conception of Horus does not represent all that is known about it, and it may well be supplemented by a passage from the Pyramid Texts,[2] which reads, "Adoration to thee, O "Osiris.[3] Rise thou up on thy left side, place thyself "on thy right side. This water which I give unto thee "is the water of youth (or rejuvenation). Adoration to "thee, O Osiris! Rise thou up on thy left side, place "thyself on thy right side. This bread which I have "made for thee is warmth. Adoration to thee, O "Osiris! The doors of heaven are opened to thee, the "doors of the streams are thrown wide open to thee. "The gods in the city of Pe come [to thee], Osiris, at "the sound (or voice) of the supplication of Isis and "Nephthys. . . . . . Thy elder sister took thy body in "her arms, she chafed thy hands, she clasped thee to "her breast [when] she found thee [lying] on thy side "on the plain of Neṭȧt."[4] And in another place we

1 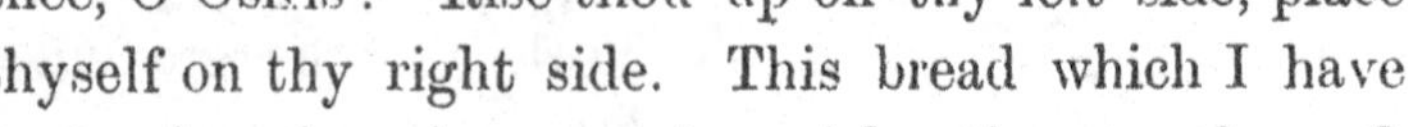

2 Mer-en-Rā, line 336; Pepi II., line 862.

3 I omit the king's names.

4 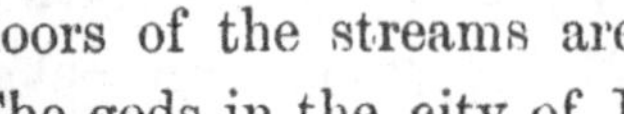

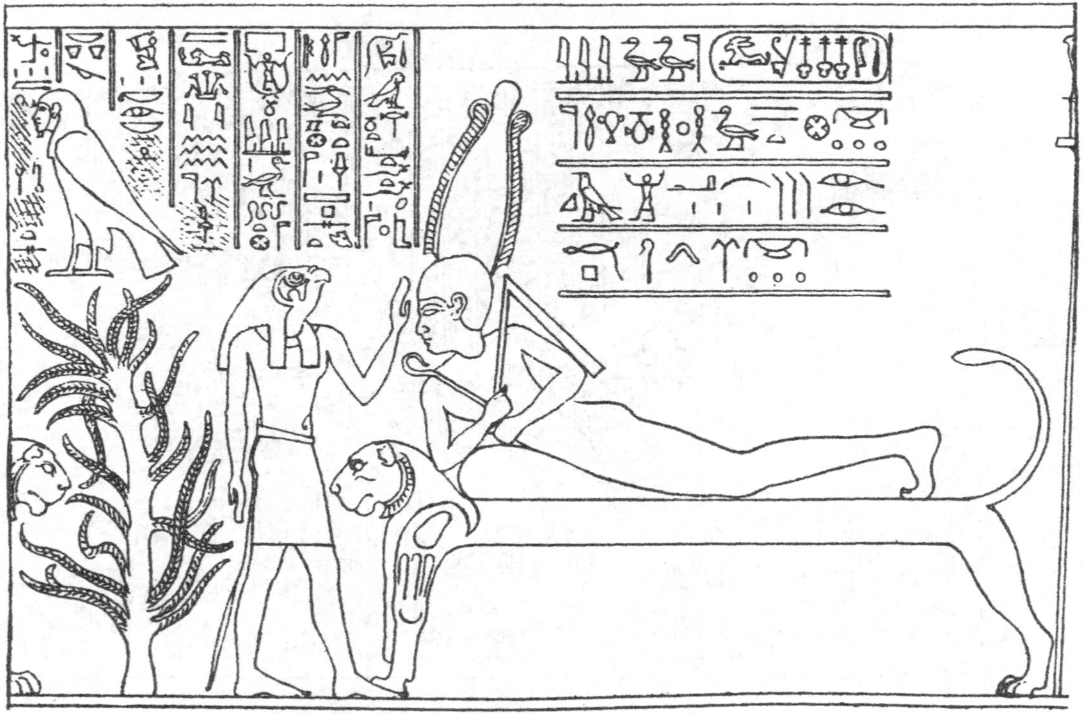

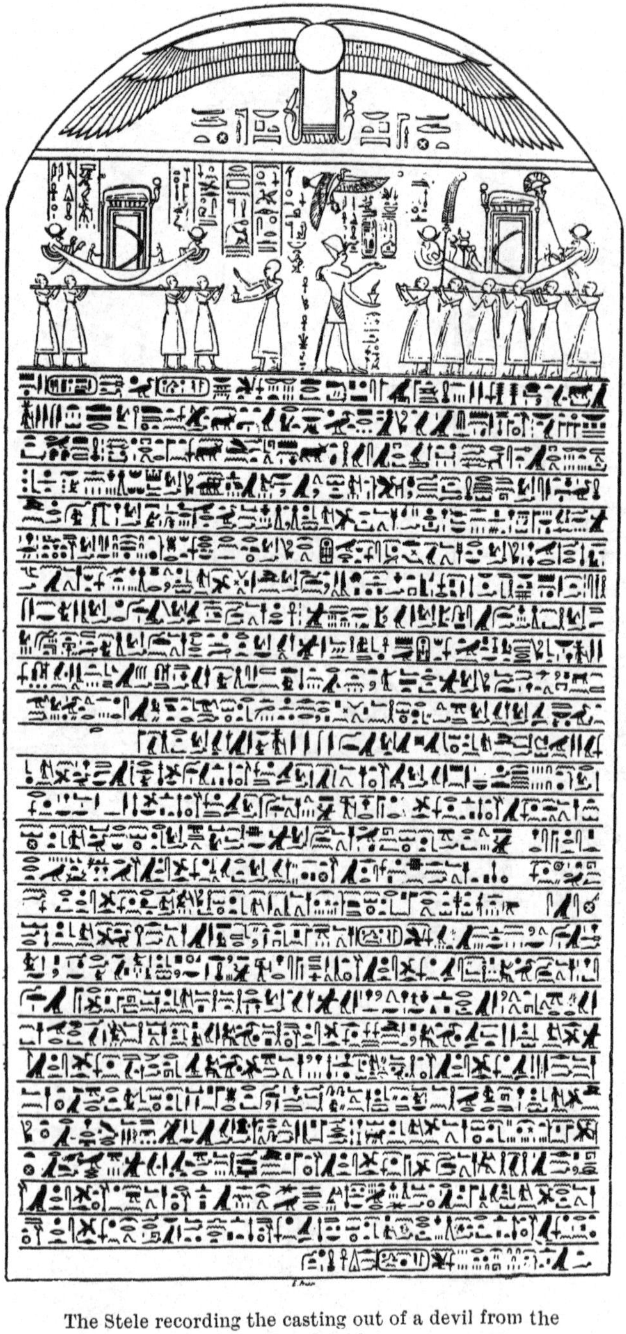

The Stele recording the casting out of a devil from the Princess of Bekhten.

read :[1] "Thy two sisters, Isis and Nephthys, came to "thee, Kam-urt, in thy name of Kam-ur, Uatchet-urt "in thy name of Uatch-ur" . . . . . . "Isis and "Nephthys weave magical protection for thee in the "city of Saut, for thee their lord, in thy name of 'Lord "of Saut,' for their god, in thy name of 'God.' They "praise thee; go not thou far from them in thy name "of 'Ṭua.' They present offerings to thee; be not "wroth in thy name of 'Tchenṭru.' Thy sister Isis "cometh to thee rejoicing in her love for thee.[2] Thou "hast union with her, thy seed entereth her. She "conceiveth in the form of the star Sepṭet (Sothis). "Horus-Sepṭ issueth from thee in the form of Horus, "dweller in the star Sepṭet. Thou makest a spirit to "be in him in his name 'Spirit dwelling in the god "Tchenṭru.' He avengeth thee in his name of 'Horus, "the son who avenged his father.' Hail, Osiris, Ḳeb "hath brought to thee Horus, he hath avenged thee, he "hath brought to thee the hearts of the gods, Horus "hath given thee his Eye, thou hast taken possession "of the Urert Crown thereby at the head of the gods. "Horus hath presented to thee thy members, he hath "collected them completely, there is no disorder in "thee. Thoth hath seized thy enemy and hath slain "him and those who were with him." The above words are addressed to dead kings in the Pyramid

[1] Tetà, line 274; Pepi I., line 27; Mer-en-Rā, line 37; and Pepi II., line 67.

[2] Pyramid Text, Tetà, l. 276.

Texts, and what the gods were supposed to do for them was believed by the Egyptians to have been actually done for Osiris. These extracts are peculiarly valuable, for they prove that the legend of Osiris which was current under the XVIIIth Dynasty was based upon traditions which were universally accepted in Egypt under the Vth and VIth Dynasties.

The hymn concludes with a reference to the accession of Horus, son of Isis, the flesh and bone of Osiris, to the throne of his grandfather Ḳeb, and to the welcome which he received from the Tchatcha, or Administrators of heaven, and the Company of the Gods, and the Lords of Truth, who assembled in the Great House of Heliopolis to acknowledge his sovereignty. His succession also received the approval of Neb-er-tcher, who, as we saw from the first legend in this book, was the Creator of the Universe.

VI.

A Legend of Khensu Nefer-ḥetep[1] and the Princess of Bekhten.

The text of this legend is cut in hieroglyphics upon a sandstone stele, with a rounded top, which was found

[1] In the headlines of this section, p. 106 ff., for Ptaḥ Nefer-ḥetep read Khensu Nefer-ḥetep.

in the temple of Khensu at Thebes, and is now preserved in the Bibliothèque Nationale at Paris; it was discovered by Champollion, and removed to Paris by Prisse d'Avennes in 1846. The text was first published by Prisse d'Avennes,[1] and it was first translated by Birch[2] in 1853. The text was republished and translated into French by E. de Rougé in 1858,[3] and several other renderings have been given in German and in English since that date.[4] When the text was first published, and for some years afterwards, it was generally thought that the legend referred to events which were said to have taken place under a king who was identified as Rameses XIII., but this misconception was corrected by Erman, who showed[5] that the king was in reality Rameses II. By a careful examination of the construction of the text he proved that the narrative on the stele was drawn up several hundreds of years after the events described in it took place, and that its author was but imperfectly acquainted with the form of the Egyptian language in use in the reign of Rameses II. In fact, the legend was written in the interests of the priests of the temple of Khensu, who

[1] *Choix de Monuments Égyptiens*, Paris, 1847, plate xxiv.

[2] *Transactions of the Royal Society of Literature*, New Series, vol. iv., p. 217 ff.

[3] *Journal Asiatique* (*Étude sur une Stèle Égyptienne*), August, 1856, August, 1857, and August-Sept., 1858, Paris, 8vo, with plate.

[4] Brugsch, *Geschichte Aegyptens*, 1877, p. 627 ff.; Birch, *Records of the Past*, Old Series, vol. iv., p. 53 ff.; Budge, *Egyptian Reading Book*, text and transliteration, p. 40 ff.; translation, p. xxviii. ff.

[5] *Aeg. Zeit.*, 1883, pp. 54–60.

wished to magnify their god and his power to cast out devils and to exorcise evil spirits; it was probably composed between B.C. 650 and B.C. 250.[1]

The legend, after enumerating the great names of Rameses II., goes on to state that the king was in the "country of the two rivers," by which we are to understand some portion of Mesopotamia, the rivers being the Tigris and Euphrates, and that the local chiefs were bringing to him tribute consisting of gold, lapis-lazuli, turquoise, and logs of wood from the Land of the God. It is difficult to understand how gold and logs of wood from Southern Arabia and East Africa came to be produced as tribute by chiefs who lived so far to the north. Among those who sent gifts was the Prince of Bekhten, and at the head of all his tribute he sent his eldest daughter, bearing his message of homage and duty. Now the maiden was beautiful, and the King of Egypt thought her so lovely that he took her to wife, and bestowed upon her the name "Rā-neferu," which means something like the "beauties of Rā." He took her back with him to Egypt, where she was installed as Queen.

During the summer of the fifteenth year of his reign, whilst Rameses II. was celebrating a festival of Åmen-Rā in the Temple of Luxor, one came to him and reported that an envoy had arrived from the Prince of Bekhten, bearing with him many gifts for the Royal Wife Rā-neferu. When the envoy had been brought

[1] Maspero, *Les Contes Populaires*, 3rd edit., p. 166.

into the presence, he addressed words of homage to the king, and, having presented the gifts from his lord, he said that he had come to beg His Majesty to send a "learned man," , i.e., a magician, to Bekhten to attend Bent-enth-resh, 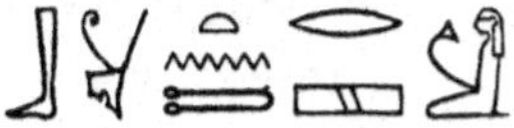, His Majesty's sister-in-law, who was stricken with some disease. Thereupon the king summoned the learned men of the House of Life, i.e., the members of the great College of Magic at Thebes, and the *qenbetu* officials, and when they had entered his presence, he commanded them to select a man of "wise heart and deft fingers" to go to Bekhten. The choice fell upon one Teḥuti-em-ḥeb, and His Majesty sent him to Bekhten with the envoy. When they arrived in Bekhten, Teḥuti-em-ḥeb found that the Princess Bent-enth-resh was possessed by an evil spirit which refused to be exorcised by him, and he was unable to cast out the devil. The Prince of Bekhten, seeing that the healing of his daughter was beyond the power of the Egyptian, sent a second envoy to Rameses II., and besought him to send a god to drive out the devil. This envoy arrived in Egypt in the summer of the twenty-sixth year of the reign of Rameses II., and found the king celebrating a festival in Thebes. When he heard the petition of the envoy, he went to the Temple of Khensu Nefer-ḥetep "a second time,"[1] and

[1] Thus the king must have invoked the help of Khensu on the occasion of the visit of the first envoy.

presented himself before the god and besought his help on behalf of his sister-in-law.

Then the priests of Khensu Nefer-ḥetep carried the statue of this god to the place where was the statue of Khensu surnamed "Pa-àri-sekher," i.e., the "Worker of destinies," who was able to repel the attacks of evil spirits and to drive them out. When the statues of the two gods were facing each other, Rameses II. entreated Khensu Nefer-ḥetep to "turn his face towards," i.e., to look favourably upon, Khensu Pa-àri-sekher, and to let him go to Bekhten to drive the devil out of the Princess of Bekhten. The text affords no explanation of the fact that Khensu Nefer-ḥetep was regarded as a greater god than Khensu Pa-àri-sekher, or why his permission had to be obtained before the latter could leave the country. It is probable that the demands made upon Khensu Nefer-ḥetep by the Egyptians who lived in Thebes and its neighbourhood were so numerous that it was impossible to let his statue go into outlying districts or foreign lands, and that a deputy-god was appointed to perform miracles outside Thebes. This arrangement would benefit the people, and would, moreover, bring much money to the priests. The appointment of a deputy-god is not so strange as it may seem, and modern African peoples are familiar with the expedient. About one hundred years ago the priests of the god Bobowissi of Winnebah, in the Tshi region of West Africa, found their business so large that it was absolutely necessary for them to appoint a deputy. The priests therefore selected Brahfo, i.e., "deputy," and gave out that Bobowissi had deputed all minor matters to him, and that his utterances were to be regarded as those of Bobowissi. Delegates were ordered to be sent to Winnebah in Ashanti, where they would be shown the "deputy" god by the priests, and afterwards he would be taken to Mankassim, where he would reside, and do for the people all that Bobowissi had done hitherto.[1]

When Rameses II. had made his petition to Khensu Nefer-ḥetep, the statue of the god bowed its head twice, in token of assent. Here it is clear that we have an example of the use of statues with movable limbs, which were worked, when occasion required, by the priests. The king then made a second petition to the god to transfer his *sa*, , or magical power, to Khensu Pa-àri-sekher so that when he had arrived in Bekhten he would be able to heal the Princess. Again the statue of Khensu Nefer-ḥetep bowed its head twice, and the petition of the king was granted. The text goes on to say that the magical power of the greater god was transferred to the lesser god four times, or in a fourfold measure, but we are not told how this was effected. We know from many passages in the texts that every god was believed to possess this magical power, which is called the "*sa* of life," , or the "*sa* of the god," .[2] This *sa* could be transferred by

[1] Ellis, *Tshi-speaking Peoples*, p. 55. [2] Text of Unàs, line 562.

a god or goddess to a human being, either by an embrace or through some offering which was eaten. Thus Temu transferred the magical power of his life to Shu and Tefnut by embracing them,[1] and in the Ritual of the Divine Cult [2] the priest says, "The two vessels of milk of Temu are the *sa*, 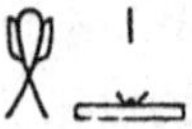, of my limbs." The man who possessed this *sa* could transfer it to his friend by embracing him and then "making passes" with his hands along his back. The *sa* could be received by a man from a god and then transmitted by him to a statue by taking it in his arms, and this ceremony was actually performed by the king in the Ritual of the Divine Cult.[3] The primary source of this *sa* was Rā, who bestowed it without measure on the blessed dead,[4] and caused them to live for ever thereby. These facts make it tolerably certain that the magical power of Khensu Nefer-ḥetep was transferred to Khensu Pa-àri-sekher in one of two ways: either the statue of the latter was brought near to that of the former and it received the *sa* by contact, or the high priest first received the *sa* from the greater god and then transmitted it to the lesser god by embraces and "passes" with his hands. Be this as it may,

[1] Pyramid Texts, Pepi I., l. 466. [2] Ed. Moret, p. 21.

[3] *Ibid.*, p. 99.

[4] 
, Pepi I., line 666.

Khensu Pa-àri-sekher received the magical power, and having been placed in his boat, he set out for Bekhten, accompanied by five smaller boats, and chariots and horses which marched on each side of him.

When after a journey of seventeen months Khensu Pa-àri-sekher arrived in Bekhten, he was cordially welcomed by the Prince, and, having gone to the place where the Princess who was possessed of a devil lived, he exercised his power to such purpose that she was healed immediately. Moreover, the devil which had been cast out admitted that Khensu Pa-àri-sekher was his master, and promised that he would depart to the place whence he came, provided that the Prince of Bekhten would celebrate a festival in his honour before his departure. Meanwhile the Prince and his soldiers stood by listening to the conversation between the god and the devil, and they were very much afraid. Following the instructions of Khensu Pa-àri-sekher the Prince made a great feast in honour of the supernatural visitors, and then the devil departed to the "place which he loved," and there was general rejoicing in the land. The Prince of Bekhten was so pleased with the Egyptian god that he determined not to allow him to return to Egypt. When the statue of Khensu Pa-àri-sekher had been in Bekhten for three years and nine months, the Prince in a vision saw the god, in the form of a golden hawk, come forth from his shrine, and fly up into the air and direct his course to Egypt. Realizing that the statue of the god was useless without its indwelling spirit, the Prince of Bekhten permitted the priests of Khensu Pa-åri-sekher to depart with it to Egypt, and dismissed them with gifts of all kinds. In due course they arrived in Egypt and the priests took their statue to the temple of Khensu Nefer-ḥetep, and handed over to that god all the gifts which the Prince of Bekhten had given them, keeping back nothing for their own god. After this Khensu Pa-åri-sekher returned to his temple in peace, in the thirty-third year of the reign of Rameses II., having been absent from it about eight years.

VII.

A Legend of Khnemu and of a Seven Years' Famine.

The text of this most interesting legend is found in hieroglyphics on one side of a large rounded block of granite some eight or nine feet high, which stands on the south-east portion of Sâḥal, a little island lying in the First Cataract, two or three miles to the south of Elephantine Island and the modern town of Aswân. The inscription is not cut into the rock in the ordinary way, but was "stunned" on it with a blunted chisel, and is, in some lights, quite invisible to anyone standing near the rock, unless he is aware of its existence. It is in full view of the river-path which leads from Mahallah to Philae, and yet it escaped the notice of scores of travellers who have searched the rocks and islands in the Cataract for graffiti and inscriptions. The inscription, which covers a space six feet by five feet, was discovered accidentally on February 6th, 1889, by the late Mr. C. E. Wilbour, a distinguished American gentleman who spent many years in research in Egypt. He first copied the text, discovering in the course of his work the remarkable nature of its contents and then his friend Mr. Maudslay photographed it. The following year he sent prints from Mr. Maudslay's negatives to Dr. Brugsch, who in the course of 1891 published a transcript of the text with a German translation and notes in a work entitled *Die biblischen sieben Jahre der Hungersnoth*, Leipzig, 8vo.

The legend contained in this remarkable text describes a terrible famine which took place in the reign of Tcheser, a king of the IIIrd Dynasty, and lasted for seven years. Insufficient Nile-floods were, of course, the physical cause of the famine, but the legend shows that the "low Niles" were brought about by the neglect of the Egyptians in respect of the worship of the god of the First Cataract, the great god Khnemu. When, according to the legend, king Tcheser had been made to believe that the famine took place because men had ceased to worship Khnemu in a manner appropriate to his greatness, and when he had taken steps to remove the ground of complaint, the Nile rose to its accustomed height, the crops became abundant once more, and all misery caused by scarcity of provisions ceased. In other words, when Tcheser restored the offerings of Khnemu, and re-endowed his sanctuary and his priesthood, the god allowed Ḥāpi to pour forth his streams from the caverns in the Cataract, and to flood the land with abundance. The general character of the legend, as we have it here, makes it quite certain that it belongs to a late period, and the forms of the hieroglyphics and the spellings of the words indicate that the text was "stunned" on the rock in the reign of one of the Ptolemies, probably at a time when it was to the interest of some men to restore the worship of Khnemu, god of the First Cataract. These interested people could only have been the priests of Khnemu, and the probability that this was so becomes almost a certainty when we read in the latter part of the text the list of the tolls and taxes which they were empowered to levy on the merchants, farmers, miners, etc., whose goods passed down the Cataract into Egypt. Why, if this be the case, they should have chosen to connect the famine with the reign of Tcheser is not clear. They may have wished to prove the great antiquity of the worship of Khnemu, but it would have been quite easy to select the name of some king of the Ist Dynasty, and had they done this, they would have made the authority of Khnemu over the Nile coaeval with Dynastic civilization. It is impossible to assume that no great famine took place in Egypt between the reign of Tcheser and the period when the inscription was made, and when we consider this fact the choice by the editor of the legend of a famine which took place under the IIIrd Dynasty to illustrate the power of Khnemu seems inexplicable.

Of the famines which must have taken place in the Dynastic period the inscriptions tell us nothing, but the story of the seven years' famine mentioned in the Book of Genesis shows that there is nothing improbable in a famine lasting so long in Egypt. Arab historians also mention several famines which lasted for seven years. That which took place in the years 1066–1072 nearly ruined the whole country. A cake of bread was sold for 15 *dînânîr* (the *dînâr* = 10*s.*), a horse was sold for 20, a dog for 5, a cat for 3, and an egg for 1 *dînâr*. When all the animals were eaten men began to eat each other, and human flesh was sold in public. "Passengers were caught in the streets by hooks let "down from the windows, drawn up, killed, and "cooked."[1] During the famine which began in 1201 people ate human flesh habitually. Parents killed and cooked their own children, and a wife was found eating her husband raw. Baby fricassee and haggis of children's heads were ordinary articles of diet. The graves even were ransacked for food. An ox sold for 70 *dînânîr*.[2]

[1] Lane Poole, *Middle Ages*, p. 146. [2] *Ibid.*, p. 216.

The legend begins with the statement that in the 18th year of the reign of King Tcheser, when Maṭâr, the Erpā Prince and Ḥā, was the Governor of the temple properties of the South and North, and was also the Director of the Khenti men at Elephantine (Aswân), a royal despatch was delivered to him, in which the king said: "I am in misery on my throne. "My heart is very sore because of the calamity which "hath happened, for the Nile hath not come forth[1] for "seven years. There is no grain, there are no vege-"tables, there is no food, and every man is robbing his "neighbour. Men wish to walk, but they are unable "to move; the young man drags along his limbs, the "hearts of the aged are crushed with despair, their legs "fail them, they sink to the ground, and they clutch "their bodies with their hands in pain. The councillors "are dumb, and nothing but wind comes out of the "granaries when they are opened. Everything is in a "state of ruin." A more graphic picture of the misery caused by the famine could hardly be imagined. The king then goes on to ask Maṭâr where the Nile is born? what god or goddess presides over it? and what is his [or her] form? He says he would like to go to the temple of Thoth to enquire of that god, to go to the College of the Magicians, and search through the sacred books in order to find out these things.

When Maṭâr had read the despatch, he set out to go to the king, and explained to him the things which

[1] I.e., there have been insufficient Nile-floods.

he wished to know. He told him that the Nile rose near the city of Elephantine, that it flowed out of two caverns, which were the breasts of the Nile-god, that it rose to a height of twenty-eight cubits at Elephantine, and to the height of seven cubits at Sma-Beḥuṭet, or, Diospolis Parva in the Delta. He who controlled the Nile was Khnemu, and when this god drew the bolt of the doors which shut in the stream, and smote the earth with his sandals, the river rushed forth. Maṭâr also described to the king the form of Khnemu, which was that of Shu, and the work which he did, and the wooden house in which he lived, and its exact position, which was near the famous granite quarries. The gods who dwelt with Khnemu were the goddess Sepṭ (Sothis, or the Dog-star), the goddess Ānqet, Ḥāp (or Ḥep), the Nile-god, Shu, Ḳeb, Nut, Osiris, Isis, Nephthys, and Horus. Thus we see that the priests of Khnemu made him to be the head of a Company of Gods. Finally Maṭâr gave the king a list of all the stones, precious and otherwise, which were found in and about Elephantine.

When the king, who had, it seems, come to Elephantine, heard these things he rejoiced greatly, and he went into the temple of Khnemu. The priests drew back the curtains and sprinkled him with holy water, and then he passed into the shrine and offered up a great sacrifice of bread-cakes, beer, geese, oxen, and all kinds of good things, to the gods and goddesses who dwelt at Elephantine, in the place called "Couch of the heart in life and power." Suddenly he found himself standing face to face with the god Khnemu, whom he placated with a peace-offering and with prayer. Then the god opened his eyes, and bent his body towards the king, and spake to him mighty words, saying, "I am "Khnemu, who made thee. My hands knitted together "thy body and made it sound, and I gave thee thy "heart." Khnemu then went on to complain that, although the ground under the king's feet was filled with stones and metal, men were too inert to work them and to employ them in repairing or rebuilding of the shrines of the gods, or in doing what they ought to do for him, their Lord and Creator. These words were, of course, meant as a rebuke for the king, who evidently, though it is not so stated in the text, was intended by Khnemu to undertake the rebuilding of his shrine without delay. The god then went on to proclaim his majesty and power, and declared himself to be Nu, the Celestial Ocean, and the Nile-god, "who "came into being at the beginning, and riseth at his "will to give health to him that laboureth for Khnemu." He described himself as the Father of the gods, the Governor of the earth and of men, and then he promised the king to make the Nile rise yearly, regularly, and unceasingly, to give abundant harvests, to give all people their heart's desire, to make misery to pass away, to fill the granaries, and to make the whole land of Egypt yellow with waving fields of full ripe grain. When the king, who had been in a dream, heard the god mention crops, he woke up, and his courage returned to him, and having cast away despair from his heart he issued a decree by which he made ample provision for the maintenance of the worship of the god in a fitting state. In this decree, the first copy of which was cut upon wood, the king endowed Khnemu with 20 schoinoi of land on each side of the river, with gardens, etc. It was further enacted that every man who drew water from the Nile for his land should contribute a portion of his crops to the god. Fishermen, fowlers, and hunters were to pay an octroi duty of one-tenth of the value of their catches when they brought them into the city, and a tithe of the cattle was to be set apart for the daily sacrifice. The masters of caravans coming from the Sûdân were to pay a tithe also, but they were not liable to any further tax in the country northwards. Every metal-worker, ore-crusher, miner, mason, and handicraftsman of every kind, was to pay to the temple of the god one-tenth of the value of the material produced or worked by his labour. The decree provided also for the appointment of an inspector whose duty it would be to weigh the gold, silver, and copper which came into the town of Elephantine, and to assess the value both of these metals and of the precious stones, etc., which were to be devoted to the service of Khnemu. All materials employed in making the images of the gods, and all handicraftsmen employed in the work were exempted from tithing. In short, the worship of the god and his company was to be maintained according to ancient use and wont, and the people were to supply the temple with everything necessary in a generous spirit and with a liberal hand. He who failed in any way to comply with the enactments was to be beaten with the rope, and the name of Tcheser was to be perpetuated in the temple.

VIII.

The Legend of the Death and Resurrection of Horus, and other Magical Texts.

The magical and religious texts of the Egyptians of all periods contain spells intended to be used against serpents, scorpions, and noxious reptiles of all kinds, and their number, and the importance which was attached to them, suggest that Egypt must always have produced these pests in abundance, and that the Egyptians were always horribly afraid of them. The text of Unȧs, which was written towards the close of the Vth Dynasty, contains many such spells, and in the Theban and Saïte Books of the Dead several Chapters consist of nothing but spells and incantations, many of which are based on archaic texts, against crocodiles, serpents, and other deadly reptiles, and insects of all kinds. All such creatures were regarded

The Metternich Stele—Obverse.

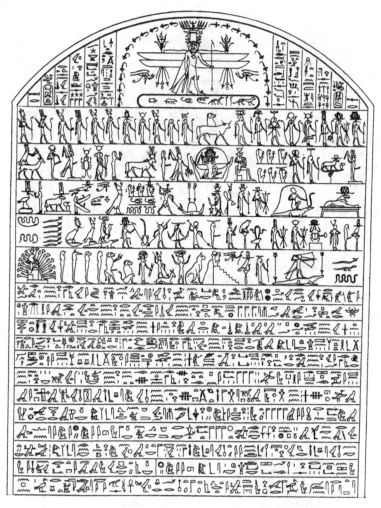

The Metternich Stele—Reverse.

as incarnations of evil spirits, which attack the dead as well as the living, and therefore it was necessary for the well-being of the former that copies of spells against them should be written upon the walls of tombs, coffins, funerary amulets, etc. The gods were just as open to the attacks of venomous reptiles as man, and Rā himself, the king of the gods, nearly died from the poison of a snake-bite. Now the gods were, as a rule, able to defend themselves against the attacks of Set and his fiends, and the poisonous snakes and insects which were their emissaries, by virtue of the "fluid of life," 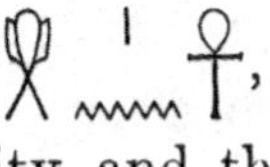, which was the peculiar attribute of divinity, and the efforts of Egyptians were directed to the acquisition of a portion of this magical power, which would protect their souls and bodies and their houses and cattle, and other property, each day and each night throughout the year. When a man cared for the protection of himself only he wore an amulet of some kind, in which the  was localized. When he wished to protect his house against invasion by venomous reptiles he placed statues containing the  in niches in the walls of various chambers, or in some place outside but near the house, or buried them in the earth with their faces turned in the direction from which he expected the attack to come.

Towards the close of the XXVIth Dynasty, when superstition in its most exaggerated form was general in Egypt, it became the custom to make house talismans in the form of small stone stelae, with rounded tops, which rested on bases having convex fronts. On the front of such a talisman was sculptured in relief a figure of Horus the Child (Harpokrates), standing on two crocodiles, holding in his hands figures of serpents, scorpions, a lion, and a horned animal, each of these being a symbol of an emissary or ally of Set, the god of Evil. Above his head was the head of Bes, and on each side of him were solar symbols, i.e., the lily of Nefer-Tem, figures of Rā and Harmakhis, the Eyes of Rā (the Sun and Moon), etc. The reverse of the stele and the whole of the base were covered with magical texts and spells, and when a talisman of this kind was placed in a house, it was supposed to be directly under the protection of Horus and his companion gods, who had vanquished all the hosts of darkness and all the powers of physical and moral evil. Many examples of this talisman are to be seen in the great Museums of Europe, and there are several fine specimens in the Third Egyptian Room in the British Museum. They are usually called "Cippi of Horus." The largest and most important of all these "cippi" is that which is commonly known as the "Metternich Stele," because it was given to Prince Metternich by Muḥammad 'Ali Pâshâ; it was dug up in 1828 during the building of a cistern in a Franciscan Monastery in Alexandria, and was first published, with a translation of a large part of the text, by Professor

Golénischeff.[1] The importance of the stele is enhanced by the fact that it mentions the name of the king in whose reign it was made, viz., Nectanebus I., who reigned from B.C. 378 to B.C. 360.

The obverse, reverse, and two sides of the Metternich Stele have cut upon them nearly three hundred figures of gods and celestial beings. These include figures of the great gods of heaven, earth, and the Other World, figures of the gods of the planets and the Dekans, figures of the gods of the days of the week, of the weeks, and months, and seasons of the year, and of the year. Besides these there are a number of figures of local forms of the gods which it is difficult to identify. On the rounded portion of the obverse the place of honour is held by the solar disk, in which is seen a figure of Khnemu with four ram's heads, which rests between a pair of arms, 𓂓, and is supported on a lake of celestial water; on each side of it are four of the spirits of the dawn, and on the right stands the symbol of the rising sun, Nefer-Temu, and on the left stands Thoth. Below this are five rows of small figures of gods. Below these is Harpokrates in relief, in the attitude already described. He stands on two crocodiles under a kind of canopy, the sides of which are supported by Thoth and Isis, and holds Typhonic animals and reptiles. Above the canopy are the two Eyes of Rā,

[1] See *Metternichstele*, Leipzig, 1877. The Stele was made for Ānkh-Psemthek, son of the lady Tent-Ḥet-nub, prophet of Nebun, overseer of Temt and scribe of Ḥet (see line 87).

each having a pair of human arms and hands. On the right of Harpokrates are Seker and Horus, and on his left the symbol of Nefer-Temu. On the left and right are the goddesses Nekhebet and Uatchet, who guard the South of Egypt and the North respectively. On the reverse and sides are numerous small figures of gods. This stele represented the power to protect man possessed by all the divine beings in the universe, and, however it was placed, it formed an impassable barrier to every spirit of evil and to every venomous reptile. The spells, which are cut in hieroglyphics on all the parts of the stele not occupied by figures of gods, were of the most potent character, for they contained the actual words by which the gods vanquished the powers of darkness and evil. These spells form the texts which are printed on p. 142 ff., and may be thus summarized:—

The first spell is an incantation directed against reptiles and noxious creatures in general. The chief of these was Āpep, the great enemy of Rā, who took the form of a huge serpent that "resembled the intestines," and the spell doomed him to decapitation, and burning, and hacking in pieces. These things would be effected by Serqet, the Scorpion-goddess. The second part of the spell was directed against the poison of Āpep, and was to be recited over anyone who was bitten by a snake. When uttered by Horus it made Āpep to vomit, and when used by a magician properly qualified would make the bitten person to vomit, and so free his body from the poison.

The next spell is directed to be said to the Cat, i.e., a symbol of the daughter of Rā, or Isis, who had the head of Rā, the eyes of the uraeus, the nose of Thoth, the ears of Neb-er-tcher, the mouth of Tem, the neck of Neḥeb-ka, the breast of Thoth, the heart of Rā, the hands of the gods, the belly of Osiris, the thighs of Menthu, the legs of Khensu, the feet of Åmen-Horus, the haunches of Horus, the soles of the feet of Rā, and the bowels of Meḥ-urit. Every member of the Cat contained a god or goddess, and she was able to destroy the poison of any serpent, or scorpion, or reptile, which might be injected into her body. The spell opens with an address to Rā, who is entreated to come to his daughter, who has been stung by a scorpion on a lonely road, and to cause the poison to leave her body. Thus it seems as if Isis, the great magician, was at some time stung by a scorpion.

The next section is very difficult to understand. Rā-Harmakhis is called upon to come to his daughter, and Shu to his wife, and Isis to her sister, who has been poisoned. Then the Aged One, i.e., Rā, is asked to let Thoth turn back Neḥa-ḥer, or Set. "Osiris is "in the water, but Horus is with him, and the Great "Beetle overshadows him," and every evil spirit which dwells in the water is adjured to allow Horus to proceed to Osiris. Rā, Sekhet, Thoth, and Ḥeka, this last-named being the spell personified, are the four great gods who protect Osiris, and who will blind and choke his enemies, and cut out their tongues. The cry of the Cat is again referred to, and Rā is asked if he does not remember the cry which came from the bank of Neṭit. The allusion here is to the cries which Isis uttered when she arrived at Neṭit near Abydos, and found lying there the dead body of her husband.

At this point on the Stele the spells are interrupted by a long narrative put into the mouth of Isis, which supplies us with some account of the troubles that she suffered, and describes the death of Horus through the sting of a scorpion. Isis, it seems, was shut up in some dwelling by Set after he murdered Osiris, probably with the intention of forcing her to marry him, and so assist him to legalize his seizure of the kingdom. Isis, as we have already seen, had been made pregnant by her husband after his death, and Thoth now appeared to her, and advised her to hide herself with her unborn child, and to bring him forth in secret, and he promised her that her son should succeed in due course to his father's throne. With the help of Thoth she escaped from her captivity, and went forth accompanied by the Seven Scorpion-goddesses, who brought her to the town of Per-Sui, on the edge of the Reed Swamps. She applied to a woman for a night's shelter, but the woman shut her door in her face. To punish her one of the Scorpion-goddesses forced her way into the woman's house, and stung her child to death. The grief of the woman was so bitter and sympathy-compelling that Isis laid her hands on the child, and, having uttered one of her most potent spells over him, the poison of the scorpion ran out of his body, and the child came to life again. The words of the spell are cut on the Stele, and they were treasured by the Egyptians as an infallible remedy for scorpion stings. When the woman saw that her son had been brought back to life by Isis, she was filled with joy and gratitude, and, as a mark of her repentance, she brought large quantities of things from her house as gifts for Isis, and they were so many that they filled the house of the kind, but poor, woman who had given Isis shelter.

Now soon after Isis had restored to life the son of the woman who had shown churlishness to her, a terrible calamity fell upon her, for her beloved son Horus was stung by a scorpion and died. The news of this event was conveyed to her by the gods, who cried out to her to come to see her son Horus, whom the terrible scorpion Uḥāt had killed. Isis, stabbed with pain at the news, as if a knife had been driven into her body, ran out distraught with grief. It seems that she had gone to perform a religious ceremony in honour of Osiris in a temple near Ḥetep-ḥemt, leaving her child carefully concealed in Sekhet-Ȧn. During her absence the scorpion Uḥāt, which had been sent by Set, forced its way into the hiding-place of Horus, and there stung him to death. When Isis came and found the dead body, she burst forth in lamentations, the sound of which brought all the people from the neighbouring districts to her side. As she related to them the history of her sufferings they endeavoured to console her, and when they found this to be impossible they lifted up their voices and wept with her. Then Isis placed her nose in the mouth of Horus so that she might discover if he still breathed, but there was no breath in his throat; and when she examined the wound in his body made by the fiend Ȧun-ȧb she saw in it traces of poison. No doubt about his death then remained in her mind, and clasping him in her arms she lifted him up, and in her transports of grief leaped about like fish when they are laid on red-hot coals. Then she uttered a series of heart-breaking laments, each of which begins with the words "Horus is bitten." The heir of heaven, the son of Un-Nefer, the child of the gods, he who was wholly fair, is bitten! He for whose wants I provided, he who was to avenge his father, is bitten! He for whom I cared and suffered when he was being fashioned in my womb, is bitten! He whom I tended so that I might gaze upon him, is bitten! He whose life I prayed for is bitten! Calamity hath overtaken the child, and he hath perished.

Whilst Isis was saying these and many similar words, her sister Nephthys, who had been weeping bitterly for her nephew Horus as she wandered about among the swamps, came, in company with the Scorpion-goddess Serqet, and advised Isis to pray to heaven for help. Pray that the sailors in the Boat of Rā may cease from rowing, for the Boat cannot travel onwards whilst Horus lies dead. Then Isis cried out to heaven, and her voice reached the Boat of Millions of Years, and the Disk ceased to move onward, and came to a standstill. From the Boat Thoth descended, being equipped with words of power and spells of all kinds, and bearing with him the "great command of *maā-kheru*," i.e., the WORD, whose commands were performed, instantly and completely, by every god, spirit, fiend, human being, and by every thing, animate and inanimate, in heaven, earth, and the Other World. Then he came to Isis and told her that no harm could possibly have happened to Horus, for he was under the protection of the Boat of Rā; but his words failed to comfort Isis, and though she acknowledged the greatness of his designs, she complained that they savoured of delay. "What is the good," she asks, "of all thy "spells, and incantations, and magical formulae, and the "great command of *maā-kheru*, if Horus is to perish "by the poison of a scorpion, and to lie here in the "arms of Death? Evil, evil is his destiny, for it hath "entailed the deepest misery for him and death."

In answer to these words Thoth, turning to Isis and Nephthys, bade them to fear not, and to have no anxiety about Horus, "For," said he, "I have come "from heaven to heal the child for his mother." He then pointed out that Horus was under protection as the Dweller in his Disk (Åten), the Great Dwarf, the Mighty Ram, the Great Hawk, the Holy Beetle, the Hidden Body, the Divine Bennu, etc., and proceeded to utter the great spell which restored Horus to life. By his words of power Thoth transferred the "fluid of life" of Rā, and as soon as this came upon the child's body the poison of the scorpion flowed out of him, and he once more breathed and lived. When this was done Thoth returned to the Boat of Rā, the gods who formed its crew resumed their rowing, and the Disk passed on its way to make its daily journey across the sky. The gods in heaven, who were amazed and uttered cries of terror when they heard of the death of Horus, were made happy once more, and sang songs of joy over his recovery. The happiness of Isis in her child's restoration to life was very great, for she could again hope that he would avenge his father's murder, and occupy his throne. The final words of Thoth comforted her greatly, for he told her that he would take charge of the case of Horus in the Judgment Hall of Ȧnu, wherein Osiris had been judged, and that as his advocate he would make any accusations which might be brought against Horus to recoil on him that brought them. Furthermore, he would give Horus power to repulse any attacks which might be made upon him by beings in the heights above, or fiends in the depths below, and would ensure his succession to the Throne of the Two Lands, i.e., Egypt. Thoth also promised Isis that Rā himself should act as the advocate of Horus, even as he had done for his father Osiris. He was also careful to allude to the share which Isis had taken in the restoration of Horus to life, saying, "It is the words "of power of his mother which have lifted up his face, "and they shall enable him to journey wheresoever "he pleaseth, and to put fear into the powers above. "I myself hasten [to obey them]." Thus everything turned on the power of the spells of Isis, who made the sun to stand still, and caused the dead to be raised.

Such are the contents of the texts on the famous Metternich Stele. There appears to be some confusion in their arrangement, and some of them clearly are misplaced, and, in places, the text is manifestly corrupt. It is impossible to explain several passages, for we do not understand all the details of the system of magic which they represent. Still, the general meaning of the texts on the Stele is quite clear, and they record a legend of Isis and Horus which is not found so fully described on any other monument.

IX.

The History of Isis and Osiris.

The history of Isis and Osiris given on pp. 198–248 is taken from the famous treatise of Plutarch entitled *De Iside et Osiride,* and forms a fitting conclusion to this volume of Legends of the Gods. It contains all the essential facts given in Plutarch's work, and the only things omitted are his derivations and mythological speculations, which are really unimportant for the Egyptologist. Egyptian literature is full of allusions to events which took place in the life of Osiris, and to his persecution, murder, and resurrection, and numerous texts of all periods describe the love and devotion of his sister and wife Isis, and the filial piety of Horus. Nowhere, however, have we in Egyptian a connected account of the causes which led to the murder by Set of Osiris, or of the subsequent events which resulted in his becoming the king of heaven and judge of the dead. However carefully we piece together the fragments of information which we can extract from native Egyptian literature, there still remains a series of gaps which can only be filled by guesswork. Plutarch, as a learned man and a student of comparative religion and mythology, was most anxious to understand the history of Isis and Osiris, which Greek and Roman scholars talked about freely, and which none of them comprehended, and he made enquiries of priests and others, and examined critically such information as he could obtain, believing and hoping that he would penetrate the mystery in which these gods were wrapped. As a result of his labours he collected a number of facts about the form of the Legend of Isis and Osiris as it was known to the learned men of his day, but there is no evidence that he had the slightest knowledge of the details of the original African Legend of these gods as it was known to the Egyptians, say, under the VIth Dynasty. Moreover, he never realized that the characteristics and attributes of both Isis and Osiris changed several times during the long history of Egypt, and that a thousand years before he lived the Egyptians themselves had forgotten what the original form of the legend was. They preserved a number of ceremonies, and performed very carefully all the details of an ancient ritual at the annual commemoration festival of Osiris which was held in November and December, but the evidence of the texts makes it quite clear that the meaning and symbolism of nearly all the details were unknown alike to priests and people.

An important modification of the cult of Isis and Osiris took place in the third century before Christ, when the Ptolemies began to consolidate their rule in Egypt. A form of religion which would be acceptable both to Egyptians and Greeks had to be provided, and this was produced by modifying the characteristics of Osiris and calling him Sarapis, and identifying him with the Greek Pluto. To Isis were added many of the attributes of the great Greek goddesses, and into her worship were introduced "mysteries" derived from non-Egyptian cults, which made it acceptable to the people everywhere. Had a high priest of Osiris who lived at Abydos under the XVIIIth Dynasty witnessed the celebration of the great festival of Isis and Osiris in any large town in the first century before Christ, it is tolerably certain that he would have regarded it as a lengthy act of worship of strange gods, in which there appeared, here and there, ceremonies and phrases which reminded him of the ancient Abydos ritual. When the form of the cult of Isis and Osiris introduced by the Ptolemies into Egypt extended to the great cities of Greece and Italy, still further modifications took place in it, and the characters of Isis and Osiris were still further changed. By degrees Osiris came to be regarded as the god of death pure and simple, or as the personification of Death, and he ceased to be regarded as the great protecting ancestral spirit, and the all-powerful protecting Father of his people. As the importance of Osiris declined that of Isis grew, and men came to regard her as the great Mother-goddess of the world. The priests described from tradition the great facts of her life according to the Egyptian legends, how she had been a loving and devoted wife, how she had gone forth after her husband's murder by Set to seek for his body, how she had found it and brought it home, how she revivified it by her spells and had union with Osiris and conceived by him, and how in due course she brought forth her son, in pain and sorrow and loneliness in the Swamps of the Delta, and how she reared him and watched over him until he was old enough to fight and vanquish his father's murderer, and how at length she seated him in triumph on his father's throne. These things endeared Isis to the people everywhere, and as she herself had not suffered death like Osiris, she came to be regarded as the eternal mother of life and of all living things. She was the creatress of crops, she produced fruit, vegetables, plants of all kinds and trees, she made cattle prolific, she brought men and women together and gave them offspring, she was the authoress of all love, virtue, goodness and happiness. She made the light to shine, she was the spirit of the Dog-star which heralded the Nile-flood, she was the source of the power in the beneficent light of the moon; and finally she took the dead to her bosom and gave them peace, and introduced them to a life of immortality and happiness similar to that which she had bestowed upon Osiris.

The message of the cult of Isis as preached by her priests was one of hope and happiness, and coming to the Greeks and Romans, as it did, at a time when men were weary of their national cults, and when the speculations of the philosophers carried no weight with the general public, the people everywhere welcomed it with the greatest enthusiasm. From Egypt it was carried to the Islands of Greece and to the mainland, to Italy, Germany, France, Spain and Portugal, and then crossing the western end of the Mediterranean it entered North Africa, and with Carthage as a centre spread east and west along the coast. Wherever the cult of Isis came men accepted it as something which supplied what they thought to be lacking in their native cults; rich and poor, gentle and simple, all welcomed it, and the philosopher as well as the ignorant man rejoiced in the hope of a future life which it gave to them. Its Egyptian origin caused it to be regarded with the profoundest interest, and its priests were most careful to make the temples of Isis quite different from those of the national gods, and to decorate them with obelisks, sphinxes, shrines, altars, etc., which were either imported from temples in Egypt, or were copied from Egyptian originals. In the temples of Isis services were held at daybreak and in the early afternoon daily, and everywhere these were attended by crowds of people. The holy water used in the libations and for sprinkling the people was Nile water, specially imported from Egypt, and to the votaries of the goddess it symbolized the seed of the god Osiris, which germinated and brought forth fruit through the spells of the goddess Isis. The festivals and processions of Isis were everywhere most popular, and were enjoyed by learned and unlearned alike. In fact, the Isis-play which was acted annually in November, and the festival of the blessing of the ship, which took place in the spring, were the most important festivals of the year. Curiously enough, all the oldest gods and goddesses of Egypt passed into absolute oblivion, with the exception of Osiris (Sarapis), Isis, Anubis the physician, and Harpokrates, the child of Osiris and Isis, and these, from being the ancestral spirits of a comparatively obscure African tribe in early dynastic times, became for several hundreds of years the principal objects of worship of some of the most cultured and intellectual nations. The treatise of Plutarch *De Iside* helps to explain how this came about, and for those who study the Egyptian Legend of Isis and Osiris the work has considerable importance.

LEGENDS OF EGYPTIAN GODS

THE HISTORY OF CREATION—A.

[1] *Kheperu.* The verb KHEPER means "to make, to form, to produce, to become, and to roll"; *kheperu* here means "the things which come into being through the rollings of the ball of the god Kheper (the roller)," i.e., the Sun.

[2] I.e., serpents and snakes, or perhaps plants.

THE HISTORY OF CREATION—A.

The Book of knowing the evolutions[1] of Rā, and of overthrowing Āpep. [These are] the words which the god Neb-er-tcher spake after he had come into being:—"I am he who came into being in "the form of the god Kheperȧ, and I am the creator "of that which came into being, that is to say, I am "the creator of everything which came into being; "now the things which I created, and which came "forth out of my mouth after that I had come into "being myself were exceedingly many. The sky (or, "heaven) had not come into being, the earth did not "exist, and the children of the earth,[2] and the creep-"ing things, had not been made at that time. I "myself raised them up from out of Nu,[3] from a state "of helpless inertness. I found no place whereon I "could stand. I worked a charm[4] upon my own "heart (or, will), I laid the foundation [of things] by "Maāt,[5] and I made everything which had form. I "was [then] one by myself, for I had not emitted from "myself the god Shu, and I had not spit out from "myself the goddess Tefnut; and there existed no

[3] The primeval watery mass which was the source and origin of all beings and things. [4] I.e., he uttered a magical formula.

[5] I.e., by exact and definite rules.

"other who could work with me. I laid the "foundations [of things] in my own heart, and "there came into being multitudes of created "things, which came into being from the created "things which were born from the created things "which arose from what they brought forth. I "had union with my closed hand, and I embraced "my shadow as a wife, and I poured seed into "my own mouth, and I sent forth from myself "issue in the form of the gods Shu and Tefnut. "Saith my father Nu:—My Eye was covered up "behind them (i.e., Shu and Tefnut), but after "two *hen* periods had passed from the time when "they departed from me, from being one god I "became three gods, and I came into being in "the earth. Then Shu and Tefnut rejoiced from "out of the inert watery mass wherein they "were, and they brought to me my Eye (i.e., "the Sun). Now after these things I gathered "together my members, and I wept over them, "and men and women sprang into being from "the tears which came forth from my Eye. "And when my Eye came to me, and found "that I had made another [Eye] in place where "it was (i.e., the Moon), it was wroth with (or, "raged at) me, whereupon I endowed it (i.e., the "second Eye) with [some of] the splendour which "I had made for the first [Eye], and I made it "to occupy its place in my Face, and henceforth

THE HISTORY OF CREATION—B.

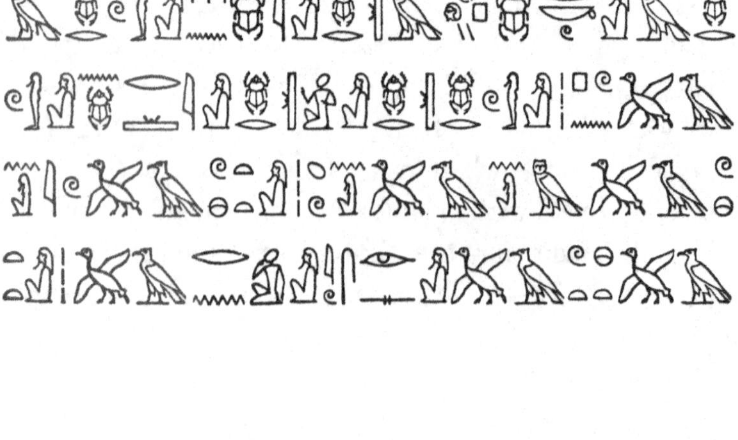

"it ruled throughout all this earth. When there fell "on them their moment[1] through plant-like clouds, "I restored what had been taken away from them, "and I appeared from out of the plant-like clouds. "I created creeping things of every kind, and every "thing which came into being from them. Shu and "Tefnut brought forth [Seb and] Nut; and Seb and "Nut brought forth Osiris, and Ḥeru-khent-ȧn-maati,[2] "and Set, and Isis, and Nephthys at one birth,[3] one "after the other, and they produced their multitudinous "offspring in this earth."

THE HISTORY OF CREATION—B.

The Book of knowing the evolutions of Rā, and of overthrowing Āpep. [These are] the words of the god Neb-er-tcher, who said:— "I am the creator of what hath come into being, "and I myself came into being under the form "of the god Kheperȧ, and I came into being in "primeval time. I came into being in the form of "Kheperȧ, and I am the creator of what did come "into being, that is to say, I formed myself out "of the primeval matter, and I made and formed "myself out of the substance which existed in "primeval time. My name is Ȧusȧres (i.e., Osiris), "who is the primeval matter of primeval matter.

[1] I.e., the period of calamity wherein their light was veiled through plant-like clouds.
[2] I.e., the Blind Horus.
[3] I.e., these five gods were all born at one time.

"I have done my will in everything in this earth. "I have spread myself abroad therein, and I have "made strong my hand. I was ONE by myself, for "they (i.e., the gods) had not been brought forth, "and I had emitted from myself neither Shu nor "Tefnut. I brought my own name[1] into my mouth "as a word of power, and I forthwith came into "being under the form of things which are and under "the form of Kheperȧ. I came into being from "out of primeval matter, and from the beginning I "appeared under the form of the multitudinous "things which exist; nothing whatsoever existed at "that time in this earth, and it was I who made "whatsoever was made. I was ONE by myself, and "there was no other being who worked with me in "that place. I made all the things under the forms "of which I appeared then by means of the Soul-God "which I raised into firmness at that time from out "of Nu, from a state of inactivity. I found no place "whatsoever there whereon I could stand, I worked "by the power of a spell by means of my heart, I laid "a foundation [for things] before me, and whatsoever "was made, I made. I was ONE by myself, and I laid "the foundation of things [by means of] my heart, and "I made the other things which came into being, and "the things of Kheperȧ which were made were mani-"fold, and their offspring came into existence from "the things to which they gave birth. I it was who

[1] I.e., I uttered my own name from my own mouth as a word of power.

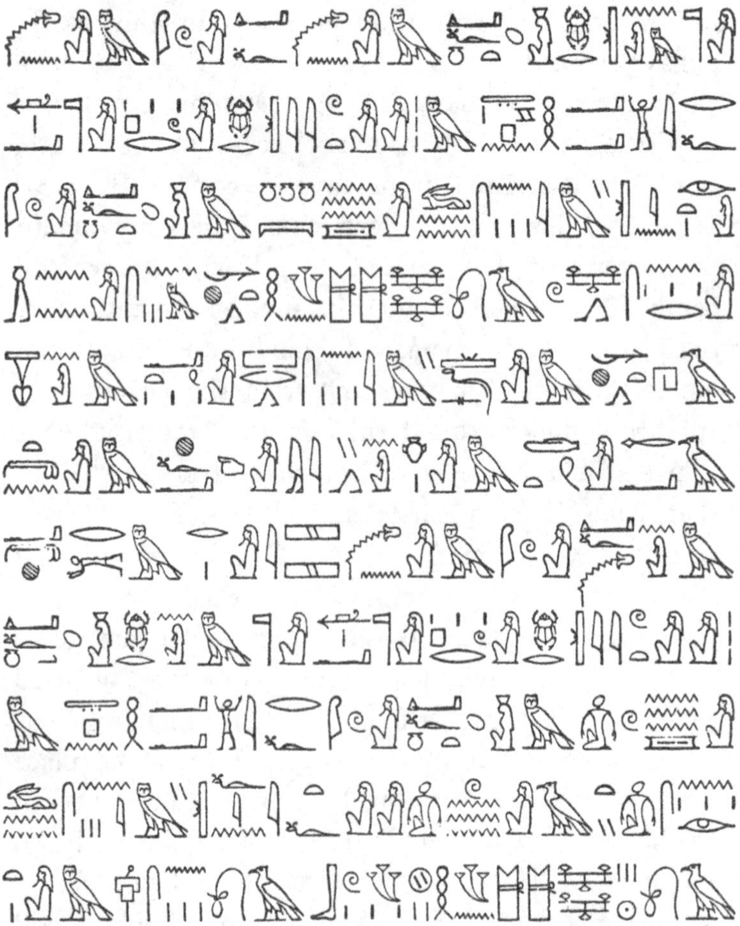

"emitted Shu, and I it was who emitted Tefnut, "and from being the ONE god (or, the only god) "I became three gods; the two other gods who "came into being on this earth sprang from me, "and Shu and Tefnut rejoiced (or, were raised "up) from out of Nu in which they were. Now "behold, they brought my Eye to me after two "*ḥen* periods since the time when they went forth "from me. I gathered together my members "which had appeared in my own body, and after-"wards I had union with my hand, and my heart "(or, will) came unto me from out of my hand, "and the seed fell into my mouth, and I emitted "from myself the gods Shu and Tefnut, and so "from being the ONE god (or, the only god) I "became three gods; thus the two other gods "who came into being on this earth sprang from "me, and Shu and Tefnut rejoiced (or, were raised "up) from out of Nu in which they were. My "father Nu saith:—They covered up (or, concealed) "my Eye with the plant-like clouds which were "behind them (i.e., Shu and Tefnut) for very many "*ḥen* periods. Plants and creeping things [sprang "up] from the god REM, through the tears which "I let fall. I cried out to my Eye, and men and "women came into existence. Then I bestowed "upon my Eye the uraeus of fire, and it was wroth "with me when another Eye (i.e., the Moon) came "and grew up in its place; its vigorous power fell

"on the plants, on the plants which I had placed "there, and it set order among them, and it took up "its place in my face, and it doth rule the whole "earth. Then Shu and Tefnut brought forth Osiris, "and Ḥeru-khenti-ȧn-maa, and Set, and Isis, and "Nephthys, and behold, they have produced off- "spring, and have created multitudinous children in "this earth, by means of the beings which came into "existence from the creatures which they produced. "They invoke my name, and they overthrow their "enemies, and they make words of power for the "overthrowing of Apep, over whose hands and arms "AKER keepeth ward. His hands and arms shall "not exist, his feet and legs shall not exist, and he is "chained in one place whilst Rā inflicts upon him "the blows which are decreed for him. He is thrown "upon his accursed back, his face is slit open by "reason of the evil which he hath done, and he shall "remain upon his accursed back."

THE LEGEND OF THE DESTRUCTION OF MANKIND.

THE LEGEND OF THE DESTRUCTION OF MANKIND.

[Here is the story of Rā,] the god who was self-begotten and self-created, after he had assumed the sovereignty over men and women, and gods, and things, the ONE god. Now men and women were speaking words of complaint, saying:—"Behold, "his Majesty (Life, Strength, and Health to him!) "hath grown old, and his bones have become like "silver, and his members have turned into gold and "his hair is like unto real lapis-lazuli." His Majesty heard the words of complaint which men and women were uttering, and his Majesty (Life, Strength, and Health to him!) said unto those who were in his train:—"Cry out, and bring to me my Eye, and "Shu, and Tefnut, and Seb, and Nut, and the "father-gods, and the mother-gods who were with "me, even when I was in Nu side by side with my "god Nu. Let there be brought along with my Eye "his ministers, and let them be led to me hither "secretly, so that men and women may not perceive "them [coming] hither, and may not therefore take "to flight with their hearts. Come thou[1] with them

[1] The god here addressed appears to have been Nu.

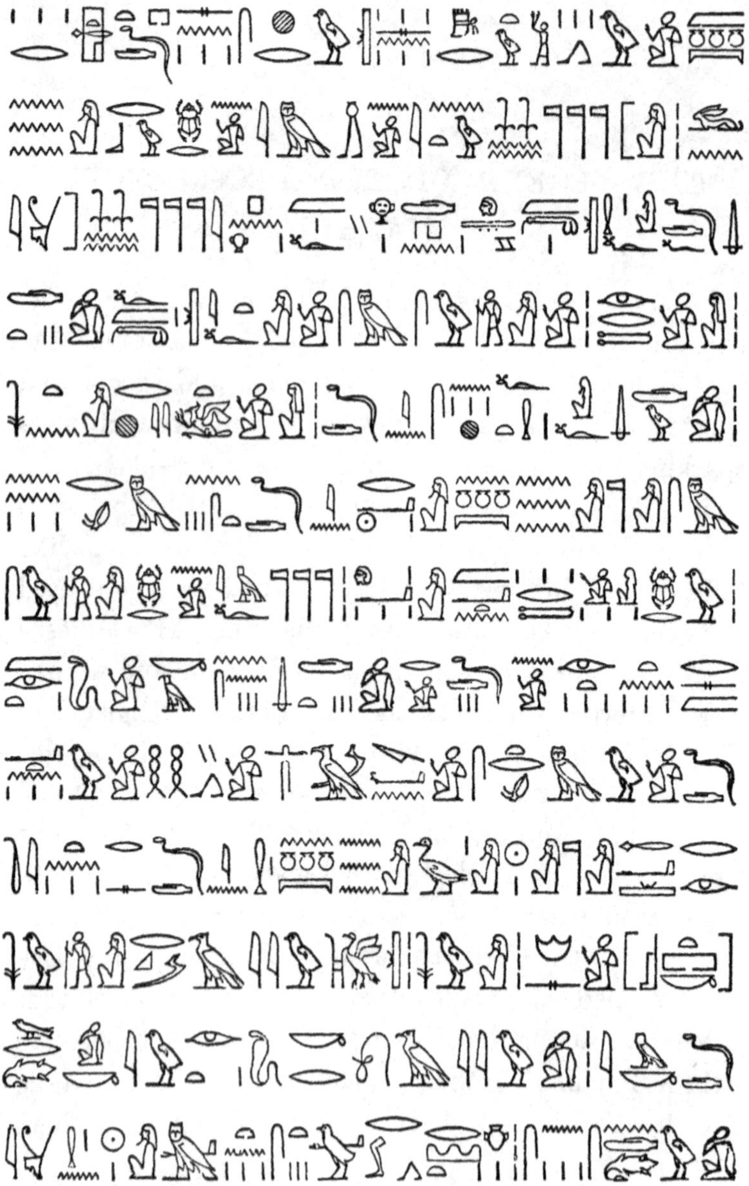

"to the Great House, and let them declare their "plans (or, arrangements) fully, for I will go from "Nu into the place wherein I brought about my own "existence, and let those gods be brought unto me "there." Now the gods were drawn up on each side of Rā, and they bowed down before his Majesty until their heads touched the ground, and the maker of men and women, the king of those who have knowledge, spake his words in the presence of the Father of the first-born gods. And the gods spake in the presence of his Majesty, saying:—"Speak unto us, "for we are listening to them" (i.e., thy words). Then Rā spake unto Nu, saying:—"O thou first-"born god from whom I came into being, O ye gods "of ancient time, my ancestors, take ye heed to what "men and women [are doing]; for behold, those who "were created by my Eye are uttering words of com-"plaint against me. Tell me what ye would do in "the matter, and consider this thing for me, and seek "out [a plan] for me, for I will not slay them until I "have heard what ye shall say to me concerning it."

Then the Majesty of Nu, to son Rā, spake, saying:—"Thou art the god who art greater than he "who made thee, thou art the sovereign of those who "were created with thee, thy throne is set, and the "fear of thee is great; let thine Eye go against those "who have uttered blasphemies against thee." And the Majesty of Rā said:—"Behold, they have betaken "themselves to flight into the mountain lands, for their

"hearts are afraid because of the words which they "have uttered." Then the gods spake in the presence of his Majesty, saying:—"Let thine Eye go forth "and let it destroy for thee those who revile thee "with words of evil, for there is no eye whatsoever "that can go before it and resist thee and it when it "journeyeth in the form of Hathor." Thereupon this goddess went forth and slew the men and the women who were on the mountain (or, desert land). And the Majesty of this god said, "Come, come in "peace, O Hathor, for the work is accomplished." Then this goddess said, "Thou hast made me to "live, for when I gained the mastery over men and "women it was sweet to my heart;" and the Majesty of Rā said, "I myself will be master over them as "[their] king, and I will destroy them." And it came to pass that Sekhet of the offerings waded about in the night season in their blood, beginning at Suten-ḥenen.[1] Then the Majesty of Rā spake [saying], "Cry out, and let there come to me swift "and speedy messengers who shall be able to run "like the wind . . . .;" and straightway messengers of this [kind were brought unto him. And the Majesty of this god spake [saying], "Let these "messengers go to Ābu,[2] and bring unto me man-"drakes in great numbers;" and [when] these

[1] Or, Ḥenen-su, חָנֵס, i.e., Herakleopolis Magna.

[2] I.e., Elephantine, or Syene, a place better known by the Arabic name Aswân.

mandrakes were brought unto him the Majesty of this god gave them to Sekhet, the goddess who dwelleth in Ȧnnu (Heliopolis) to crush. And behold, when the maidservants were bruising the grain for [making] beer, these mandrakes were placed in the vessels which were to hold the beer, and some of the blood of the men and women [who had been slain]. Now they made seven thousand vessels of beer. Now when the Majesty of Rā, the King of the South and North, had come with the gods to look at the vessels of beer, and behold, the daylight had appeared after the slaughter of men and women by the goddess in their season as she sailed up the river, the Majesty of Rā said, "It is good, it is "good, nevertheless I must protect men and women "against her." And Rā said, "Let them take up "the vases and carry them to the place where the "men and women were slaughtered by her." Then the Majesty of the King of the South and North in the three-fold beauty of the night caused to be poured out these vases of beer which make [men] to lie down (or, sleep), and the meadows of the Four Heavens[1] were filled with beer (or, water) by reason of the Souls of the Majesty of this god. And it came to pass that when this goddess arrived at the dawn of day, she found these [Heavens] flooded [with beer], and she was pleased thereat; and

[1] I.e., the South, North, West, and East of the sky.

[1] I.e., "the fair and gracious goddess."

[2] Literally, "My heart hath stopped greatly."

she drank [of the beer and blood], and her heart rejoiced, and she became drunk, and she gave no further attention to men and women. Then said the Majesty of Rā to this goddess, "Come in peace, come "in peace, O Amit,"[1] and thereupon beautiful women came into being in the city of Amit (or, Amem). And the Majesty of Rā spake [concerning] this goddess, [saying], "Let there be made for her vessels "of the beer which produceth sleep at every holy "time and season of the year, and they shall be in "number according to the number of my hand- "maidens;" and from that early time until now men have been wont to make on the occasions of the festival of Hathor vessels of the beer which make them to sleep in number according to the number of the handmaidens of Rā. And the Majesty of Rā spake unto this goddess, [saying], "I am smitten "with the pain of the fire of sickness; whence "cometh to me [this] pain?" And the Majesty of Rā said, "I live, but my heart hath become exceed- "ingly weary[2] with existence with them (i.e., with "men); I have slain [some of] them, but there is "a remnant of worthless ones, for the destruction "which I wrought among them was not as great "as my power." Then the gods who were in his following said unto him, "Be not overcome by thy "inactivity, for thy might is in proportion to thy "will." And the Majesty of this god said unto the Majesty of Nu, "My members are weak for (or, as

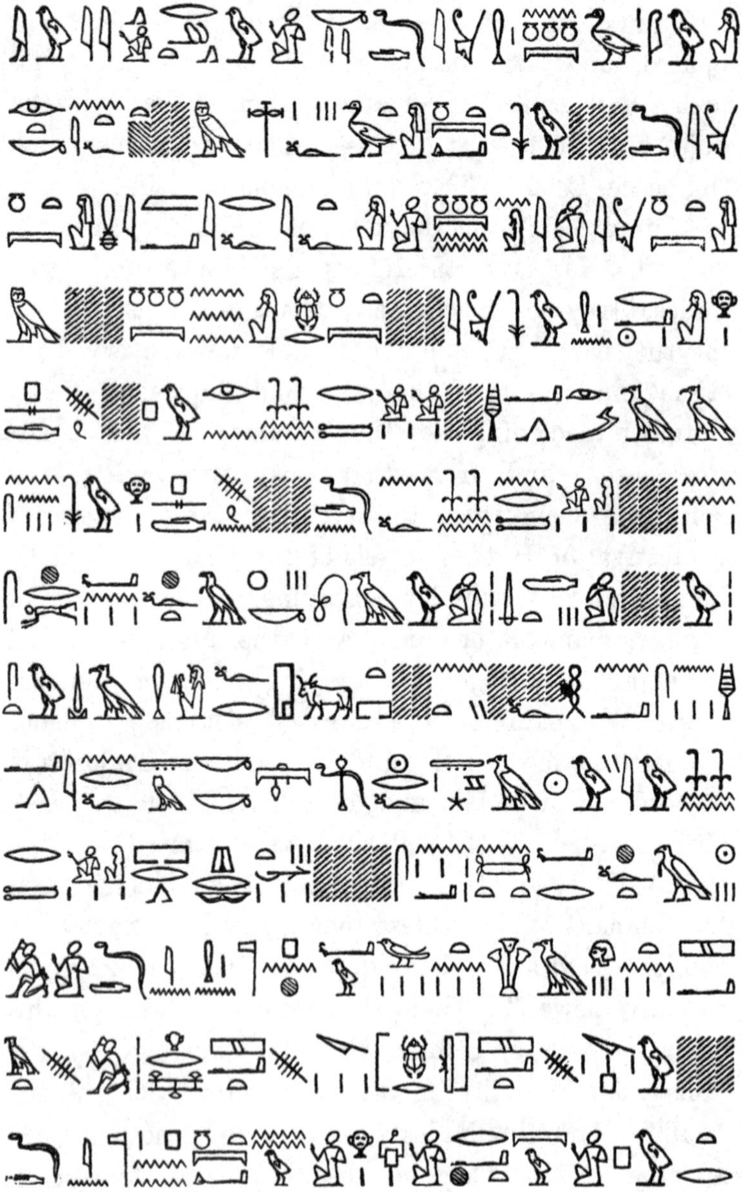

"at) the first time; I will not permit this to come "upon me a second time." And the Majesty of the god Nu said, "O son Shu, be thou the Eye "for thy father . . . . . and avenge (?) him, and "thou goddess Nut, place him . . . . . ." And the goddess Nut said, "How can this be then, "O my father Nu?" "Hail," said Nut . . . . . to the god Nu, and the goddess straightway became [a cow], and she set the Majesty of Rā upon [her] back . . . . . And when these things had been done, men and women saw the god Rā upon the back [of the cow]. Then these men and women said, "Remain with us, and we will overthrow "thine enemies who speak words of blasphemy "[against thee], and [destroy them]." Then his Majesty [Rā] set out for the Great House, and [the gods who were in the train of Rā remained] with them (i.e., the men); during that time the earth was in darkness. And when the earth became light [again], and the morning had dawned, the men came forth with their bows and their [weapons], and they set their arms in motion to shoot the enemies [of Rā]. Then said the Majesty of this god, "Your "transgressions of violence are placed behind you, "for the slaughtering of the enemies is above the "slaughter [of sacrifice];" thus came into being the slaughter [of sacrifice]. And the Majesty of this god said unto Nut, "I have placed myself upon my back "in order to stretch myself out." What then is the

meaning of this? It meaneth that he united (?) himself with Nut. [Thus came into being] . . . . . . Then said the Majesty of this god, "I am departing "from them (i.e., from men), and he must come after "me who would see me;" thus came into being . . . . . Then the Majesty of this god looked forth from its interior, saying, "Gather together [men for "me], and make ready for me an abode for multi-"tudes;" thus came into being . . . . . . And his Majesty (life, health, and strength be to him!) said, "Let a great field (*sekhet*) be produced (*ḥetep*);" thereupon Sekhet-ḥetep came into being. [And the god said], "I will gather herbs (*ȧarȧṭ*) therein;" thereupon Sekhet-ȧaru came into being. [And the god said], "I will make it to contain as dwellers things (*khet*) "like stars of all sorts;" thereupon the stars (*ȧkhekha*) came into being. Then the goddess Nut trembled because of the height. And the Majesty of Rā said, "I decree that supports be to bear [the "goddess up];" thereupon the props of heaven (*ḥeḥ*) came into being. And the Majesty of Rā said, "O "my son Shu, I pray thee to set thyself under [my] "daughter Nut, and guard thou for me the supports "(*ḥeḥ*) of the millions (*ḥeḥ*) which are there, and "which live in darkness. Take thou the goddess "upon thy head, and act thou as nurse for her;" thereupon came into being [the custom] of a son nursing a daughter, and [the custom] of a father carrying a son upon his head.

II. THIS CHAPTER SHALL BE SAID OVER [A FIGURE OF] THE COW.—The supporters [called] Ḥeḥ-enti shall be by her shoulder. The supporters [called] Ḥeḥ-enti shall be at her side, and one cubit and four spans of hers shall be in colours, and nine stars shall be on her belly, and Set shall be by her two thighs and shall keep watch before her two legs, and before her two legs shall be Shu, under her belly, and he shall be made (i.e., painted) in green *qenȧt* colour. His two arms shall be under the stars, and his name shall be made (i.e., written) in the middle of them, namely, "Shu himself." A boat with a rudder and a double shrine shall be therein, and Ȧten (i.e., the Disk) shall be above it, and Rā shall be in it, in front of Shu, near his hand, or, as another reading hath, behind him, near his hand. And the udders of the Cow shall be made to be between her legs, towards the left side. And on the two flanks, towards the middle of the legs, shall be done in writing [the words], "The exterior heaven," and "I am what is "in me," and "I will not permit them to make her "to turn." That which is [written] under the boat which is in front shall read, "Thou shalt not be "motionless, my son;" and the words which are written in an opposite direction shall read, "Thy "support is like life," and "The word is as the "word there," and "Thy son is with me," and "Life, strength, and health be to thy nostrils!" And that which is behind Shu, near his shoulder,

shall read, "They keep ward," and that which is behind him, written close to his feet in an opposite direction, shall read, "Maāt," and "They come in," and "I protect daily." And that which is under the shoulder of the divine figure which is under the left leg, and is behind it shall read, "He who sealeth all "things." That which is over his head, under the thighs of the Cow, and that which is by her legs shall read, "Guardian of his exit." That which is behind the two figures which are by her two legs, that is to say, over their heads, shall read, "The "Aged One who is adored as he goeth forth," and "The Aged One to whom praise is given when he "goeth in." That which is over the head of the two figures, and is between the two thighs of the Cow, shall read, "Listener," "Hearer," "Sceptre of the "Upper Heaven," and "Star" (?).

III. Then the Majesty of this god spake unto Thoth, [saying], "Let a call go forth for me to the "Majesty of the god Seb, saying, 'Come, with the "'utmost speed, at once.'" And when the Majesty of Seb had come, the Majesty of this god said unto him, "Let war be made against thy worms (or, "serpents) which are in thee; verily, they shall "have fear of me as long as I have being; but thou "knowest their magical powers. Do thou go to the "place where my father Nu is, and say thou unto "him, 'Keep ward over the worms (or, serpents) "'which are in the earth and water.' And more-

"over, thou shalt make a writing for each of the "nests of thy serpents which are there, saying, "'Keep ye guard [lest ye] cause injury to anything.' "They shall know that I am removing myself [from "them], but indeed I shall shine upon them. Since, "however, they indeed wish for a father, thou shalt "be a father unto them in this land for ever. More-"over, let good heed be taken to the men who have "my words of power, and to those whose mouths "have knowledge of such things; verily my own "words of power are there, verily it shall not happen "that any shall participate with me in my protection, "by reason of the majesty which hath come into "being before me. I will decree them to thy son "Osiris, and their children shall be watched over, "the hearts of their princes shall be obedient (or, "ready) by reason of the magical powers of those "who act according to their desire in all the earth "through their words of power which are in their "bodies."

IV. AND THE MAJESTY OF THIS GOD SAID, "Call "to me the god Thoth," and one brought the god to him forthwith. And the Majesty of this god said unto Thoth, "Let us depart to a distance from "heaven, from my place, because I would make "light and the god of light (KHU) in the Ṭuat "and [in] the Land of Caves. Thou shalt write "down [the things which are] in it, and thou shalt "punish those who are in it, that is to say, the

[1] I.e., the "North-lords," that is to say, the peoples who lived in the extreme north of the Delta, and on its sea-coasts, and perhaps in the Islands of the Mediterranean.

"workers who have worked iniquity (or, rebellion). "Through thee I will keep away from the servants "whom this heart [of mine] loatheth. Thou shalt be "in my place (*ȧst*) ÅSTI, and thou shalt therefore be "called, O Thoth, the 'ÅSTI of Rā.' Moreover, I give "thee power to send (*hab*) forth . . . . .; thereupon "shall come into being the Ibis (*habi*) bird of Thoth. "I moreover give thee [power] to lift up thine hand "before the two Companies of the gods who are "greater than thou, and what thou doest shall be "fairer than [the work of] the god KHEN; therefore "shall the divine bird *tekni* of Thoth come into "being. Moreover, I give thee [power] to embrace "(*ȧnḥ*) the two heavens with thy beauties, and with "thy rays of light; therefore shall come into being the "Moon-god (*Ȧāḥ*) of Thoth. Moreover, I give thee "[power] to drive back (*ānān*) the Ha-nebu;[1] therefore "shall come into being the dog-headed Ape (*ānān*) "of Thoth, and he shall act as governor for me. "Moreover, thou art now in my place in the sight of "all those who see thee and who present offerings to "thee, and every being shall ascribe praise unto thee, "O thou who art God."

V. WHOSOEVER SHALL RECITE the words of this composition over himself shall anoint himself with olive oil and with thick unguent, and he shall have propitiatory offerings on both his hands of incense, and behind his two ears shall be pure natron, and sweet-smelling salve shall be on his lips.

He shall be arrayed in a new double tunic, and his body shall be purified with the water of the nile-flood, and he shall have upon his feet a pair of sandals made of white [leather], and a figure of the goddess Maāt shall be drawn upon his tongue with green-coloured ochre. Whensoever Thoth shall wish to recite this composition on behalf of Rā, he must perform a sevenfold (?) purification for three days, and priests and [ordinary] men shall do likewise. Whosoever shall recite the above words shall perform the ceremonies which are to be performed when this book is being read. And he shall make his place of standing (?) in a circle (or, at an angle) . . . . . which is beyond [him], and his two eyes shall be fixed upon himself, all his members shall be [composed], and his steps shall not carry him away [from the place]. Whosoever among men shall recite [these] words shall be like Rā on the day of his birth; and his possessions shall not become fewer, and his house shall never fall into decay, but shall endure for a million eternities.

Then the Aged One himself (i.e., Rā) embraced (?) the god Nu, and spake unto the gods who came forth in the east of the sky, "Ascribe ye praise to "the god, the Aged One, from whom I have come "into being. I am he who made the heavens, and I "set in order [the earth, and created the gods, and] "I was with them for an exceedingly long period; "then was born the year and . . . . . . but my "soul is older than it (i.e., time). It is the Soul of

"Shu, it is the Soul of Khnemu (?),[1] it is the Soul of "Ḥeḥ, it is the Soul of Kek and Ḳerḥ (i.e., Night and "Darkness), it is the Soul of Nu and of Rā, it is the "Soul of Osiris, the lord of Ṭeṭṭu, it is the Soul of "the *Sebàk* Crocodile-gods and of the Crocodiles, "it is the Soul of every god [who dwelleth] in the "divine Snakes, it is the Soul of Āpep in Mount "Bakhau (i.e., the Mount of Sunrise), and it is the "Soul of Rā which pervadeth the whole world."

Whosoever sayeth [these words] worketh his own protection by means of the words of power, "I am "the god Ḥekau (i.e., the divine Word of power), "and [I am] pure in my mouth, and [in] my belly; "[I am] Rā from whom the gods proceeded. I am "Rā, the Light-god (Khu)." When thou sayest [this], step forth in the evening and in the morning on thine own behalf if thou wouldst make to fall the enemies of Rā. I am his Soul, and I am Ḥeka.

Hail, thou lord of eternity, thou creator of everlastingness, who bringest to nought the gods who came forth from Rā, thou lord of thy god, thou prince who didst make what made thee, who art beloved by the fathers of the gods, on whose head are the pure words of power, who didst create the woman (*erpit*) that standeth on the south side of thee, who didst create the goddess who hath her face on her breast, and the serpent which standeth

[1] There are mistakes in the text here.

on his tail, with her eye on his belly, and with his tail on the earth, to whom Thoth giveth praises, and upon whom the heavens rest, and to whom Shu stretcheth out his two hands, deliver thou me from those two great gods who sit in the east of the sky, who act as wardens of heaven and as wardens of earth, and who make firm the secret places, and who are called "Āaiu-su," and "Per-f-er-maa-Nu." Moreover [there shall be] a purifying on the . . . . . day of the month . . . ., even according to the performance of the ceremonies in the oldest time.

Whosoever shall recite this Chapter shall have life in Neter-kher (i.e., Underworld), and the fear of him shall be much greater than it was formerly [upon earth] . . . . and they shall say, "Thy names "are 'Eternity' and 'Everlastingness.'" They are called, they are called, "Åu-peḥ-nef-n-āa-em-ta-uat-åpu," and "Rekh-kuå-[tut]-en-neter-pui- . . . . . en en-ḥrå-f-Ḥer-shefu." I am he who hath strengthened the boat with the company of the gods, and his Shenit, and his Gods, by means of words of power.

THE LEGEND OF RĀ AND ISIS.

THE LEGEND OF RĀ AND ISIS.

THE CHAPTER of the divine (or, mighty) god, who created himself, who made the heavens and the earth, and the breath of life, and fire, and the gods, and men, and beasts, and cattle, and reptiles, and the fowl of the air, and the fish, who is the king of men and gods, [who existeth] in one Form, [to whom] periods of one hundred and twenty years are as single years, whose names by reason of their multitude are unknowable, for [even] the gods know them not. Behold, the goddess Isis lived in the form of a woman, who had the knowledge of words [of power]. Her heart turned away in disgust from the millions of men, and she chose for herself the millions of the gods, but esteemed more highly the millions of the spirits. Was it not possible to become even as was Rā in heaven and upon earth, and to make [herself] mistress of the earth, and a [mighty] goddess—thus she meditated in her heart—by the knowledge of the Name of the holy god? Behold, Rā entered [heaven] each day at the head of his mariners, stablishing himself upon the double throne of the two horizons. Now the divine one had become old, he dribbled at

the mouth, and he let his emissions go forth from him upon the earth, and his spittle fell upon the ground. This Isis kneaded in her hand,[1] with [some] dust, and she fashioned it in the form of a sacred serpent, and made it to have the form of a dart, so that none might be able to escape alive from it, and she left it lying upon the road whereon the great god travelled, according to his desire, about the two lands. Then the holy god rose up in the tabernacle of the gods in the great double house (life, strength, health!) among those who were in his train, and [as] he journeyed on his way according to his daily wont, the holy serpent shot its fang into him, and the living fire was departing from the god's own body, and the reptile destroyed the dweller among the cedars. And the mighty god opened his mouth, and the cry of His Majesty (life, strength, health!) reached unto the heavens, and the company of the gods said, "What is it?" and his gods said, "What is the matter?" And the god found [no words] wherewith to answer concerning himself. His jaws shook, his lips trembled, and the poison took possession of all his flesh just as Ḥāpi (i.e., the Nile) taketh possession of the land

[1] Here we have another instance of the important part which the spittle played in magical ceremonies that were intended to produce evil effects. The act of spitting, however, was intended sometimes to carry a curse with it, and sometimes a blessing, for a man spat in the face of his enemy in order to lay the curse of impurity upon him, and at the present time men spit upon money to keep the devils away from it.

through which he floweth. Then the great god made firm his heart (i.e., took courage) and he cried out to those who were in his following:—" Come ye unto me, " O ye who have come into being from my members,[1] " ye gods who have proceeded from me, for I would " make you to know what hath happened. I have been " smitten by some deadly thing, of which my heart hath " no knowledge, and which I have neither seen with " my eyes nor made with my hand; and I have no " knowledge at all who hath done this to me. I have " never before felt any pain like unto it, and no pain " can be worse than this [is]. I am a Prince, the son " of a Prince, and the divine emanation which was pro- " duced from a god. I am a Great One, the son of a " Great One, and my father hath determined for me my " name. I have multitudes of names, and I have multi- " tudes of forms, and my being existeth in every god. " I have been invoked (or, proclaimed ?) by Temu and " Ḥeru-Ḥekennu. My father and my mother uttered " my name, and [they] hid it in my body at my birth so " that none of those who would use against me words of " power might succeed in making their enchantments " have dominion over me.[2] I had come forth from my " tabernacle to look upon that which I had made, and " was making my way through the two lands which I

[1] The gods were, according to one belief, nothing more than the various names of Rā, who had taken the forms of the various members of his body.

[2] Thus the god's own name became his most important talisman.

"had made, when a blow was aimed at me, but I know "not of what kind. Behold, is it fire? Behold, is it "water? My heart is full of burning fire, my limbs "are shivering, and my members have darting pains in "them. Let there be brought unto me my children the "gods, who possess words of magic, whose mouths are "cunning [in uttering them], and whose powers reach "up to heaven." Then his children came unto him, and every god was there with his cry of lamentation; and Isis[1] came with her words of magic, and the place of her mouth [was filled with] the breath of life, for the words which she putteth together destroy diseases, and her words make to live those whose throats are choked (i.e., the dead). And she said, "What is this, O divine "father? What is it? Hath a serpent shot his "venom into thee? Hath a thing which thou hast "fashioned lifted up its head against thee? Verily "it shall be overthrown by beneficent words of power, "and I will make it to retreat in the sight of thy "rays." The holy god opened his mouth, [saying], "I was going along the road and passing through "the two lands of my country, for my heart wished "to look upon what I had made, when I was

[1] The position of Isis as the "great enchantress" is well defined, and several instances of her magical powers are recorded. By the utterance of her words of power she succeeded in raising her dead husband Osiris to life, and she enabled him by their means to beget Horus of her. Nothing could withstand them, because they were of divine origin, and she had learned them from Thoth, the intelligence of the greatest of the gods.

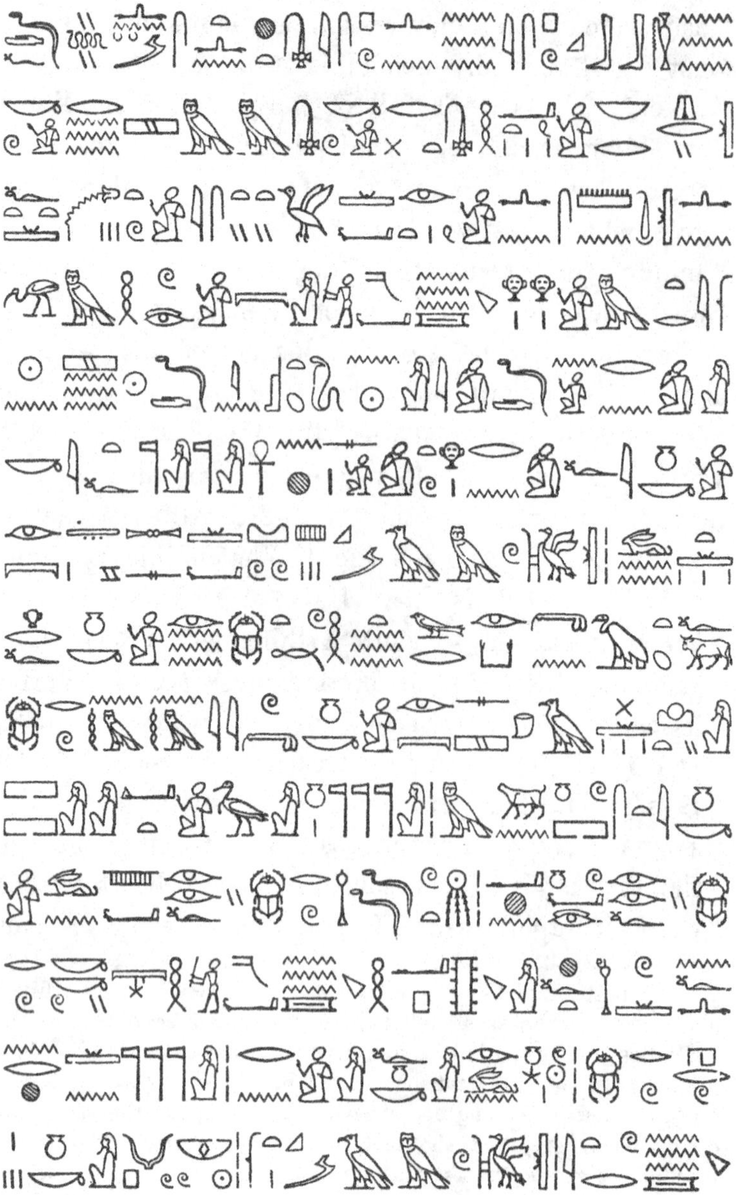

"bitten by a serpent which I did not see; behold, is "it fire? Behold, is it water? I am colder than "water, I am hotter than fire, all my members sweat, "I myself quake, mine eye is unsteady. I cannot look "at the heavens, and water forceth itself on my face "as in the time of the Inundation."[1] And Isis said unto Rā, "O my divine father, tell me thy name, for he "who is able to pronounce his name liveth." [And Rā said], "I am the maker of the heavens and the earth, "I have knit together the mountains, and I have "created everything which existeth upon them. I "am the maker of the Waters, and I have made "Meḥt-ur to come into being; I have made the Bull "of his Mother, and I have made the joys of love to "exist. I am the maker of heaven, and I have made "to be hidden the two gods of the horizon, and I "have placed the souls of the gods within them. I "am the Being who openeth his eyes and the light "cometh; I am the Being who shutteth his eyes and "there is darkness. I am the Being who giveth "the command, and the waters of Ḥāpi (the Nile) "burst forth, I am the Being whose name the gods "know not. I am the maker of the hours and "the creator of the days. I am the opener (i.e., "inaugurator) of the festivals, and the maker of the "floods of water. I am the creator of the fire of life

[1] Or, "the period of the summer." The season Shemmu, 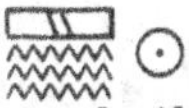, began soon after the beginning of April and lasted until nearly the end of July.

"whereby the works of the houses are caused to come "into being. I am Kheperȧ in the morning, and Rā "at the time of his culmination (i.e., noon), and Temu "in the evening."[1] Nevertheless the poison was not driven from its course, and the great god felt no better. Then Isis said unto Rā, "Among the things "which thou hast said unto me thy name hath not "been mentioned. O declare thou it unto me, and "the poison shall come forth; for the person who "hath declared his name shall live." Meanwhile the poison burned with blazing fire and the heat thereof was stronger than that of a blazing flame. Then the Majesty of Rā said, "I will allow myself to be "searched through by Isis, and my name shall come "forth from my body and go into hers." Then the divine one hid himself from the gods, and the throne in the Boat of Millions of Years[2] was empty. And it came to pass that when it was the time for the heart to come forth [from the god], she said unto her son Horus, "The great god shall bind "himself by an oath to give his two eyes."[3] Thus was the great god made to yield up his name, and

[1] Khepera, Rā, and Temu were the three principal forms of the Sun-god according to the theological system of the priests of Heliopolis.

[2] The name by which the Boat of Rā is generally known in Egyptian texts. It was this boat which was stopped in its course when Thoth descended from the sky to impart to Isis the words of power that were to raise her dead child Horus to life.

[3] I.e., the  of the sun, and the  of the moon. The sun and the moon were the visible, material symbols of the Sun-god.

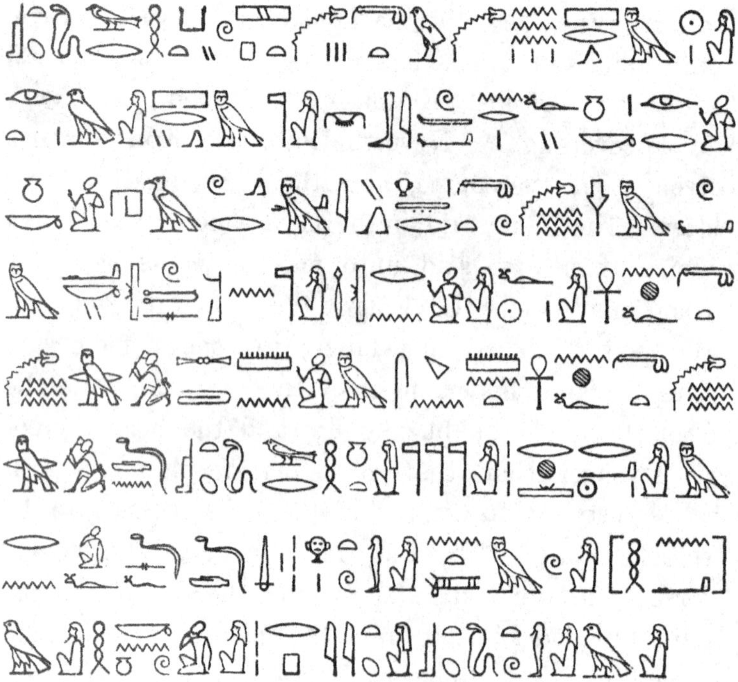

Isis, the great lady of enchantments, said, "Flow on, "poison, and come forth from Rā; let the Eye of "Horus come forth from the god and shine (?) outside "his mouth. I have worked, and I make the poison "to fall on the ground, for the venom hath been "mastered. Verily the name hath been taken away "from the great god. Let Rā live, and let the poison "die; and if the poison live then Rā shall die. And "similarly, a certain man, the son of a certain man, "shall live and the poison shall die." These were the words which spake Isis, the great lady, the mistress of the gods, and she had knowledge of Rā in his own name. The above words shall be said over an image of Temu and an image of Ḥeru-Ḥekennu,[1] and over an image of Isis and an image of Horus.

[1] The attributes of this god are not well defined. He was a god of the Eastern Delta, and was associated with the cities where Temu was worshipped.

THE LEGEND OF HORUS OF BEḤUṬET AND THE WINGED DISK.

[1] I.e., in Nubia, probably the portion of it which lies round about the modern Kalâbsha. In ancient days Ta-kens appears to have included a portion of the Nile Valley to the north of Aswân.

[2] I.e., Apollinopolis, the modern Edfû.

THE LEGEND OF HORUS OF BEḤUṬET AND THE WINGED DISK.

XII. 2. In the three hundred and sixty-third year of Rā-(Ḥeru-Khuti), who liveth for ever and for ever, His Majesty was in TA-KENS,[1] and his soldiers were with him; [the enemy] did not conspire (*auu*) against their lord, and the land [is called] UAUATET unto this day. **3.** And Rā set out on an expedition in his boat, and his followers were with him, and he arrived at UTHES-ḤERU,[2] [which lay to] the west of this nome, and to the east of the canal PAKHENNU, which is called [. . . . . to this day]. And Ḥeru-Beḥuṭet was **4** in the boat of Rā, and he said unto his father Rā-Ḥeru-Khuti (i.e., Rā-Harmachis), "I see that the enemies are conspiring against their "lord; let thy fiery serpent gain the mastery . . . . . "over them." **XIII. 1.** Then the Majesty of Rā-Harmachis said unto thy divine KA, O Ḥeru-Beḥuṭet, "O son of Rā, thou exalted one, who didst proceed "from me, overthrow thou the enemies who are before "thee straightway." And Ḥeru-Beḥuṭet flew up into the horizon in the form of the great Winged Disk, for which reason he is called "Great god, lord of

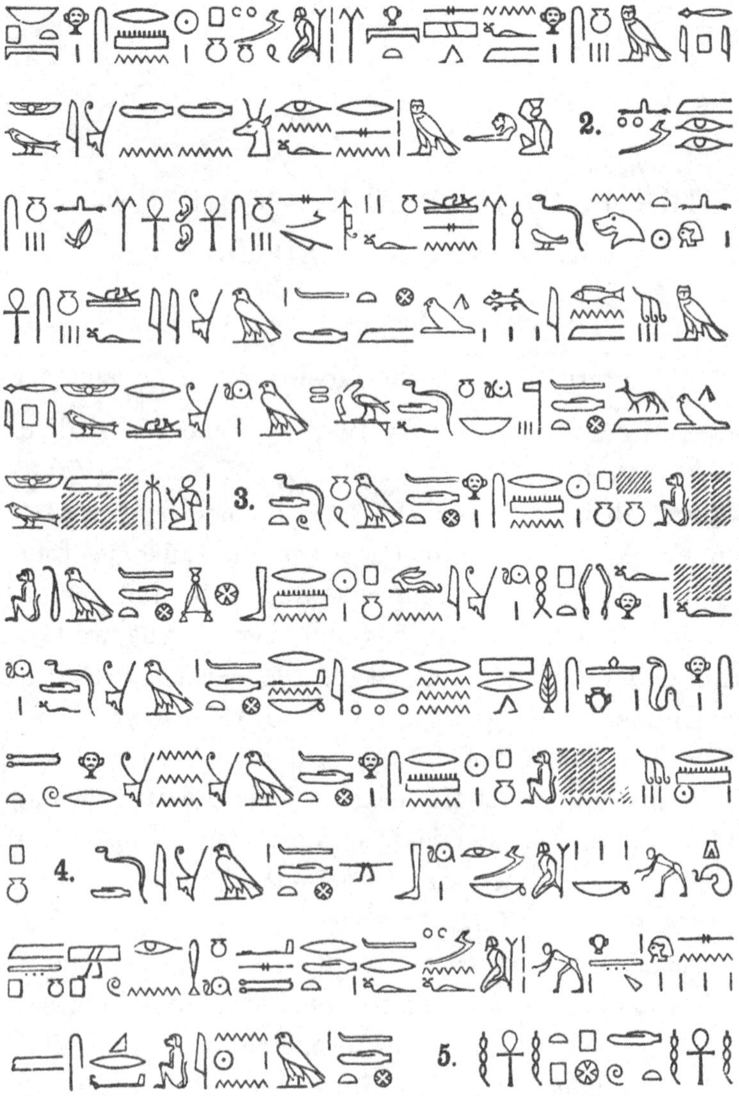

[1] I.e., drops of blood.

[2] I.e., from the city.

heaven," unto this day. And when he saw the enemies in the heights of heaven he set out to follow after them in the form of the great Winged Disk, and he attacked with such terrific force those who opposed him, **2** that they could neither see with their eyes nor hear with their ears, and each of them slew his fellow. In a moment of time there was not a single creature left alive. Then Ḥeru Beḥuṭet, shining with very many colours, came in the form of the great Winged Disk to the Boat of Rā-Harmachis, and Thoth said unto Rā, "O Lord of the gods, Beḥuṭet hath returned "in the form of the great Winged Disk, shining "[with many colours] . . . . . . children;" **3** for this reason he is called Ḥeru-Beḥuṭet unto this day. And Thoth said, "The city Ṭeb shall be called the city of "Ḥeru-Beḥuṭet," and thus is it called unto this day. And Rā embraced the . . . . . of Rā, and said unto Ḥeru-Beḥuṭet, "Thou didst put grapes[1] into the "water which cometh forth from it,[2] and thy heart "rejoiced thereat;" and for this reason the water (or, canal) of Ḥeru-Beḥuṭet is called "[Grape-Water]" unto this day, and the . . . . unto this day. **4.** And Ḥeru-Beḥuṭet said, "Advance, O Rā, and look "thou upon thine enemies who are lying under thee "on this land;" thereupon the Majesty of Rā set out on the way, and the goddess ĀSTHERṬET ('Ashtoreth?) was with him, and he saw the enemies overthrown on the ground, each one of them being fettered. Then said Rā to Ḥeru-Beḥuṭet, **5** "There is sweet

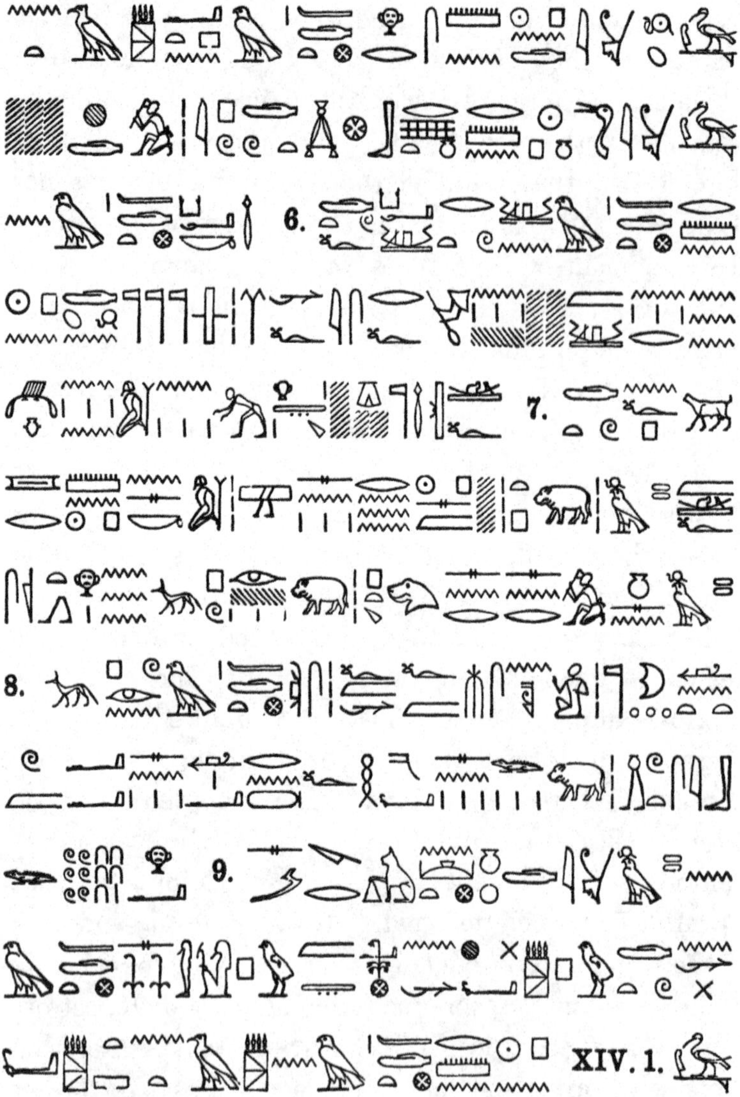

[1] I.e., Edfu. [2] I.e., Great Protector. [3] I.e., "Great Canal."

"life in this place," and for this reason the abode of the palace of Ḥeru-Beḥuṭet is called "Sweet Life" unto this day. And Rā said unto Thoth, "[Here was "the slaughter] of mine enemies;" and the place is called ṬEB[1] unto this day. And Thoth said unto Ḥeru-Beḥuṭet, "Thou art a great protector (*mākāa*);" and **6** the Boat of Ḥeru-Beḥuṭet is called MĀKĀA[2] unto this day. Then said Rā unto the gods who were in his following, "Behold now, let us sail in our boat "upon the water, for our hearts are glad because our "enemies have been overthrown on the earth;" and the water where the great god sailed is **7** called P-KHEN-UR[3] unto this day. And behold the enemies [of Rā] rushed into the water, and they took the forms of [crocodiles and] hippopotami, but nevertheless Rā-Ḥeru-Khuti sailed over the waters in his boat, and when the crocodiles and the hippopotami had come nigh unto him, they opened wide their jaws in order to destroy Rā-Ḥeru-Khuti. **8.** And when Ḥeru-Beḥuṭet arrived and his followers who were behind him in the forms of workers in metal, each having in his hands an iron spear and a chain, according to his name, they smote the crocodiles and the hippopotami; and there were brought in there straightway six hundred and fifty-one crocodiles, **9** which had been slain before the city of Edfû. Then spake Rā-Harmachis unto Ḥeru-Beḥuṭet, "My Image shall be [here] in the land of the South, "which is a house of victory (or, strength);" and the House of Ḥeru-Beḥuṭet is called NEKHT-ḤET unto this

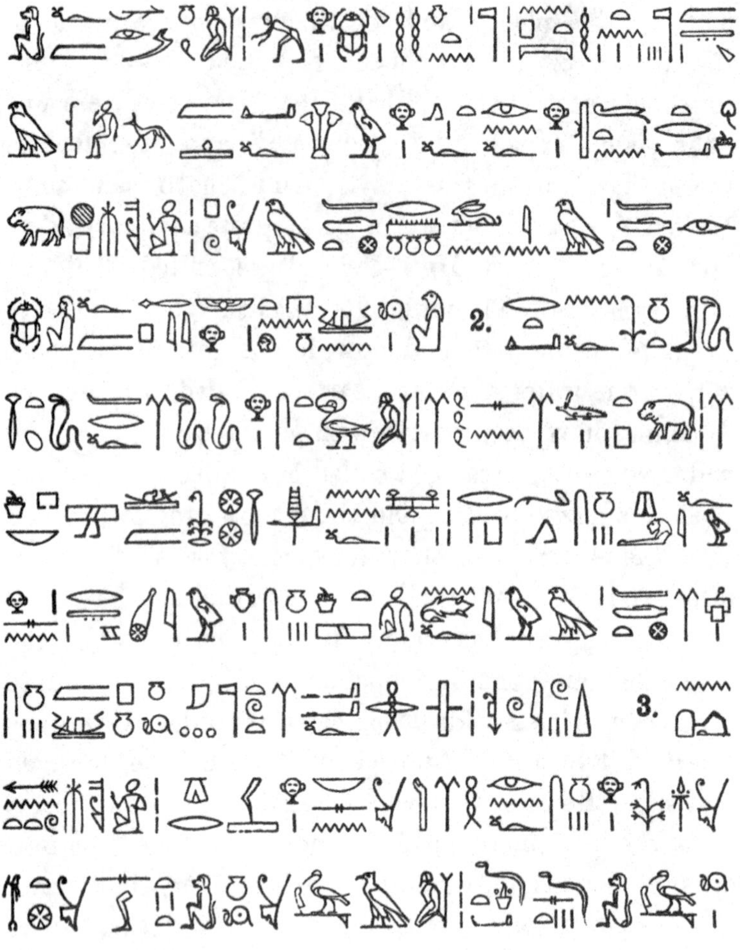

[1] The goddess Nekhebet was incarnate in a special kind of serpent, and the centre of her worship was in the city of Nekheb, which the Greeks called Eileithyiaspolis, and the Arabs Al-Kâb.

[2] The centre of the worship of Uatchet, or Uatchit, was at Per-Uatchet, a city in the Delta.

[3] I.e., the enemies.

day. **XIV. 1.** Then the god Thoth spake, after he had looked upon the enemies lying upon the ground, saying, "Let your hearts rejoice, O ye gods of heaven! Let "your hearts rejoice, O ye gods who are in the earth! "Horus, the Youthful One, cometh in peace, and he "hath made manifest on his journey deeds of very "great might, which he hath performed according to "the Book of Slaying the Hippopotamus." And from that day figures of Ḥeru-Beḥuṭet in metal have existed.

Then Ḥeru-Beḥuṭet took upon himself the form of the Winged Disk, and he placed himself upon the front of the Boat of Rā. **2.** And he placed by his side the goddess Nekhebet[1] and the goddess Uatchet,[2] in the form of two serpents, that they might make the enemies to quake in [all] their limbs when they were in the forms of crocodiles and hippopotami in every place wherein he came in the Land of the South and in the Land of the North. Then those enemies rose up to make their escape from before him, and their face was towards the Land of the South. And their hearts were stricken down through fear of him. And Ḥeru-Beḥuṭet was at the back (or, side) of them in the Boat of Rā, and there were in his hands a metal lance and a metal chain; and the metal workers who were with their lord were equipped **3** for fighting with lances and chains. And Ḥeru-Beḥuṭet saw them[3] to the south-east of the city of Uast (Thebes) some distance away. Then Rā said to Thoth, "Those enemies "shall be smitten with blows that kill;" and Thoth

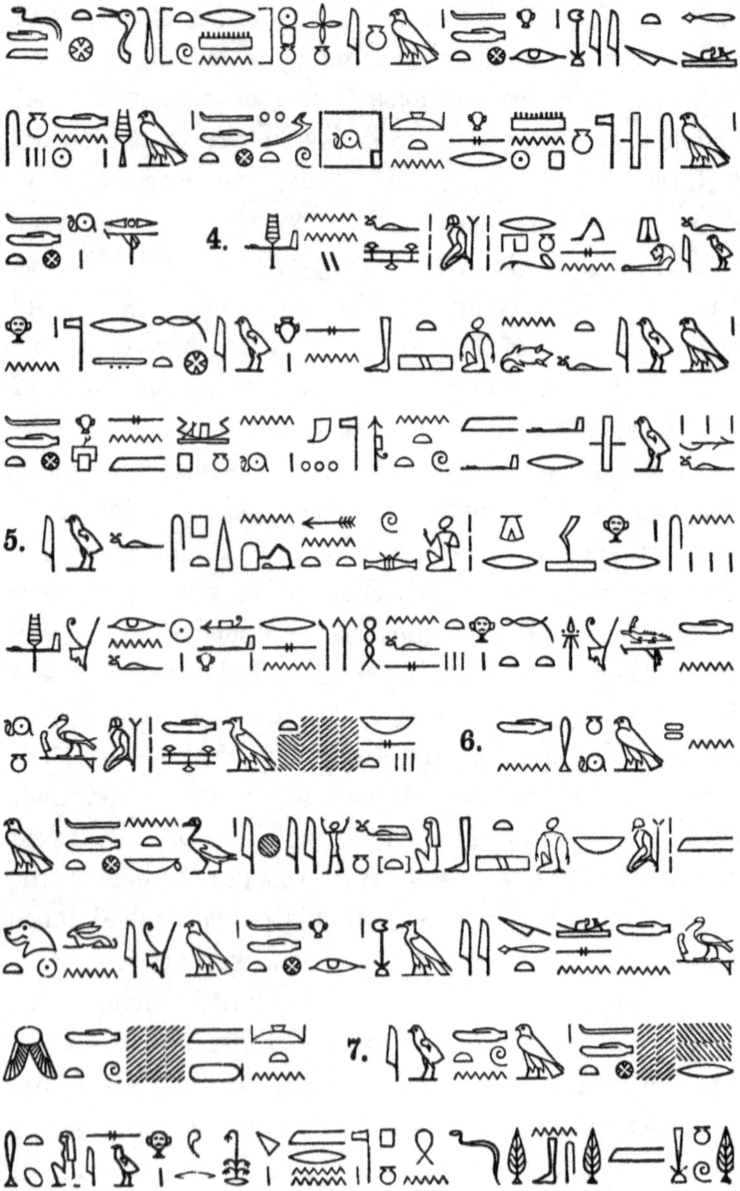

4.
5.
6.
7.

said to Rā, "[That place] is called the city TCHEṬ-"MET unto this day." And Ḥeru-Beḥuṭet made a great overthrow among them, and Rā said, "Stand still, O Ḥeru-Beḥuṭet," and [that place] is called "ḤET-RĀ" to this day, and the god who dwelleth therein is Ḥeru - Beḥuṭet - Rā - Ȧmsu (or, Min). **4.** Then those enemies rose up to make their escape from before him, and the face of the god was towards the Land of the North, and their hearts were stricken through fear of him. And Ḥeru-Beḥuṭet was at the back (or, side) of them in the Boat of Rā, and those who were following him had spears of metal and chains of metal in their hands; **5** and the god himself was equipped for battle with the weapons of the metal workers which they had with them. And he passed a whole day before he saw them to the north-east of the nome of TENTYRA (Dendera). Then Rā said unto Thoth, "The enemies are resting . . . . their "lord." **6.** And the Majesty of Rā-Harmachis said to Ḥeru-Beḥuṭet, "Thou art my exalted son who "didst proceed from Nut. The courage of the "enemies hath failed in a moment." And Ḥeru-Beḥuṭet made great slaughter among them. And Thoth said, "The Winged Disk shall be called ". . . . . in the name of this Ȧat;" **7** and is called Ḥeru-Beḥuṭet . . . . . its mistress. His name is to the South in the name of this god, and the acacia and the sycamore shall be the trees of the sanctuary.

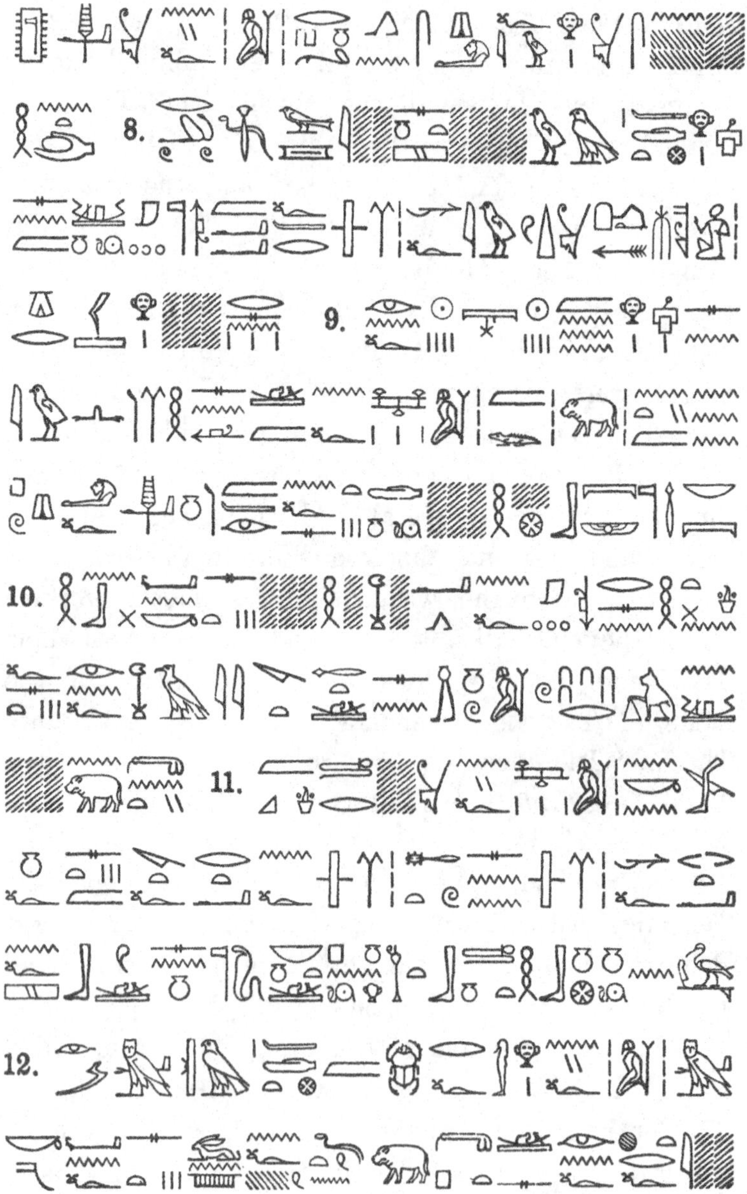

Then the enemies turned aside to flee from before him, and their faces were [towards the North, and they went] to **8** the swamps of Uatch-ur (i.e., the Mediterranean), and [their courage failed through fear of him]. And Ḥeru-Beḥuṭet was at the back (or, side) of them in the Boat of Rā, and the metal spear was in his hands, and those who were in his following were equipped with the weapons for battle of the metal workers. **9**. And the god spent four days and four nights in the water in pursuit of them, but he did not see one of the enemies, who fled from before him in the water in the forms of crocodiles and hippopotami. At length he found them and saw them. And Rā said unto Horus of Ḥeben, "O Winged Disk, "thou great god and lord of heaven, **10** seize thou "them . . . . . . ;" and he hurled his lance after them, and he slew them, and worked a great overthrow of them. And he brought one hundred and forty-two enemies to the forepart of the Boat [of Rā], and with them was a male hippopotamus **11** which had been among those enemies. And he hacked them in pieces with his knife, and he gave their entrails to those who were in his following, and he gave their carcases to the gods and goddesses who were in the Boat of Rā on the river-bank of the city of Ḥeben. Then Rā said unto Thoth, **12** "See what mighty things Ḥeru-Beḥuṭet "hath performed in his deeds against the enemies: "verily he hath smitten them! And of the male "hippopotamus he hath opened the mouth, and he

13.

XV. 1.

2.

¹ I.e., the Mediterranean.

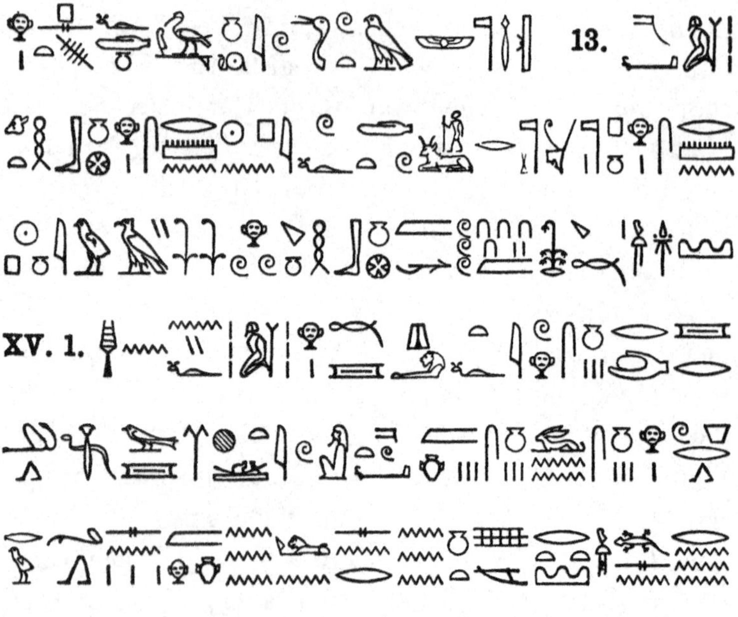

"hath speared it, and he hath mounted upon its back." Then said Thoth to Rā, "Horus shall be called "'Winged Disk, Great God, **13** Smiter of the ene-"mies in the town of Ḥeben' from this day forward, "and he shall be called 'He who standeth on the "back' and 'prophet of this god,' from this day "forward." These are the things which happened in the lands of the city of Ḥeben, in a region which measured three hundred and forty-two measures on the south, and on the north, on the west, and on the east.

XV. 1. Then the enemies rose up before him by the Lake of the North, and their faces were set towards Uatch-ur,[1] which they desired to reach by sailing; but the god smote their hearts and they turned and fled in the water, and they directed their course to the water of the nome of Mertet-Åment, and they gathered themselves together in the water of Mertet in order to join themselves with the enemies [who serve] Set and who are in this region. And Ḥeru-Beḥuṭet followed them, being equipped with all his weapons of war to fight against them. **2.** And Ḥeru-Beḥuṭet made a journey in the Boat of Rā, together with the great god who was in his boat with those who were his followers, and he pursued them on the Lake of the North twice, and passed one day and one night sailing down the river in pursuit of them before he perceived and overtook them, for he knew not the place where they were. Then he arrived at the city of Per-Reḥu. And the

3.
4.
5.
6.

Majesty of Rā said unto Ḥeru-Beḥuṭet, "What hath "happened to the enemies? They have gathered "together themselves in the water to the west (?) "of the nome of Mertet in order to unite themselves "with the enemies [who serve] Set, and who are in "this region, **3** at the place where are our staff and "sceptre." And Thoth said unto Rā, "Uast in the "nome of Mertet is called Uaseb because of this unto "this day, and the Lake which is in it is called TEMPT." Then Ḥeru-Beḥuṭet spake in the presence of his father Rā, saying, "I beseech thee to set thy boat against "them, so that I may be able to perform against them "that which Rā willeth;" and this was done. Then he made an attack upon them on the Lake which was at the west of this district, and he perceived them on the bank of the city . . . . . . which belongeth to the Lake of Mertet. **4**. Then Ḥeru-Beḥuṭet made an expedition against them, and his followers were with him, and they were provided with weapons of all kinds for battle, and he wrought a great overthrow among them, and he brought in three hundred and eighty-one enemies, and he slaughtered them in the forepart of the Boat of Rā, **5** and he gave one of them to each of those who were in his train. Then Set rose up and came forth, and raged loudly with words of cursing and abuse because of the things which Ḥeru-beḥutet had done in respect of the slaughter of the enemies. And Rā said unto Thoth, "This fiend Neḥaḥa-ḥrå "uttereth words at the top of his voice because of

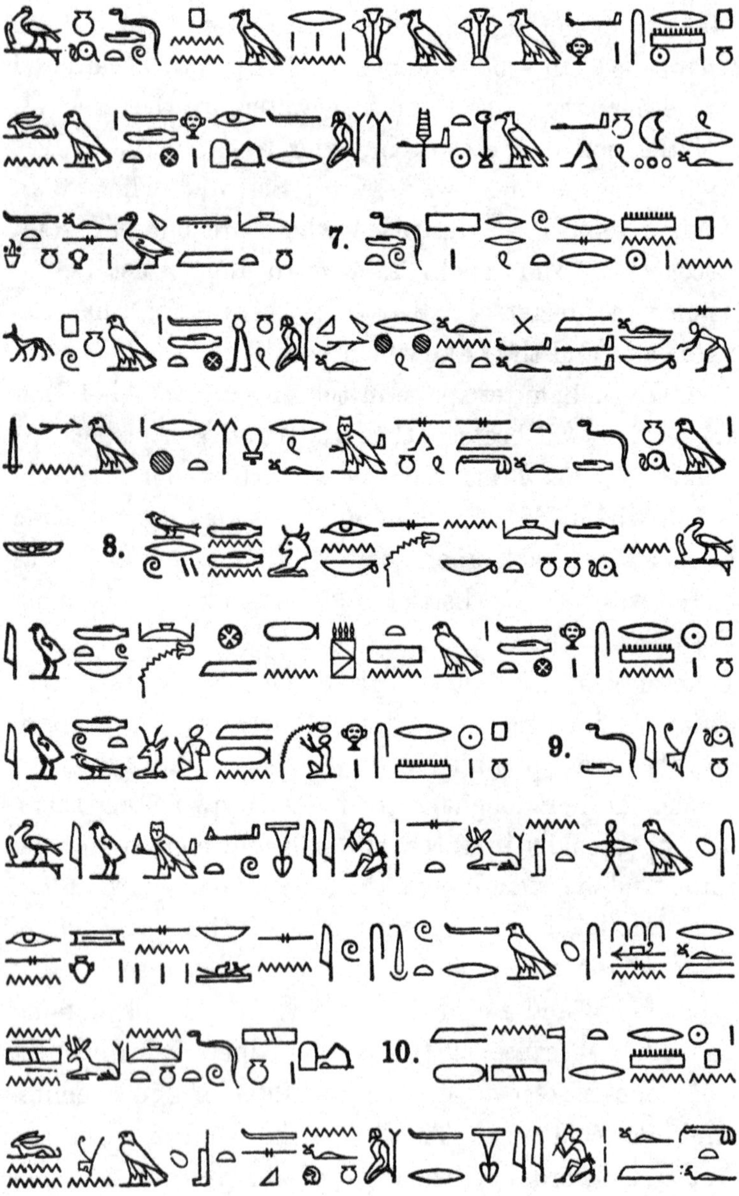

"the things which 6 Ḥeru-Beḥuṭet hath done unto "him;" and Thoth said unto Rā, "Cries of this kind "shall be called Neḥaḥa-ḥrȧ unto this day." And Ḥeru-Beḥuṭet did battle with the Enemy for a period of time, and he hurled his iron lance at him, and he threw him down on the ground in this region, 7 which is called Pa-Rereḥtu unto this day. Then Ḥeru-Beḥuṭet came and brought the Enemy with him, and his spear was in his neck, and his chain was round his hands and arms, and the weapon of Horus had fallen on his mouth and had closed it; and he went with him before his father Rā, who said, "O Horus, "thou Winged Disk, 8 twice great (Urui-Ṭenṭen) is "the deed of valour which thou hast done, and thou "hast cleansed the district." And Rā said unto Thoth, "The palace of Ḥeru-Beḥuṭet shall be called, "'Lord of the district which is cleansed' because of "this;" and [thus is it called] unto this day. And the name of the priest thereof is called Ur-Ṭenṭen unto this day. 9. And Rā said unto Thoth, "Let the "enemies and Set be given over to Isis and her son "Horus, and let them work all their heart's desire "upon them." And she and her son Horus set themselves in position with their spears in him at the time when there was storm (or, disaster) in the district, and the Lake of the god was 10 called SHE-EN-ĀḤA from that day to this. Then Horus the son of Isis cut off the head of the Enemy [Set], and the heads of his fiends in the presence of father Rā and of

11.
XVI. 1.
2.

the great company of the gods, and he dragged him by his feet through his district with his spear driven through his head and back. And Rā said unto Thoth, 11 "Let the son of Osiris drag the being of disaster "through his territory;" and Thoth said, "It shall be "called ÅTEḤ," and this hath been the name of the "region from that day to this. And Isis, the divine lady, spake before Rā, saying, "Let the exalted Winged "Disk become the amulet of my son Horus, who hath cut "off the head of the Enemy and the heads of his fiends."

XVI. 1. Thus Ḥeru-Beḥuṭet and Horus, the son of Isis, slaughtered that evil Enemy, and his fiends, and the inert foes, and came forth with them to the water on the west side of this district. And Ḥeru-Beḥuṭet was in the form of a man of mighty strength, and he had the face of a hawk, and his head was crowned with the White Crown and the Red Crown, and with two plumes and two uraei, and he had the back of a hawk, and his spear and his chain were in his hands. And Horus, the son of Isis, transformed himself into a similar shape, even as Ḥeru-Beḥuṭet had done before him. **2.** And they slew the enemies all together on the west of Per-Reḥu, on the edge of the stream, and this god hath sailed over the water wherein the enemies had banded themselves together against him from that day to this. Now these things took place on the 7th day of the first month of the season PERT. And Thoth said, "This region shall be called ÅAT-SHĀTET," and this hath been the name of the region from that day

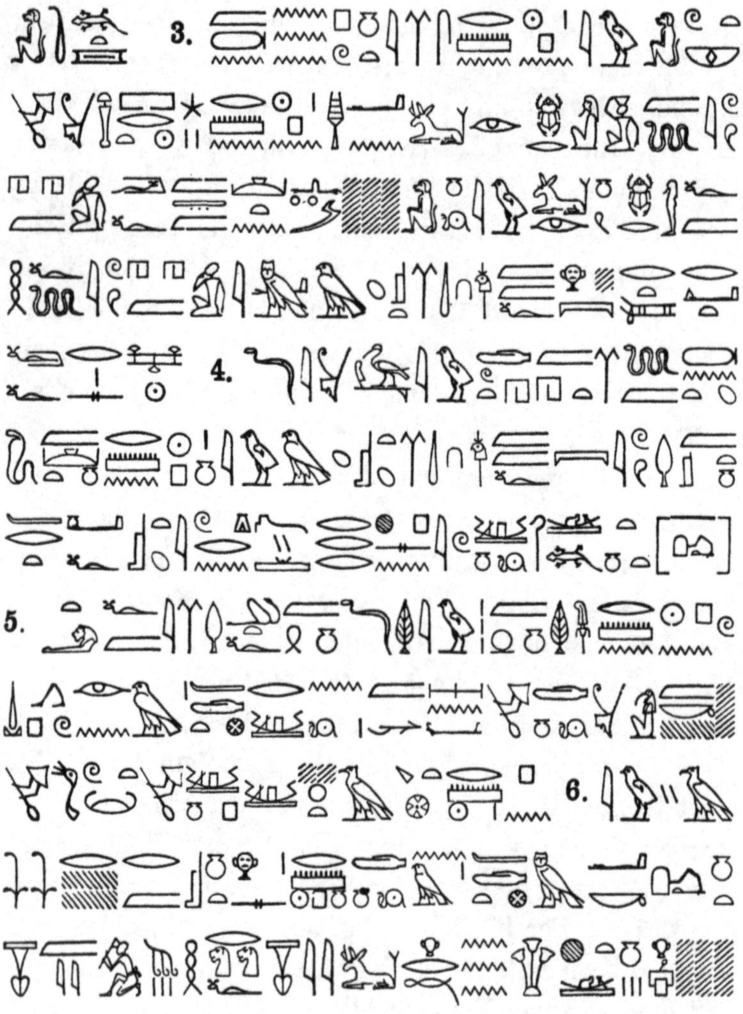

[1] This name means "the place of the Roarer," Hemhemti, , being a well-known name of the Evil One. Some texts seem to indicate that peals of thunder were caused by the fiend Set.

unto this; and the Lake which is close by it **3** hath been called ṬEMT from that day to this, and the 7th day of the first month of the season PERT hath been called the FESTIVAL OF SAILING from that day to this.

Then Set took upon himself the form of a hissing serpent, and he entered into the earth in this district without being seen. And Rā said, "Set hath taken "upon himself the form of a hissing serpent. Let "Horus, the son of Isis, in the form of a hawk-headed "staff, set himself over the place where he is, so that "the serpent may never more appear." **4**. And Thoth said, "Let this district be called HEMHEMET[1] by name;" and thus hath it been called from that day to this. And Horus, the son of Isis, in the form of a hawk-headed staff, took up his abode there with his mother Isis; in this manner did these things happen.

Then the Boat of Rā arrived at the town of Ḥet-Āḥa; **5** its forepart was made of palm wood, and the hind part was made of acacia wood; thus the palm tree and the acacia tree have been sacred trees from that day to this. Then Ḥeru-Beḥuṭet embarked in the Boat of Rā, after he had made an end of fighting, and sailed; and Rā said unto Thoth, "Let this Boat be called . . . .;" and thus hath it been called from that day to this, **6** and these things have been done in commemoration in this place from that day to this.

And Rā said unto Ḥeru-Beḥuṭet, "Behold the "fighting of the Smait fiend and his two-fold strength, "and the Smai fiend Set, are upon the water of the

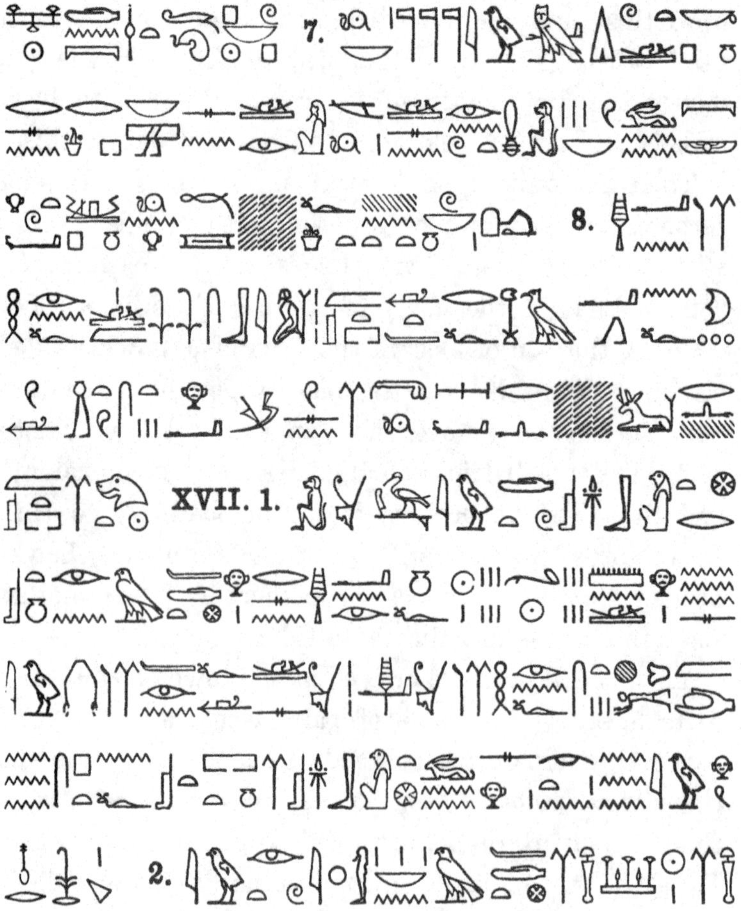

[1] It is probable that the Lake of Meḥ, i.e., the Lake of the North, was situated in the north-east of the Delta, not far from Lake Manzâlah.

[2] "Sebáu" is a common name for the associates of Set, and this fiend is himself called "Sebá," a word which means something like "rebel."

[3] I.e., place of the desire of Horus.

[4] The month Thoth.

"North, and they will sail down stream upon . . . . . ." [And] Ḥeru-Beḥuṭet said, "Whatsoever thou com-"mandest shall take place, 7 O Rā, Lord of the gods. "Grant thou, however, that this thy Boat may pursue "them into every place whithersoever they shall go, and "I will do to them whatsoever pleaseth Rā." And everything was done according to what he had said. Then this Boat of Rā was brought by the winged Sun-disk upon the waters of the Lake of Meḥ,[1] [and] Ḥeru-Beḥuṭet took in his hands his weapons, his darts, and his harpoon, and all the chains [which he required] for the fight.

8. And Ḥeru-Beḥuṭet looked and saw one [only] of these Sebȧu[2] fiends there on the spot, and he was by himself. And he threw one metal dart, and brought (or, dragged) them along straightway, and he slaughtered them in the presence of Rā. And he made an end [of them, and there were no more of the fiends] of Set in this place at [that] moment.

XVII. 1. And Thoth said, "This place shall be called "ȦST-ȦB-ḤERU,"[3] because Ḥeru-Beḥuṭet wrought his desire upon them (i.e., the enemy); and he passed six days and six nights coming into port on the waters thereof and did not see one of them. And he saw them fall down in the watery depths, and he made ready the place of Ȧst-ȧb-Ḥeru there. It was situated on the bank of the water, and the face (i.e., direction) thereof was full-front towards the South. **2.** And all the rites and ceremonies of Ḥeru-Beḥuṭet were performed on the first day of the first month[4] of the

[1] The month Tybi.

[2] The month Mekhir.

[3] A mythological locality originally placed near Herakleopolis. The name means "the place where nothing grows." Several forms of the name occur in the older literature, and in the Theban Recension of the Book of the Dead we find , , , and .

[4] The Crown of the South.

[5] The Crown of the North.

[6] A kind of jasper (?).

season Akhet, and on the first day of the first month[1] of the season Pert, and on the twenty-first and twenty-fourth days of the second month[2] of the season Pert. These are the festivals in the town of Ȧst-ȧb, by the side of the South, in Ȧn-ruṭ-f.[3] And he came into port and went against them, keeping watch as for a king over the Great God in Ȧn-ruṭ-f, in this place, in order to drive away the Enemy and his Smaiu fiends at his coming by night from the region of Mertet, to the west of this place. **3.**

And Ḥeru-Beḥuṭet was in the form of a man who possessed great strength, with the face of a hawk; and he was crowned with the White Crown,[4] and the Red Crown,[5] and the two plumes, and the Urerit Crown, and there were two uraei upon his head. His hand grasped firmly his harpoon to slay the hippopotamus, which was [as hard] as the *khenem*[6] stone in its mountain bed.

And Rā said unto Thoth, "Indeed [Ḥeru-]Beḥuṭet "is like a Master-fighter in the slaughter of his "enemies . . . . . ."

And Thoth said unto Rā, "He shall be called 'Neb-"Āḥau'" (i.e., Master-fighter); and for this reason he hath been thus called by the priest of this god unto this day.

4. And Isis made incantations of every kind in order to drive away the fiend Ba from Ȧn-ruṭ-f, and from the Great God in this place. And Thoth said [unto Rā], "The priestess of this god shall be called by the name "of 'Nebt-Ḥeka' for this reason."

[1] I.e., Osiris.

[2] I.e., "Beautiful Place."

[3] Or perhaps fighting men who were armed with metal weapons.

And Thoth said unto Rā, "Beautiful, beautiful is "this place wherein thou hast taken up thy seat, "keeping watch, as for a king, over the Great God who "is in Ȧn-ruṭ-f[1] in peace."

5. And Thoth said, "This Great House in this place "shall therefore be called 'Ȧst-Nefert'[2] from this day. "It is situated to the south-west of the city of "Nārt, and [covereth] a space of four schoinoi." And Rā Ḥeru-Beḥuṭet said unto Thoth, "Hast thou not "searched through this water for the enemy?" And Thoth said, "**6** The water of the God-house in this "place shall be called by the name of 'Ḥeḥ' (i.e., "sought out)." And Rā said, "Thy ship, O Ḥeru-"Beḥuṭet, is great (?) upon Ānṭ-mer (?) . . . . . ." And Thoth said, "The name of [thy ship] shall be "called 'Ur,' and this stream shall be called 'Ānṭ-"mer (?).'" **7**. As concerning (or, now) the place Ȧb-Bȧt (?) is situated on the shore of the water. "Ȧst-nefert" is the name of the Great house, "Neb-Āḥa" [is the name of] the priest, ... is the name of the priestess, "Ḥeḥ" is the name of the lake, ... [is the name] of the water, **8** "Ȧm-ḥer-neṭ" is the name of the holy (?) acacia tree, "Neter ḥet" is the name of the domain of the god, "Uru" is the name of the sacred boat, the gods therein are Ḥeru-Beḥuṭet, the smiter of the lands, Horus, the son of Isis [and] Osiris . . . . **9** his blacksmiths[3] are to him, and those who are in his following are to him in his territory, with his metal lance, with his [mace], with

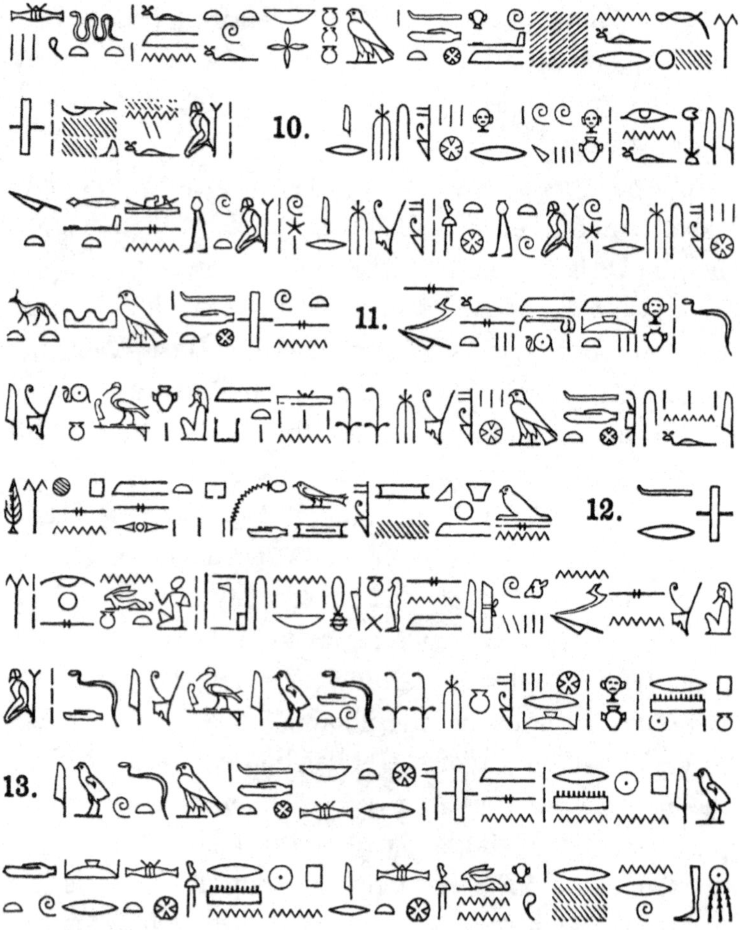

[1] In the sculptures (Naville, *Mythe*, pl. 17) Ḥeru-Beḥuṭet is seen standing in a boat spearing a crocodile, and immediately behind him in the boat is Rā-Harmachis in his shrine. The Mesentiu of the West are represented by an armed warrior in a boat, who is spearing a crocodile, and leads the way for Ḥeru-Beḥuṭet. In a boat behind the great god is a representative of the Mesentiu of the East spearing a crocodile.

his dagger, and with all his chains (or, fetters) which are in the city of Ḥeru-Beḥuṭet.

[And when he had reached the land of the North with his followers, he found the enemy.] **10**. Now as for the blacksmiths who were over the middle regions, they made a great slaughter of the enemy, and there were brought back one hundred and six of them. Now as for the blacksmiths of the West, they brought back one hundred and six of the enemy. Now as for the blacksmiths of the East, among whom was Ḥeru-Beḥuṭet, **11** he slew them (i.e., the enemy) in the presence of Rā in the Middle Domains.[1]

And Rā said unto Thoth, "My heart [is satisfied] "with the works of these blacksmiths of Ḥeru-Beḥuṭet "who are in his bodyguard. They shall dwell in "sanctuaries, and libations and purifications and "offerings shall be made to their images, and **12** [there "shall be appointed for them] priests who shall "minister by the month, and priests who shall minister "by the hour, in all their God-houses whatsoever, as their "reward because they have slain the enemies of the god."

And Thoth said, "The [Middle] Domains shall be "called after the names of these blacksmiths from this "day onwards, **13** and the god who dwelleth among "them, Ḥeru-Beḥuṭet, shall be called the 'Lord of "Mesent' from this day onwards, and the domain shall "be called 'Mesent of the West' from this day onwards."

As concerning Mesent of the West, the face (or, front) thereof shall be towards [the East], towards the place

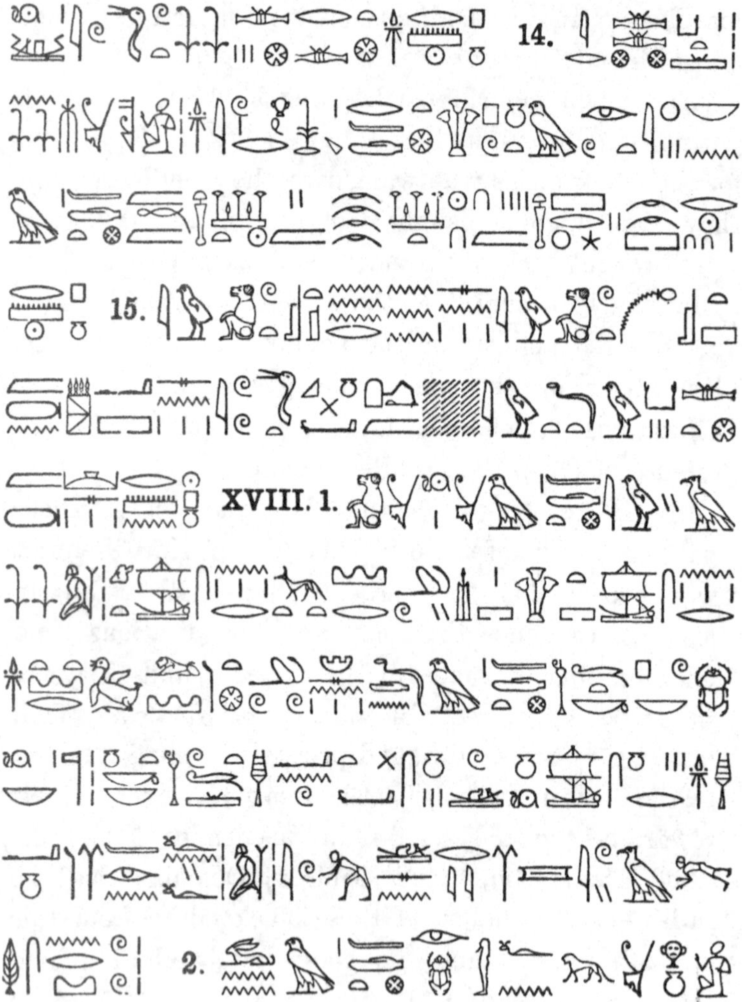

[1] The month Thoth.
[2] The month Choiak.
[3] The month Tybi.
[4] The month Mechir.
[5] Zoan-Tanis.

where Rā riseth, and this Mesent shall be called "Mesent of the East" from this day onwards. **14**. As concerning the double town of Mesent, the work of these blacksmiths of the East, the face (or, front) thereof shall be towards the South, towards the city of Beḥuṭet, the hiding-place of Ḥeru-Beḥuṭet. And there shall be performed therein all the rites and ceremonies of Ḥeru-Beḥuṭet on the second day of the first month[1] of the season of Akhet, and on the twenty-fourth day of the fourth month[2] of the season of Akhet, and on the seventh day of the first month[3] of the season Pert, and on the twenty-first day of the second month[4] of the season Pert, from this day onwards. **15**. Their stream shall be called "Åsti," the name of their Great House shall be called "Ābet," the [priest (?)] shall be called "Qen-āḥa," and their domain shall be called "Kau-Mesent" from this day onwards.

XVIII. 1. And Rā said unto Ḥeru-Beḥuṭet, "These "enemies have sailed up the river, to the country of "Setet, to the end of the pillar-house of Ḥat, and they "have sailed up the river to the east, to the country of "Tchalt (or, Tchart),[5] which is their region of swamps."

And Ḥeru-Beḥutet said, "Everything which thou "hast commanded hath come to pass, Rā, Lord of the "gods; thou art the lord of commands." And they untied the Boat of Rā, and they sailed up the river to the east. Then he looked upon those enemies whereof some of them had fallen into the sea (or, river), and the others had fallen headlong on the mountains. **2**.

And Ḥeru-Beḥuṭet transformed himself into a lion

[1] In the sculpture (Naville, *Mythe*, pl. 18), we see a representation of this lion, which is standing over the bodies of slain enemies upon a rectangular pedestal, or block. He is called 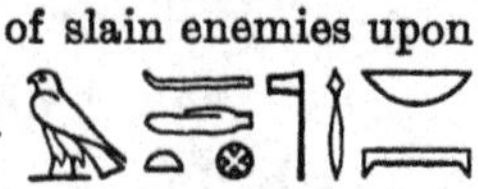 .

which had the face of a man, and which was crowned with the triple crown.[1] His paw was like unto a flint knife, and he went round and round by the side of them, and brought back one hundred and forty-two [of the enemy], and he rent them in pieces with his claws. He tore out their tongues, and their blood flowed on the ridges of the land in this place; and he made them the property of those who were in his following [whilst] he was upon the mountains.

And Rā said unto Thoth, "Behold, Ḥeru-Beḥuṭet is "like unto a lion in his lair [when] he is on the back "of the enemy who have given unto him their tongues."

3. And Thoth said, "This domain shall be called "'Khent-åbt,' and it shall [also] be called 'Tchalt' (or, "Tchart) from this day onwards. And the bringing "of the tongues from the remote places of Tchalt "(or, Tchart) [shall be commemorated] from this day "onwards. And this god shall be called 'Ḥeru-"Beḥuṭet, Lord of Mesent,' from this day onwards."

And Rā said unto Ḥeru-Beḥutet, "Let us sail to the "south up the river, and let us smite the enemies [who "are] in the forms of crocodiles and hippopotami in the "face of Egypt."

4. And Ḥeru-Beḥuṭet said, "Thy divine KA, O Rā, "Lord of the gods! Let us sail up the river against the "remainder—one third—of the enemies who are in the "water (or, river)." Then Thoth recited the Chapters of protecting the Boat [of Rā] and the boats of the blacksmiths, **5** [which he used] for making tranquil the sea at the moment when a storm was raging on it.

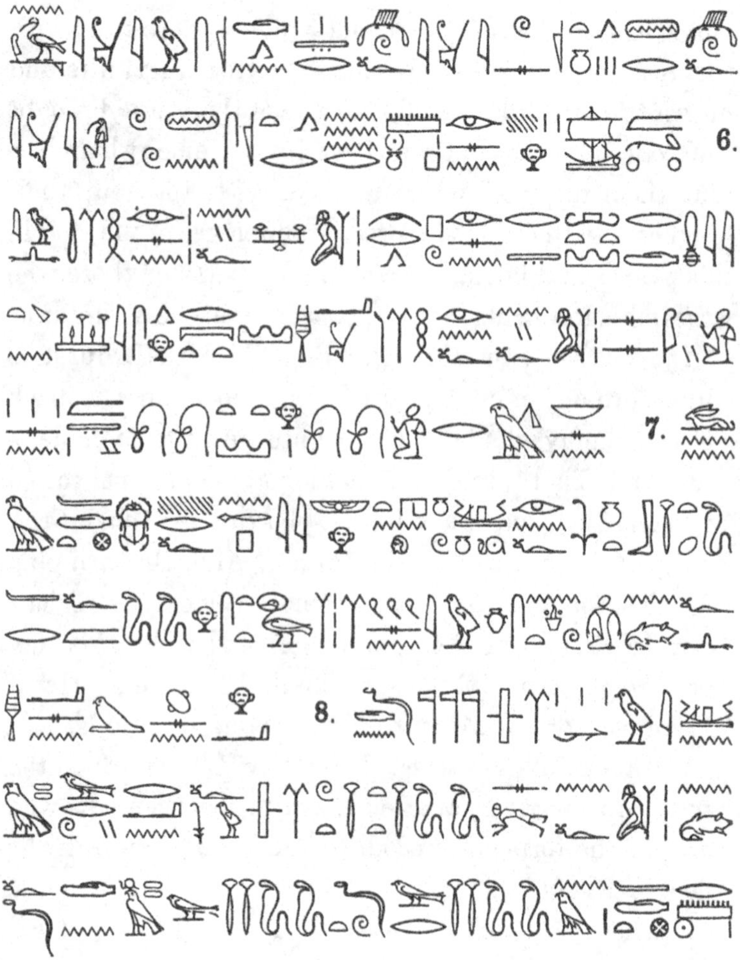

[1] Northern Nubia; the name means "Land of the Bow."

[2] A portion of Northern Nubia.

[3] The goddess of the South.

[4] The goddess of the North.

[5] I.e., Nekhebit and Uatchit.

[6] "Great one of the Two Uraei-goddesses;" these goddesses had their places above the brow of the god, or at the right and left of the solar disk.

And Rā said unto Thoth, "Have we not journeyed "throughout the whole land? Shall we not journey "over the whole sea in like manner?" And Thoth said, "This water shall be called the 'Sea of journey-"ing' from this day onward."

And they sailed about over the water during the night, **6** and they did not see any of those enemies at all.

Then they made a journey forth and arrived in the country of Ta-sti,[1] at the town of Shas-ḥertet, and he perceived the most able of their enemies in the country of Uaua,[2] and they were uttering treason against Horus their Lord.

7 And Ḥeru-Beḥuṭet changed his form into that of the Winged Disk, [and took his place] above the bow of the Boat of Rā. And he made the goddess Nekhebit[3] and the goddess Uatchit[4] to be with him in the form of serpents, so that they might make the Sebȧu fiends to quake in [all] their limbs (or, bodies). Their boldness (i.e., that of the fiends) subsided through the fear of him, they made no resistance whatsoever, and they died straightway.

8 Then the gods who were in the following of the Boat of Ḥeru-khuti said, "Great, great is that which "he hath done among them by means of the two "Serpent Goddesses,[5] for he hath overthrown the "enemy by means of their fear of him."

And Rā Ḥeru-khuti said, "The great one of the two "Serpent Goddesses of Ḥeru-Beḥuṭet shall be called "'Ur-Uatchti'[6] from this day onwards."

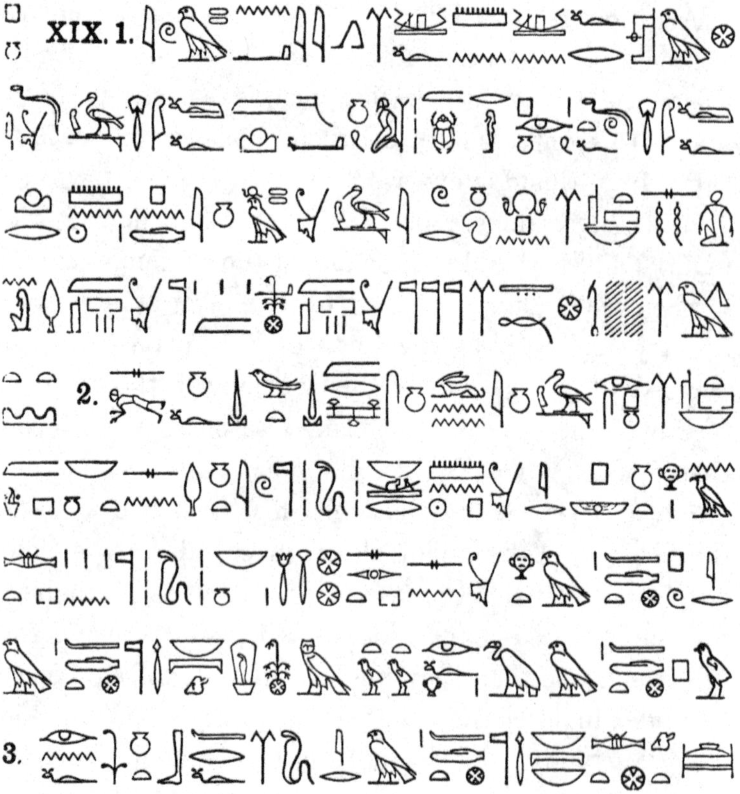

[1] In the sculpture (Naville, *Mythe*, pl. 19) we see the god, who is hawk-headed, and wears the crowns of the South and North, seated in a shrine set upon a pedestal. In the right hand he holds the sceptre , and in the left the *ānkh* . His titles are: 

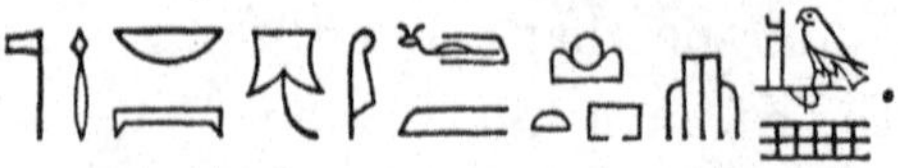.

[2] I.e., the North, especially the Delta.

[3] I.e., the South.

[4] I.e., the southern half of heaven.

[5] I.e., the northern half of heaven.

XIX. 1. And Ḥeru-khuti travelled on in his boat, and landed at the city of Thes-Ḥeru (Apollinopolis Magna). And Thoth said, "The being of light who hath come "forth from the horizon hath smitten the enemy in the "form which he hath made, and he shall be called "'Being of light who hath come forth from the horizon' "from this day onwards."[1]

And Rā Ḥeru-khuti (Rā Harmachis) said to Thoth, "Thou shalt make this Winged Disk to be in every "place wherein I seat myself (or, dwell), and in [all] "the seats of the gods in the South, and in [all] the "seats of the gods in the Land of the North, ... "in the Country of Horus, **2** that it may drive away "the evil ones from their domains."

Then Thoth made the image of the Winged Disk to be in every sanctuary and in every temple, where they now are, wherein are all the gods and all the goddesses from this day onwards. Now through the Winged Disk which is on the temple-buildings of all the gods and all the goddesses of the Land of the Lily,[2] and the Land of the Papyrus,[3] [these buildings] become shrines of Ḥeru-Beḥuṭet.

As concerning Ḥeru-Beḥuṭet, the great god, the lord of heaven, the president of the Åter of the South,[4] he it is who is made to be on the right hand. This is Heru-Beḥuṭet **3** on whom the goddess Nekhebit is placed in the form of a serpent (or, uraeus). As concerning Ḥeru-Beḥuṭet, the great god, the lord of heaven, the lord of Mesent, the president of the Åter of the North,[5]

[1]

[1] In the sculpture which illustrates this portion of the text at Edfû, two Winged Disks are represented. The first has  on each side of it. The disk has an uraeus on each side, and its two wings are called:

1. 

2. 

The second winged symbol of the god consists of a beetle with outstretched wings, which holds between his forelegs the solar disk, and between his hind legs the symbol of the orbit of the sun, . The east wing is called:

and the west wing:

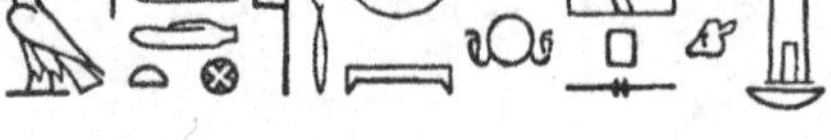

he it is who is made to be on the left hand. This Ḥeru-Beḥuṭet on whom the goddess Uatchit is placed is in the form of a serpent.

As concerning Ḥeru-Beḥuṭet, the great god, the lord of heaven, the lord of Mesent, the president of the two Ȧterti of the South and North, Rā Ḥeru-khuti set it (i.e., the Winged Disk) in his every place, to overthrow the enemies in every place wherein they are. And he shall be called President of the two Ȧterti of the South and North because of this from this day onwards.

A HYMN TO OSIRIS AND A LEGEND OF
THE ORIGIN OF HORUS.

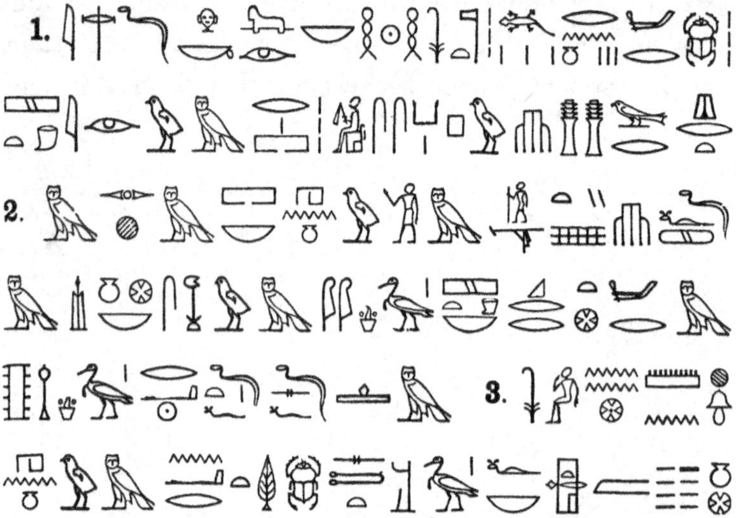

1. [hieroglyphic text]

2. [hieroglyphic text]

3. [hieroglyphic text]

[6] I.e., [hieroglyphic], a famous sanctuary in the Letopolite nome where Ptaḥ was worshipped.

[7] The region of the First Cataract, where the Nile was believed to rise.

[8] Memphis.

[9] Herakleopolis, the חָנֵס of Isaiah.

[1] A name of Herakleopolis.

[2] Khemenu or Hermopolis, the city of Thoth.

[3] These gods were: Nu and Nut; Ḥeḥu and Ḥeḥut; Kekui and Kekuit; Ḳerḥ and Ḳerḥet.

A HYMN TO OSIRIS AND A LEGEND OF THE ORIGIN OF HORUS.

1. Homage to thee, Osiris, Lord of eternity, King of the gods, whose names are manifold, whose transformations are sublime, whose form is hidden in the temples, whose KA is holy, the Governor of Ṭeṭut,[1] the mighty one of possessions (?) **2** in the shrine,[2] the Lord of praises[3] in the nome of Anetch,[4] President of the *tchefa* food in Ȧnu,[5] Lord who art commemorated in [the town of] Maāti,[6] the mysterious (or, hidden) Soul, the Lord of Qerret,[7] the sublime one in White Wall,[8] the Soul of Rā [and] his very body, who hast thy dwelling in **3** Ḥenensu,[9] the beneficent one, who art praised in Nārt,[1] who makest to rise up thy Soul, Lord of the Great House in the city[2] of the Eight Gods,[3] [who inspirest]

[1] More fully Pa-Ȧsȧr-neb-Ṭeṭut, 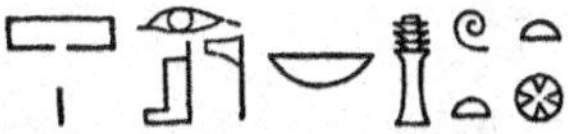, the Busiris of the Greeks; Busiris = Pa-Ȧsȧr, "House of Osiris," *par excellence*. The variant Ṭāṭāut, , also occurs.

[2] An allusion, perhaps, to the town Sekhem, , the capital of the second nome (Letopolites) of Lower Egypt.

[3] I.e., lord whose praises are sung.

[4] Letopolites.

[5] Heliopolis.

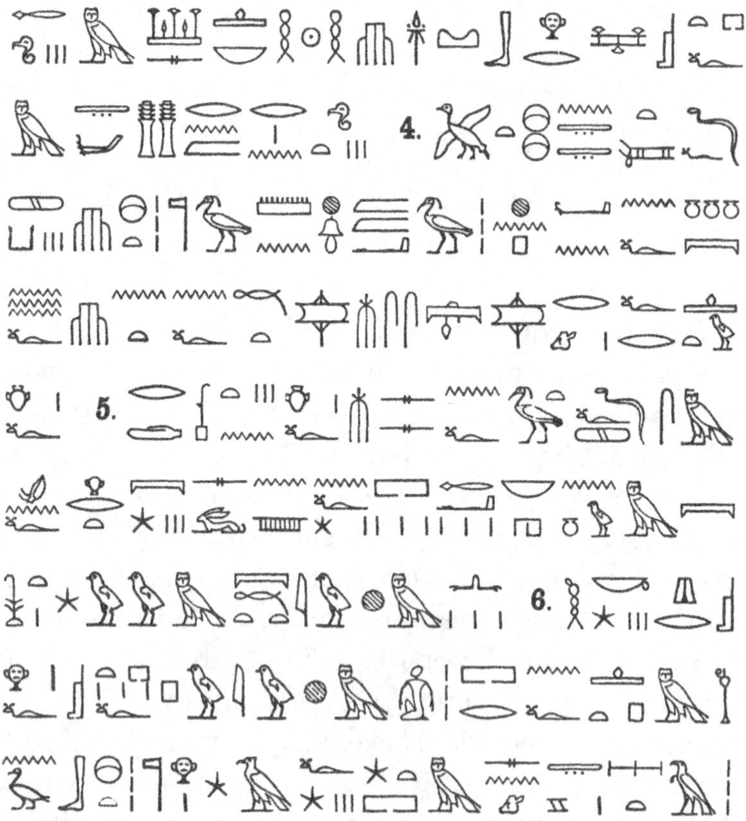

[5] Three Companies are distinguished: the gods of Heaven, the gods of Earth, and the gods of the Other World.

[6] The indestructible, immortal Spirit-soul as opposed to the Ba-soul or animal-soul.

[7] Here and in other places I have changed the pronoun of the third person into that of the second to avoid the abrupt changes of the original.

[8] I.e., they are under thy inspection and care.

[9] I.e., the stars which never set. The allusion is probably to certain circumpolar stars.

[1] I.e., do homage.

great terror in Shas-ḥetep,[1] Lord of eternity, Governor of Ȧbṭu (Abydos).

Thy seat (or, domain) reacheth far into Ta-tchesert,[2] and thy name is firmly stablished in the mouth[s] of men. **4**. Thou art the two-fold substance of the Two Lands[3] everywhere (?), and the divine food (*tchef*) of the KAU,[4] the Governor of the Companies[5] of the Gods, and the beneficent (or, perfect) Spirit-soul[6] among Spirit-souls. The god Nu draweth his waters from thee,[7] and thou bringest forth the north wind at eventide, and wind from thy nostrils to the satisfaction of thy heart. **5**. Thy heart flourisheth, and thou bringest forth the splendour of *tchef* food.

The height of heaven and the stars [thereof] are obedient unto thee, and thou makest to be opened the great gates [of the sky]. Thou art the lord to whom praises are sung in the southern heaven, thou art he to whom thanks are given in the northern heaven. The stars which never **6** diminish are under the place of thy face,[8] and thy seats are the stars which never rest.[9] Offerings appear before thee by the command of Ḳeb. The Companies of the Gods ascribe praise unto thee, the Star-gods of the Ṭuat smell the earth before thee,[1] the domains [make] bowings [before thee], and the

[1] The capital of Set, the eleventh nome of Upper Egypt; the chief local deity was Khnemu.

[2] A name of the Other World.

[3] I.e., the two Egypts, Upper and Lower.

[4] The Doubles of the beatified who are fed by Osiris in the Other World.

[1] One of the chief festivals of Osiris, during which the god made a periplus.

ends of the earth make supplication to thee **7** [when] they see thee.

Those who are among the holy ones are in terror of him, and the Two Lands, all of them, make acclamations to him when they meet His Majesty. Thou art a shining Noble at the head of the nobles, permanent in [thy] high rank, stablished in [thy] sovereignty, the beneficent Power of the Company of the Gods. Well-pleasing [is thy] face, **8** and thou art beloved by him that seeth thee. Thou settest the fear of thee in all lands, and because of their love for thee [men] hold thy name to be pre-eminent. Every man maketh offerings unto thee, and thou art the Lord who is commemorated in heaven and upon earth. Manifold are the cries of acclamation to thee in the Uaḳ[1] festival, and the **9** Two Lands shout joyously to thee with one accord. Thou art the eldest, the first of thy brethren, the Prince of the Company of the Gods, and the stablisher of Truth throughout the Two Lands. Thou settest [thy] son upon the great throne of his father Ḳeb. Thou art the beloved one of thy mother Nut, whose valour is most mighty [when] thou overthrowest the Sebȧ Fiend. **10**. Thou hast slaughtered thy enemy, and hast put the fear of thee into thy Adversary.

Thou art the bringer in of the remotest boundaries, and art stable of heart, and thy two feet are lifted up (?); thou art the heir of Ḳeb and of the sovereignty of the Two Lands, and he (i.e., Ḳeb) hath seen thy

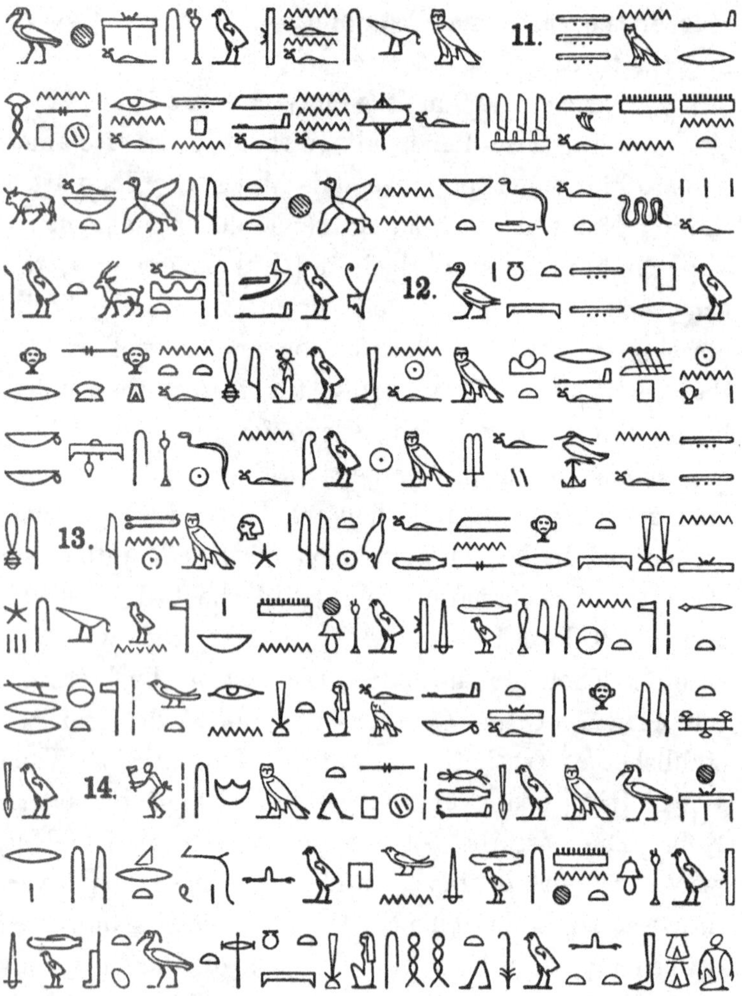

[1]  may also represent the mountainous districts of Egypt, or even foreign countries in general.

[2] To make him rise like the sun, or to enthrone him.

[3] Or, "becoming a brother to the stars," or the Star-gods.

[4] Or, beneficent.

splendid qualities, and hath commanded thee to guide **11** the lands (i.e., the world) by thy hand so long as times [and seasons] endure.

Thou hast made this earth with thy hand, the waters thereof, the winds thereof, the trees and herbs thereof, the cattle thereof of every kind, the birds thereof of every kind, the fish thereof of every kind, the creeping things thereof, and the four-footed beasts thereof. The land of the desert[1] belongeth by right to **12** the son of Nut, and the Two Lands have contentment in making him to rise[2] upon the throne of his father like Rā.

Thou rollest up into the horizon, thou settest the light above the darkness, thou illuminest [the Two Lands] with the light from thy two plumes, thou floodest the Two Lands like the **13** Disk at the beginning of the dawn. Thy White Crown pierceth the height of heaven saluting the stars,[3] thou art the guide of every god. Thou art perfect[4] in command and word. Thou art the favoured one of the Great Company of the Gods, and thou art the beloved one of the Little Company of the Gods.

Thy sister [Isis] acted as a protectress to thee. She drove [thy] enemies away, **14** she averted seasons [of calamity from thee], she recited the word (or, formula) with the magical power of her mouth, [being] skilled of tongue and never halting for a word, being perfect in command and word. Isis the magician avenged her brother. She went about seeking for him untiringly.

15.
16.
17.
18.

15. She flew round and round over this earth uttering wailing cries of grief, and she did not alight on the ground until she had found him. She made light [to come forth] from her feathers, she made air to come into being by means of her two wings, and she cried out the death cries for her brother. **16**. She made to rise up the helpless members of him whose heart was at rest, she drew from him his essence, and she made therefrom an heir. She suckled the child in solitariness and none knew where his place was, and he grew in strength. His hand is mighty (or, victorious) within the house **17** of Ḳeb, and the Company of the Gods rejoice greatly at the coming of Horus, the son of Osiris, whose heart is firmly stablished, the triumphant one, the son of Isis, the flesh and bone of Osiris. The Tchatcha[1] of Truth, and the Company of the Gods, and Neb-er-tcher[2] himself, and the Lords of Truth, gather together to him, and assemble therein.[3] **18**. Verily those who defeat iniquity rejoice[4] in the House of Ḳeb to bestow the divine rank and dignity upon him to whom it belongeth, and the sovereignty upon him whose it is by right.

[1] Literally, the "Heads," i.e., the divine sovereign Chiefs at the court of Osiris, who acted as administrators of the god, and even as task-masters.

[2] "He who is the lord to the end (or, limit) of the world," a name of Osiris.

[3] I.e., in the House of Ḳeb.

[4] Or perhaps "take their seats in the House of Ḳeb."

A LEGEND OF PTAḤ NEFER-ḤETEP AND THE PRINCESS OF BEKHTEN.

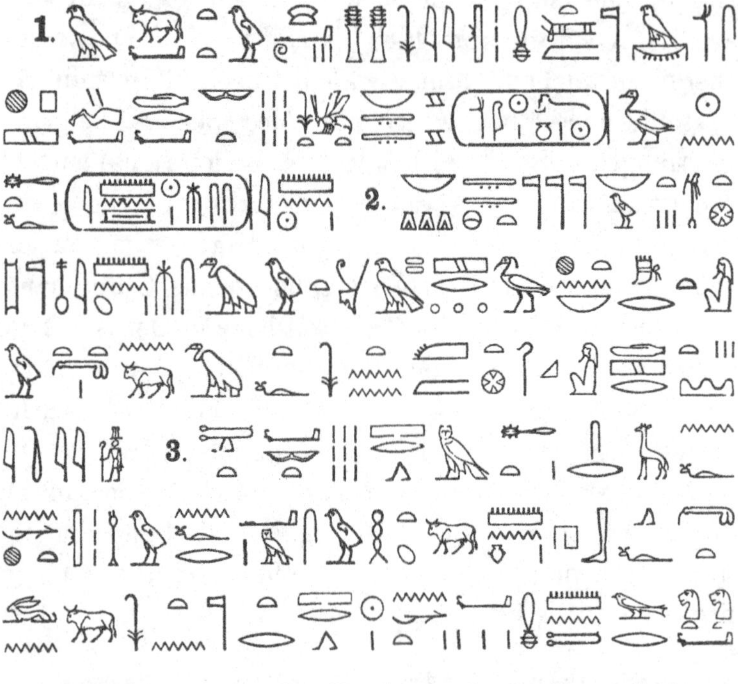

[1] I.e., the image who rises like the sun day by day, or the image of [many] crowns.

[2] Or, mighty one of the thigh, i.e., he of the mighty thigh.

[3] The nations of Nubia who fought with bows and arrows.

[4] In this version of the protocol of Rameses II. the second "strong name" of the king is omitted.

[5] I.e., Neb-er-tcher.

[6] Ka-mut-f, the Καμῆφις of the Greeks.

[7] The War-god of Thebes.

[8] I.e., Osiris.

A LEGEND OF PTAḤ NEFER-ḤETEP AND THE PRINCESS OF BEKHTEN.

1. The Horus: "Mighty Bull, the form (?) of risings,[1] stablished in sovereignty like Tem." The Golden Horus: "Mighty one of strength,[2] destroyer of the Nine Nations of the Bow."[3] King of the South and North: "The Lord of the Two Lands, (User-Maāt-Rā-setep-en-Rā)." Son of Rā: "Of his body, (Rā-meses-meri-Åmen), of Åmen-Rā;[4] **2** the Lord of the thrones of the Two Lands, and of the Company of the Gods, the Lords of Thebes, the beloved one. The beneficent god, the son of Åmen, born of Mut, begotten of Ḥeru-khuti, the glorious offspring of Neb-tchert,[5] begetting [as] the Bull of his Mother,[6] king of Egypt, Governor of the deserts, the Sovereign **3** who hath taken possession of the Nine Nations of the Bow; [who] on coming forth from the womb ordained mighty things, who gave commands whilst he was in the egg, the Bull, stable of heart, who hath sent forth his seed; the king who is a bull, [and] a god who cometh forth on the day of battle like Menthu,[7] the mighty one of strength like the son of Nut."[8]

[1] The "country of the rivers," the אֲרַם נַהֲרַיִם of Gen. xxiv. 10, the ܒܝܬ ܢܗܪܝܢ of Syrian writers.

[2] A name including Western Asia and a portion of the East Coast of Africa.

[3] The summer. The Copts called the second month of this season Paoni.

[4] The modern Temple of Luxor.

4. Behold, His Majesty was in the country of Neheru[1] according to his custom every year, and the chiefs of every land, even as far as the swamps, came [to pay] homage, bearing offerings to the Souls of His Majesty; and they brought their gifts, gold, lapis-lazuli, turquoise, **5** bars of wood of every kind of the Land of the God,[2] on their backs, and each one surpassed his neighbour.

And the Prince of Bekhten [also] caused his gifts to be brought, and he set his eldest daughter at the head of them all, and he addressed words of praise to His Majesty, and prayed to him for his life. **6**. And the maiden was beautiful, and His Majesty considered her to be the most lovely [woman] in the world, and he wrote down as her title, "Great Royal Wife, (Rā-neferu);" and when His Majesty arrived in Egypt, he did for her whatsoever was done for the Royal Wife.

On the twenty-second day of the second month of the season of Shemu,[3] in the fifteenth year [of his reign], behold, His Majesty was in Thebes, the Mighty [city], the Mistress of cities, performing **7** the praises of Father Åmen, the Lord of the thrones of the Two Lands, in his beautiful Festival of the Southern Åpt,[4] which was the seat of his heart (i.e., the chosen spot) from primaeval time, [when] one came to say to His Majesty, "An ambassador of the Prince of Bekhten "hath arrived bearing many gifts for the Royal Wife."

[1] Or, a skilled craftsman.

And having been brought into the presence of **8** His Majesty with his gifts, he spake words of adoration to His Majesty, saying, "Praise be unto thee, O thou Sun "(Rā) of the Nine Nations of the Bow, permit us to "live before thee!" And when he had spoken, and had smelt the earth before His Majesty, he continued his speech before His Majesty, saying, "I have come unto "thee, **9** my King and Lord, on behalf of Bent-Resht, "the younger sister of the Royal Wife (Rā-neferu). "[Some] disease hath penetrated into her members, "and I beseech Thy Majesty to send a man of learning "to see her."

And His Majesty said, "Bring to me the magicians '(or, scribes) of the House of Life, and the nobles **10** of "the palace." And having been brought into his presence straightway, His Majesty said unto them, "Behold, I "have caused you to be summoned [hither] in order "that ye may hear this matter. Now bring to me [one] "of your company whose heart is wise,[1] and whose "fingers are deft." And the royal scribe **11** Teḥuti-em-ḥeb came into the presence of His Majesty, and His Majesty commanded him to depart to Bekhten with that ambassador.

And when the man of learning had arrived in Bekhten, he found Bent-Resht in the condition of a woman who is possessed by a spirit, and he found **12** this spirit to be an evil one, and to be hostile in his disposition towards him.

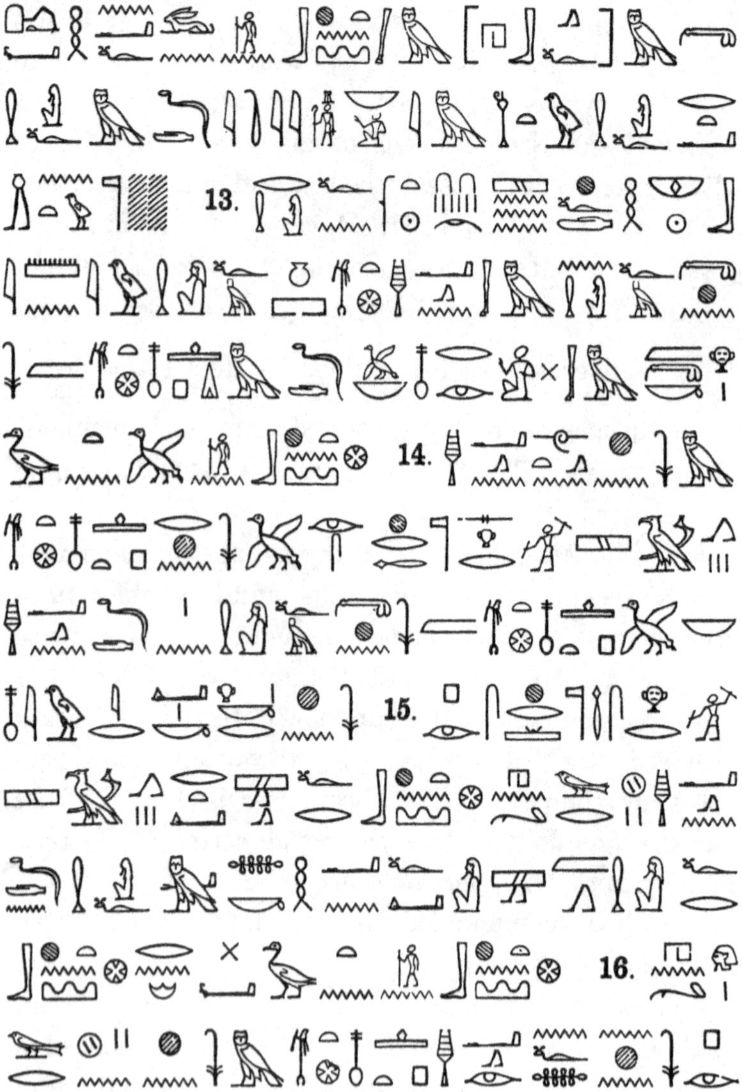

[1] The month Pakhon of the Copts.

[2] The text makes no mention of the first application to Khensu.

And the Prince of Bekhten sent a messenger a second time into the presence of His Majesty, saying, "O King, my Lord, I pray His (i.e., Thy) Majesty to "command that a god be brought hither [to contend "against the spirit."

13. Now when the messenger came] to His Majesty in the first month[1] of the season of Shemu, in the twenty-sixth year [of his reign], on the day which coincided with that of the Festival of Åmen, His Majesty was in the palace (or, temple?) of Thebes. And His Majesty spake a second time[2] in the presence of Khensu in Thebes, [called] "Nefer-Ḥetep," saying, "O my fair Lord, I present myself before thee a second "time on behalf of the daughter of the Prince of Bekhten."

14. Then Khensu in Thebes, [called] "Nefer-Ḥetep," was carried to Khensu, [called] "Pa-åri-sekher," the great god who driveth away the spirits which attack. And His Majesty spake before Khensu in Thebes, [called] "Nefer-Ḥetep," saying, "O my fair Lord, if "thou wilt give (i.e., turn) thy face to Khensu, [called] "**15** 'Pa-åri-sekher,' the great god who driveth away "the spirits which attack, permit thou that he may "depart to Bekhten;" [and the god] inclined his head with a deep inclination twice. And His Majesty said, "Let, I pray, thy protective (or, magical) power [go] "with him, so that I may make His Majesty to go to "Bekhten to deliver the daughter of the Prince of "Bekhten [from the spirit]."

16. And Khensu in Thebes, [called] "Nefer-Ḥetep,"

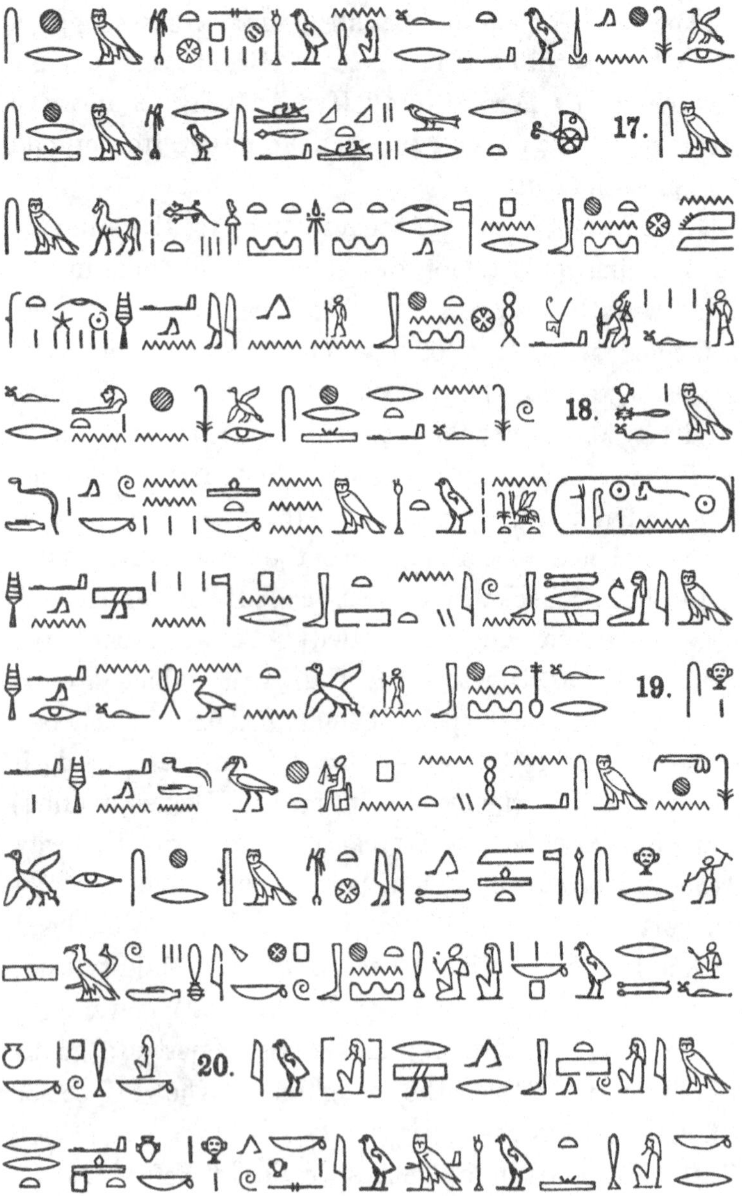
17.
18.
19.
20.

inclined his head with a deep inclination twice. And he made [his] protective power to pass into Khensu, [called] "Pa-åri-sekher-em-Uast," in a fourfold measure. Then His Majesty commanded that Khensu, [called] "Pa-åri-sekher-em-Uast," should set out on his journey in a great boat, [accompanied by] five smaller boats, and chariots, **17** and a large number of horses [which marched] on the right side and on the left.

And when this god arrived in Bekhten at the end of a period of one year and five months, the Prince of Bekhten came forth with his soldiers and his chief[s] before Khensu, [called] "Pa-åri-sekher," and he cast himself down **18** upon his belly, saying, "Thou hast "come to us, and thou art welcomed by us, by the "commands of the King of the South and North, (User-Maāt-Rā-setep-en-Rā)!"

And when this god had passed over to the place where Bent-Resht was, he worked upon the daughter of the Prince of Bekhten with his magical power, and she became better (i.e., was healed) **19** straightway. And this spirit which had been with her said, in the presence of Khensu, [called] "Pa-åri-sekher-em-Uast," "Come "in peace (i.e., Welcome!), O great god, who dost drive "away the spirits which attack! Bekhten is thy city, "the people thereof, both men and women, are thy "servants, and I myself am thy servant. **20.** I will "[now] depart unto the place whence I came, so that I "may cause thy heart to be content about the matter

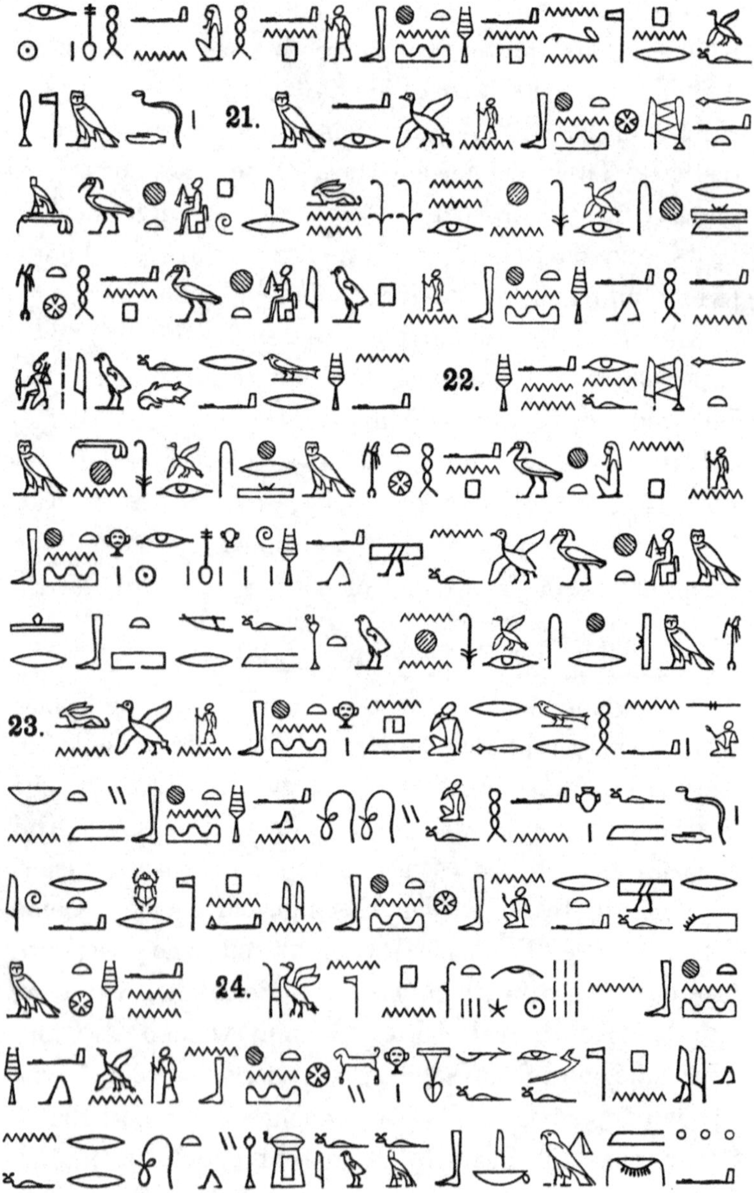
21.
22.
23.
24.

"concerning which thou hast come. I pray that Thy "Majesty will command that a happy day (i.e., a "festival, or day of rejoicing) be made with me, and "with the Prince of Bekhten." And this god inclined his head [in approval] to his priest, saying, **21** "Let "the Prince of Bekhten make a great offering in the "presence of this spirit."

Now whilst Khensu, [called] "Pa-åri-sekher-em-Uast," was arranging these [things] with the spirit, the Prince of Bekhten and his soldiers were standing there, and they feared with an exceedingly great fear. **22**. And the Prince of Bekhten made a great offering in the presence of Khensu, [called] "Pa-åri-sekher-em-Uast," and the spirit of the Prince of Bekhten, and he made a happy day (i.e., festival) on their behalf, and [then] the spirit departed in peace unto the place which he loved, by the command of Khensu, [called] "Pa-åri-sekher-em-Uast." **23**. And the Prince of Bekhten, and every person who was in the country of Bekhten, rejoiced very greatly, and he took counsel with his heart, saying, "It hath happened that this god hath been "given as a gift to Bekhten, and I will not permit him "to depart to Egypt."

24. And [when] this god had tarried for three years and nine months in Bekhten, the Prince of Bekhten, who was lying down asleep on his bed, saw this god come forth outside his shrine (now he was in the form of a golden hawk), and he flew up into the heavens and departed to Egypt; and when the Prince woke up

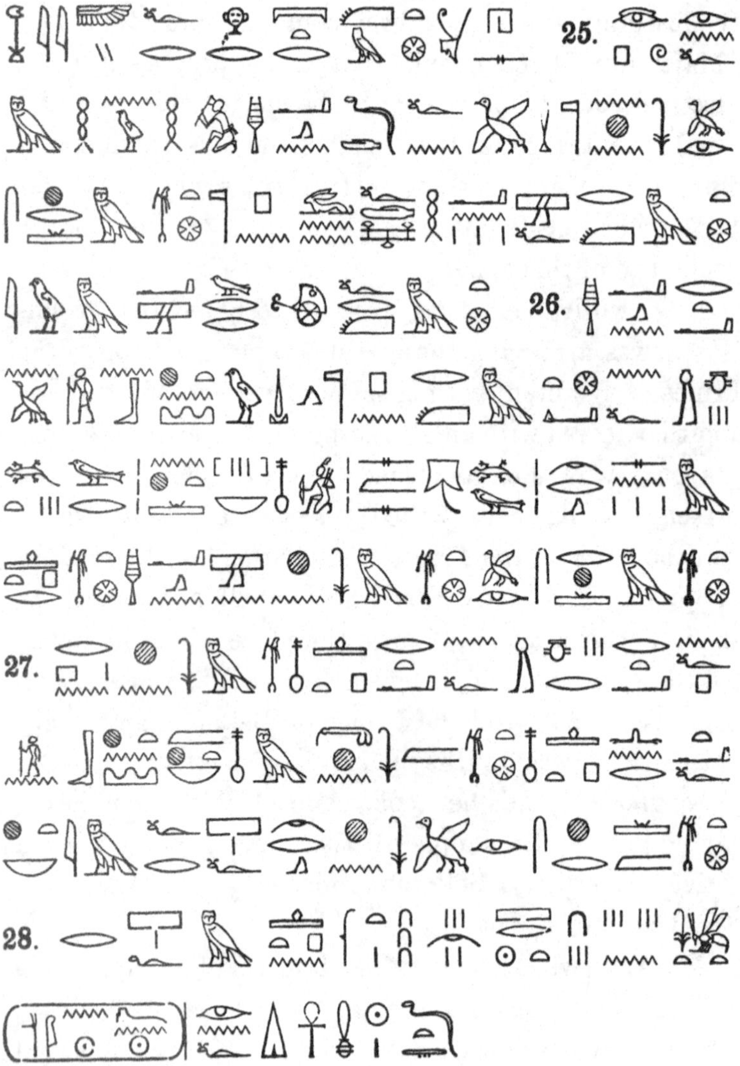
25.
26.
27.
28.

25 he was trembling. And he said unto the prophet of Khensu, [called] "Pa-åri-sekher-em-Uast," "This god "who tarried with us hath departed to Egypt; let his "chariot also depart to Egypt."

26. And the Prince of Bekhten permitted [the image of] the god to set out for Egypt, and he gave him many great gifts of beautiful things of all kinds, and a large number of soldiers and horses [went with him]. And when they had arrived in peace in Thebes, Khensu, [called] "Pa-åri-sekher-em-Uast," **27** went into the Temple of Khensu in Thebes, [called] "Nefer-Ḥetep," and he placed the offerings which the Prince of Bekhten had given unto him, beautiful things of all kinds, before Khensu in Thebes, [called] "Nefer-Ḥetep," and he gave nothing thereof whatsoever to his [own] temple.

Thus Khensu, [called] "Pa-åri-sekher-em-Uast," arrived **28** in his temple in peace, on the nineteenth day of the second month[1] of the season Pert, in the thirty-third year of the [reign of the] King of the South and North, (User-Maāt-en-Rā-setep-en-Rā), the giver of life, like Rā, for ever.

[1] The month Mekhir of the Copts; the season Pert is the Egyptian spring.

A LEGEND OF THE GOD KHNEMU AND OF A SEVEN YEARS' FAMINE.

[2] I.e., the people who were in front of, that is, to the South of Egypt, or the population of the country which lies between Daḳḳah and Aswân.

[3] The ancient Egyptian name for Elephantine Island, which appears to have gained this name because it resembled an elephant in shape.

[4] I.e., the palace.

[5] I.e., risen.

A LEGEND OF THE GOD KHNEMU AND OF A SEVEN YEARS' FAMINE.

1. In the eighteenth year of the Horus, Neter-Khat, of the King of the South and North, Neter-Khat, of the Lord of the Shrines of Uatchit and Nekhebit, Neter-Khat, of the Golden Horus (Tcheser),[1] when Maṭȧr was Ḥā Prince, and Erpā, and Governor of the temple-cities in the Land of the South, and director of the Khenti[2] folk in Abu,[3] there was brought unto him the following royal despatch: "This is to inform thee "that misery hath laid hold upon me

"**2** [as I sit] upon the great throne by reason of "those who dwell in the Great House.[4] My heart is "grievously afflicted by reason of the exceedingly great "evil [which hath happened] because Ḥāpi (i.e., the "Nile) hath not come forth[5] in my time to the [proper] "height for seven years. Grain is very scarce, vege-"tables are lacking altogether, every kind of thing "which men eat for their food hath ceased, and every "man [now] plundereth

"**3** his neighbour. Men wish to walk, but are

[1] Tcheser was a king of the IIIrd Dynasty, and is famous as the builder of the Step Pyramid at Ṣaḳḳârah. His tomb was discovered by Mr. J. Garstang at Bêt Khallâf in Upper Egypt in 1901.

[1] I.e., the high court officials and administrators.

[2] The famous priest and magician, who was subsequently deified and became one of the chief gods of Memphis.

[3] Hermopolis.

[4] Per-ānkh, or Pa-ānkh, was a name given to one of the temple-colleges of priests and scribes.

[5] I.e., the Inundation, or Nile Flood.

"unable to move, the child waileth, the young man "draggeth his limbs along, and the hearts of the aged "folk are crushed with despair; their legs give way "under them, and they sink down to the ground, and "their hands are laid upon their bodies [in pain]. The "*shennu*[1] nobles are destitute of counsel, and [when] "the storehouses which should contain supplies are "opened, there cometh forth therefrom nothing but "wind. Everything

"**4** is in a state of ruin. My mind hath remembered, "going back to former time, when I had an advocate, "to the time of the gods, and of the Ibis-god, and of "the chief Kher-ḥeb priest I-em-ḥetep,[2] the son of "Ptaḥ of his Southern Wall.

"Where is the place of birth of Ḥāpi (the Nile)? "What god, or what goddess, presideth (?) over it? "What manner of form hath he? It is he who "stablisheth

"**5** revenue for me, and a full store of grain. I "would go to the Chief of Ḥet-Sekhet,[3] whose bene-"ficence strengtheneth all men in their works. I "would enter into the House of Life,[4] I would unfold "the written rolls [therein], and I would lay my hand "upon them."

Then [Maṭâr] set out on his journey, and he returned to me straightway. He gave me instruction concerning the increase of Ḥāpi,[5] and told me

6 all things which men had written concerning it, and he revealed to me the secret doors (?) whereto my

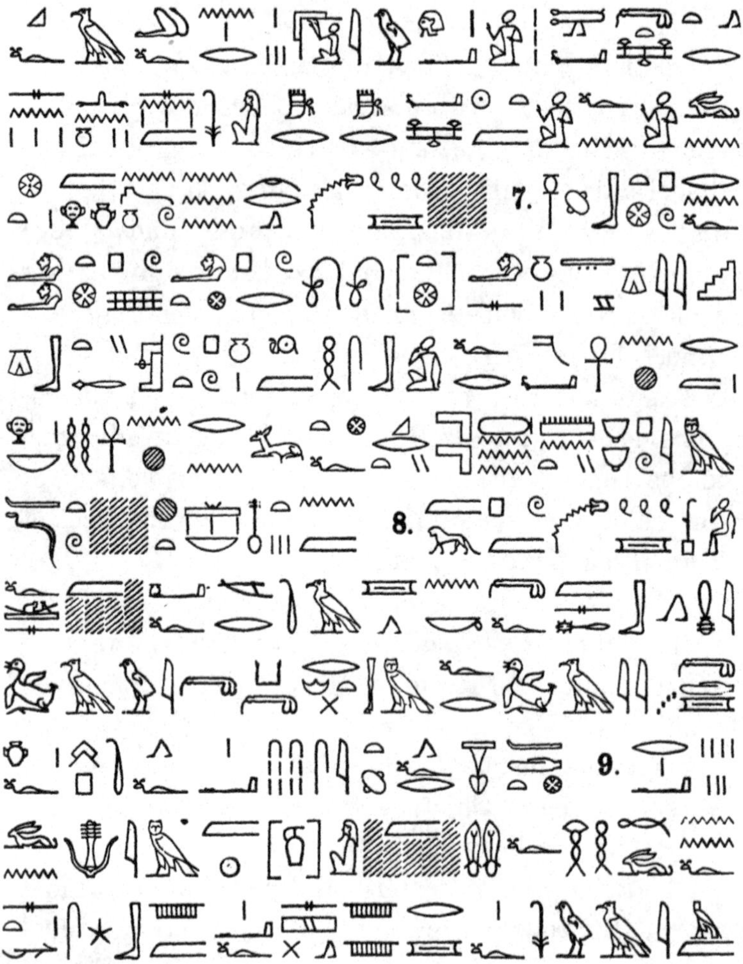

[1] The Elephant City, i.e., Elephantine.

[2] A portion of Northern Nubia.

[3] This is probably an allusion to the famous Nilometer on the Island of Philae.

[4] I.e., "Sweet, sweet life."

[5] The Qerti were the two openings through which the Nile entered this world from the great celestial ocean.

[6] Diospolis of Lower Egypt, or "Thebes of the North."

ancestors had betaken themselves quickly, the like of which has never been to [any] king since the time of Rā (?). And he said unto me: "There is a city in the middle "of the stream wherefrom Ḥāpi maketh his appearance;

"**7** 'Abu'[1] was its name in the beginning; it is the "City of the Beginning, and it is the Nome of the City "of the Beginning. [It reacheth] to Uaua,[2] which (?) "is the beginning of the land. There is too a flight of "steps,[3] which reareth itself to a great height, and is "the support of Rā, when he maketh his calculation to "prolong life to everyone; 'Netchemtchem Ānkh'[4] is "the name of its abode. 'The two Qerti'[5] is the name "of the water, and they are the two breasts from which "every good thing cometh forth (?).

"**8**. Here is the bed of Ḥāpi (the Nile), wherein he "reneweth his youth [in his season], wherein he causeth "the flooding of the land. He cometh and hath union "as he journeyeth, as a man hath union with a woman. "And again he playeth the part of a husband and "satisfieth his desire. He riseth to the height of "twenty-eight cubits [at Abu], and he droppeth at "Sma-Beḥuṭet[6]

"**9** to seven cubits. The union (?) there is that of "the god Khnemu in [Abu. He smiteth the ground] "with his sandals, and [its] fulness becometh abundant; "he openeth the bolt of the door with his hand, and he "throweth open the double door of the opening through "which the water cometh.

"Moreover, he dwelleth there in the form of the

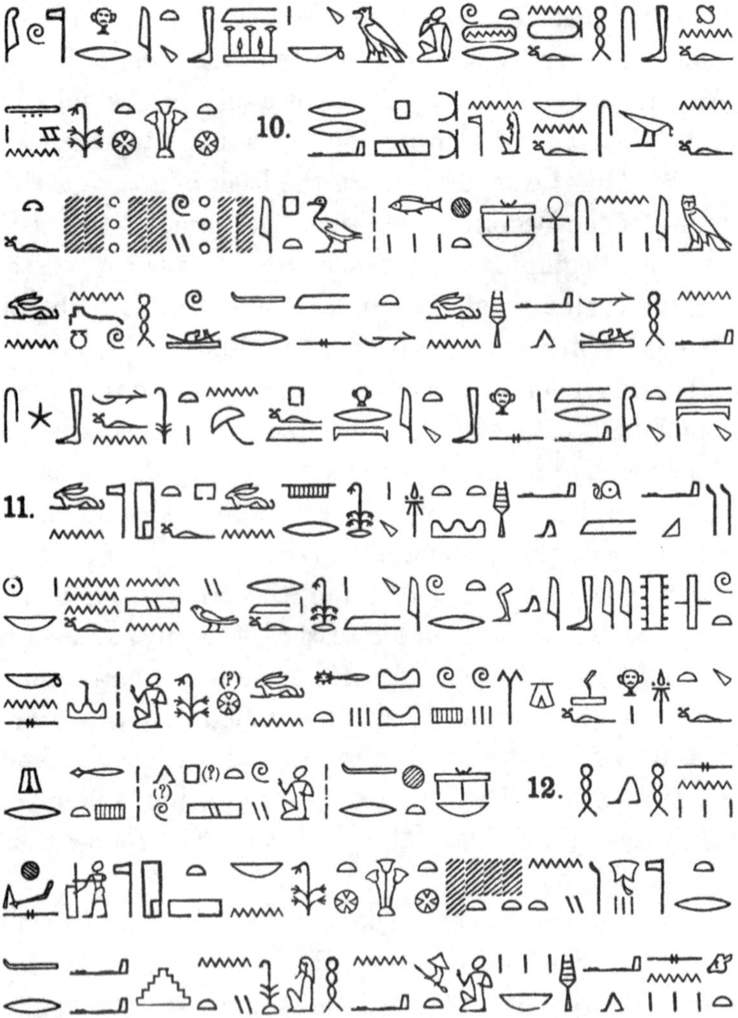

[1] The god who separated the Sky-goddess Nut from the embrace of her husband, the Earth-god Ḳeb, and who holds her above him each day.

[2] Kens extended south from Philae as far as Korosko.

"god Shu,[1] as one who is lord over his own territory, "and his homestead, the name of which is 'Ȧa' (i.e., "the 'Island'). There he keepeth an account of the "products of the Land of the South and of the Land of "the North,

"**10** in order to give unto every god his proper share, "and he leadeth to each [the metals], and the [precious "stones, and the four-footed beasts], and the feathered "fowl, and the fish, and every thing whereon they live. "And the cord [for the measuring of the land] and the "tablet whereon the register is kept are there.

"And there is an edifice of wood there, with the "portals thereof formed of reeds, wherein he dwelleth "as one who is over his own territory, and he maketh "the foliage of the trees (?) to serve as a roof.

"**11.** His God-house hath an opening towards the "south-east, and Rā (or, the Sun) standeth immediately "opposite thereto every day. The stream which floweth "along the south side thereof hath danger [for him that "attacketh it], and it hath as a defence a wall which "entereth into the region of the men of Kens[2] on the "South. Huge mountains [filled with] masses of stone "are round about its domain on the east side, and shut "it in. Thither come the quarrymen with things "(tools ?) of every kind, [when] they

"**12** seek to build a House for any god in the Land of "the South, or in the Land of the North, or [shrines] as "abodes for sacred animals, or royal pyramids, and statues "of all kinds. They stand up in front of the House of

[1] Perhaps Sunut, = the Syene of the Greeks, and the סְוֵנֵה of the Hebrews.

[2] I.e., Syene.

[3] I.e., Contra Syene.

[4] I.e., the Island of Elephantine.

"the God and in the sanctuary chamber, and their sweet-"smelling offerings are presented before the face of the god "Khnemu during his circuit, even as [when they bring]

"**13** garden herbs and flowers of every kind. The "fore parts thereof are in Abu (Elephantine), and the "hind parts are in the city of Sunt (?).[1] One portion "thereof is on the east side[2] of the river, and another "portion is on the west side[3] of the river, and another "portion is in the middle[4] of the river. The stream "decketh the region with its waters during a certain "season of the year, and it is a place of delight for "every man. And works are carried on among these "quarries [which are] on the edges [of the river ?],

"**14** for the stream immediately faceth this city of "Abu itself, and there existeth the granite, the sub-"stance whereof is hard (?); 'Stone of Abu' it is called.

"[Here is] a list of the names of the gods who dwell "in the Divine House of Khnemu. The goddess of the "star Sepṭ (Sothis), the goddess Ānqet, Ḥāp (the Nile-"god), Shu, Ḳeb, Nut, Osiris, Horus, Isis, and Nephthys.

"[Here are]

"**15** the names of the stones which lie in the heart "of the mountains, some on the east side, some on the "west side, and some in [the midst of] the stream of "Abu. They exist in the heart of Abu, they exist in "the country on the east bank, and in the country on "the west bank, and in the midst of the stream, namely, "*Bekhen*-stone, *Meri* (or Meli)-stone, *Atbekhāb* (?)-stone, "*Rāḳes*-stone, and white *Utshi*-stone; these are found

[1] I.e., the stone was very famous.

[2] The "fore part," or "front," of the land means the country lying to the south of Nubia, and probably some part of the modern Egyptian Sûdân.

"on the east bank. *Per-tchani*-stone is found on the "west bank, and the *Teshi*-stone in the river.

"**16** [Here are] the names of the hard (or, hidden) "precious stones, which are found in the upper side, "among them being the . . . . . stone, the name[1] of "which hath spread abroad through [a space of] four "*ȧtru* measures: Gold, Silver, Copper, Iron, Lapis-"lazuli, Emerald, *Theḥen* (Crystal?), *Khenem* (Ruby), "*Ḳāi*, *Mennu*, *Betḳā* (?), *Temi*, *Nā* (?). The following "come forth from the fore part[2] of the land: *Meḥi*-"stone, [*Ḥe*]*maki*-stone,

"**17** *Ȧbheti*-stone, iron ore, alabaster for statues, "mother-of-emerald, antimony, seeds (or, gum) of the "*sehi* plant, seeds (or, gum) of the *ȧmem* plant, and "seeds (or, gum) of the incense plant; these are found "in the fore parts of its double city." These were the things which I learned therefrom (i.e., from Maṭȧr).

Now my heart was very happy when I heard these things, and I entered into [the temple of Khnemu]. The overseers unrolled the documents which were fastened up, the water of purification was sprinkled [upon me], a progress was made [through] the secret places, and a great offering [consisting] of bread-cakes, beer, geese, oxen (or, bulls), and beautiful things

18 of all kinds were offered to the gods and goddesses who dwell in Abu, whose names are proclaimed at the place [which is called], "Couch of the heart in life and power."

And I found the God standing in front of me, and I

[1] He was the "builder of men, maker of the gods, the Father "who was from the beginning, the maker of things which are, the "creator of things which shall be, the source of things which exist, "Father of fathers, Mother of mothers, Father of the fathers of the "gods and goddesses, lord of created things, maker of heaven, earth, "Ṭuat, water and mountains" (Lanzone, *Dizionario*, p. 957).

made him to be at peace with me by means of the thank-offering which I offered unto him, and I made prayer and supplication before him. Then he opened his eyes, and his heart was inclined [to hear] me, and his words were strong [when he said], "I am Khnemu,[1] "who fashioned thee. My two hands were about thee "and knitted together thy body, and

"**19** made healthy thy members; and it is I who "gave thee thy heart. Yet the minerals (or, precious "stones) [lie] under each other, [and they have done "so] from olden time, and no man hath worked them "in order to build the houses of the god, or to restore "those which have fallen into ruin, or to hew out "shrines for the gods of the South and of the North, or "to do what he ought to do for his lord, notwithstand-"ing that I am the Lord and the Creator.

"I am [he] who created himself, Nu, the Great "[God], who came into being at the beginning, [and] "Ḥāpi, who riseth

"**20** according to his will, in order to give health to "him that laboureth for me. I am the Director and "Guide of all men at their seasons, the Most Great, the "Father of the Gods, Shu, the Great One, the Chief of "the Earth. The two halves of the sky (i.e., the East "and the West) are as a habitation below me. A lake "of water hath been poured out for me, [namely,] Ḥāp "(i.e., the Nile), which embraceth the field-land, and "his embrace provideth the [means of] life for

"**21** every nose (i.e., every one), according to the

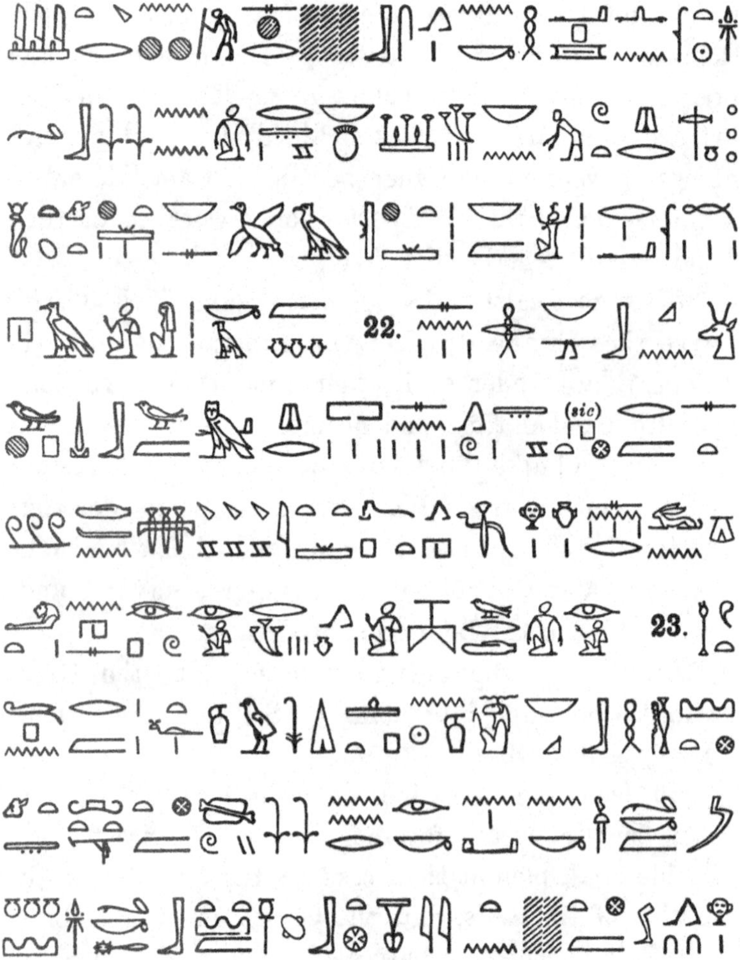

[1] The goddess of the harvest.

[2] Or perhaps, Khnemu-Rā.

[3] Qebḥet is the name given to the whole region of the First Cataract.

[4] The "Land of the Bow," i.e., the Northern Sûdân.

[5] The Land of the setting sun, the West.

"extent of his embrace of the field-land. With old age "[cometh] the condition of weakness. I will make "Ḥāp (i.e., the Nile) rise for thee, and [in] no year "shall [he] fail, and he shall spread himself out in rest "upon every land. Green plants and herbs and trees "shall bow beneath [the weight of] their produce. The "goddess Renenet[1] shall be at the head of everything, "and every product shall increase by hundreds of "thousands, according to the cubit of the year. The "people shall be filled, verily to their hearts' desire,

"**22** and everyone. Misery shall pass away, and the "emptiness of their store-houses of grain shall come "to an end. The land of Ta-Mert (i.e., Egypt) shall "come to be a region of cultivated land, the districts "[thereof] shall be yellow with grain crops, and the "grain [thereof] shall be goodly. And fertility shall "come according to the desire [of the people], more "than there hath ever been before."

Then I woke up at [the mention of] crops, my heart (or, courage) came [back], and was equal to my [former] despair, and I made the

23 following decree in the temple of my father Khnemu:—

"The king giveth an offering to Khnemu,[2] the Lord "of the city of Qebḥet,[3] the Governor of Ta-Sti,[4] in "return for those things which thou hast done for me. "There shall be given unto thee on thy right hand [the "river bank] of Manu,[5] and on thy left hand the river "bank of Abu, together with the land about the city,

24. [hieroglyphic text]

25. [hieroglyphic text]

26. [hieroglyphic text]

¹ [hieroglyphs] = schoinos.

² The inhabitants of the Northern Sûdân, probably as far to the south as Napata.

³ The people of the Island of Meroë, and probably those living on the Blue and White Niles.

"for a space of twenty measures,[1] on the east side and "on the west side, with the gardens, and the river "front

"**24** everywhere throughout the region included in "these measures. From every husbandman who tilleth "the ground, and maketh to live again the slain, and "placeth water upon the river banks and all the "islands which are in front of the region of these "measures, shall be demanded a further contribution "from the growing crops and from every storehouse, as

"**25** thy share.

"Whatsoever is caught in the nets by every fisher-"man and by every fowler, and whatsoever is taken by "the catchers of fish, and by the snarers of birds, and "by every hunter of wild animals, and by every man "who snareth lions in the mountains, when these things "enter [the city] one tenth of them shall be demanded.

"And of all the calves which are cast throughout the "regions which are included in these measures, one "tenth of their number

"**26** shall be set apart as animals which are sealed "for all the burnt offerings which are offered up daily.

"And, moreover, the gift of one tenth shall be levied "upon the gold, ivory, ebony, spices, carnelians (?), *sa* "wood, *seshes* spice, *dûm* palm fruit (?), *nef* wood, and "upon woods and products of every kind whatsoever, "which the Khentiu,[2] and the Khentiu of Ḥen-Resu,[3] "and the Egyptians, and every person whatsoever [shall "bring in].

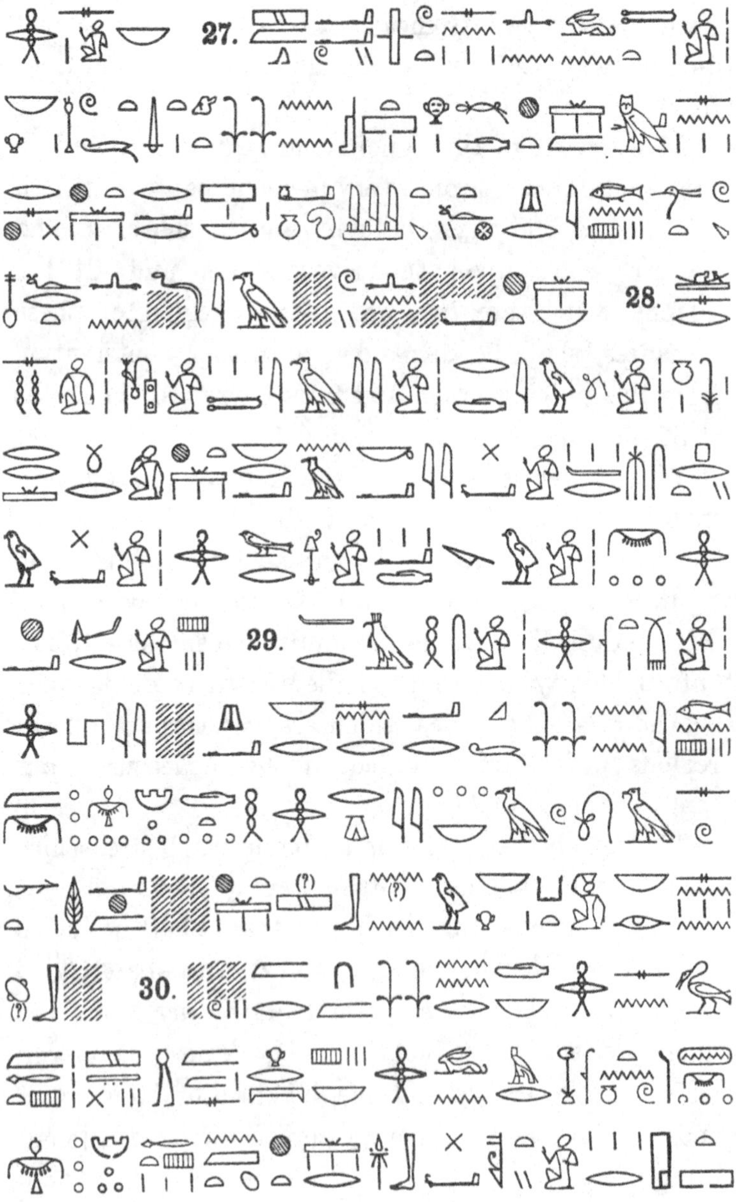
27.
28.
29.
30.

"**27**. And [every] hand shall pass them by, and no "officer of the revenue whatsoever shall utter a word "beyond these places to demand (or, levy on) things "from them, or to take things over and above [those "which are intended for] thy capital city.

"And I will give unto thee the land belonging to the "city, which beareth stones, and good land for cultiva-"tion. Nothing thereof shall be [diminished] or withheld

"**28** of all these things in order to deceive the "scribes, and the revenue officers, and the inspectors "of the king, on whom it shall be incumbent to certify "everything.

"And further, I will cause the masons, and the "hewers of ore (?), and the workers in metal, and the "smelters (?) of gold, and the sculptors in stone,

"**29** and the ore-crushers, and the furnace-men (?), "and handicraftsmen of every kind whatsoever, who "work in hewing, and cutting, and polishing these "stones, and in gold, and silver, and copper, and lead, "and every worker in wood who shall cut down any "tree, or carry on a trade of any kind, or work which "is connected with the wood trade, to

"**30** pay tithe upon all the natural products (?), and "also upon the hard stones which are brought from "their beds above, and quarried stones of all kinds.

"And there shall be an inspector over the weighing "of the gold, and silver, and copper, and real (i.e., "precious) stones, and the [other] things, which the "metal-workers require for the House of Gold,

"**31** and the sculptors of the images of the gods need "in the making and repairing of them, and [these "things] shall be exempted from tithing, and the "workmen also. And everything shall be delivered "(or, given) in front of the storehouse to their children, "a second time, for the protection of everything. And "whatsoever is before thy God-house shall be in "abundance, just as it hath ever been from the earliest "time.

"**32** And a copy of this decree shall be inscribed "upon a stele, [which shall be set up] in the holy "place, according to the writing of the [original] "document which is cut upon wood, and [figures of] "this god and the overseers of the temple shall be [cut] "thereon. Whosoever shall spit upon that which is "on it shall be admonished by the rope. And the "overseers of the priests, and every overseer of the "people of the House of the God, shall ensure the "perpetuation of my name in the House of the god "Khnemu-Rā, the lord of Abu (Elephantine), for ever."

THE LEGEND OF THE DEATH OF HORUS THROUGH THE STING OF A SCORPION AND OF HIS RESURRECTION THROUGH THOTH, AND OTHER MAGICAL TEXTS.

I.—Incantations against Reptiles and Noxious Creatures in general.

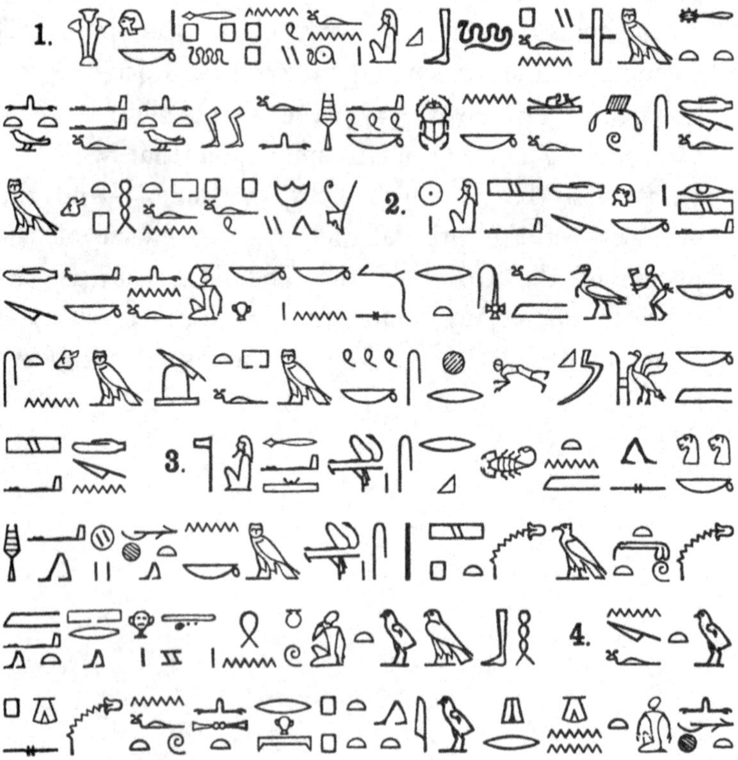

THE LEGEND OF THE DEATH OF HORUS THROUGH THE STING OF A SCORPION AND OF HIS RESURRECTION THROUGH THOTH, AND OTHER MAGICAL TEXTS.

I.—Incantations against Reptiles and Noxious Creatures in general.

1. Get thee back, Āpep, thou enemy of Rā, thou winding serpent in the form of an intestine, without arms [and] without legs. Thy body cannot stand upright so that thou mayest have therein being, long is thy[1] tail in front of thy[1] den, thou enemy; retreat before **2** Rā. Thy head shall be cut off, and the slaughter of thee shall be carried out. Thou shalt not lift up thy face, for his (i.e., Rā's) flame is in thy accursed soul. The odour which is in his chamber of slaughter is in thy members, and thy form shall be overthrown by the slaughtering knife of **3** the great god. The spell of the Scorpion-goddess Serq driveth back thy might. Stand still, stand still, and retreat through her spell.

Be vomited, O poison, I adjure thee to come forth on the earth. Horus uttereth a spell over thee, Horus hacketh **4** thee in pieces, he spitteth upon thee; thou shalt not rise up towards heaven, but shalt totter

[1] Literally, "his."

5.
6.
7.
8.
9.
10.
11.

downwards, O feeble one, without strength, cowardly, unable to fight, blind, without eyes, and with thine head turned upside down. Lift not up thy face. Get thee back quickly, and find **5** not the way. Lie down in despair, rejoice not, retreat speedily, and show not thy face because of the speech of Horus, who is perfect in words of power. The poison rejoiced, [but] the heart[s] of many were very sad thereat. **6**. Horus hath smitten it with his magical spells, and he who was in sorrow is [now] in joy. Stand still then, O thou who art in sorrow, [for] Horus hath been endowed with life. **7**. He cometh charged, appearing himself to overthrow the Sebiu fiends which bite. All men when they see Rā praise the son of Osiris. Get thee back, Worm, **8** and draw out thy poison which is in all the members of him that is under the knife. Verily the might of the word of power of Horus is against thee. Vomit thou, O Enemy, get thee back, O poison.

9. The Chapter of Casting a Spell on the Cat.

Recite [the following formula]:—

"Hail, Rā, come to thy daughter! A scorpion hath "stung her **10** on a lonely road. Her cry hath pene-"trated the heights of heaven, and is heard along the "paths. **11**. The poison hath entered into her body, and "circulateth through her flesh. She hath set her mouth "against it;[1] verily the poison is in her members.

[1] I.e., she hath directed her words against it.

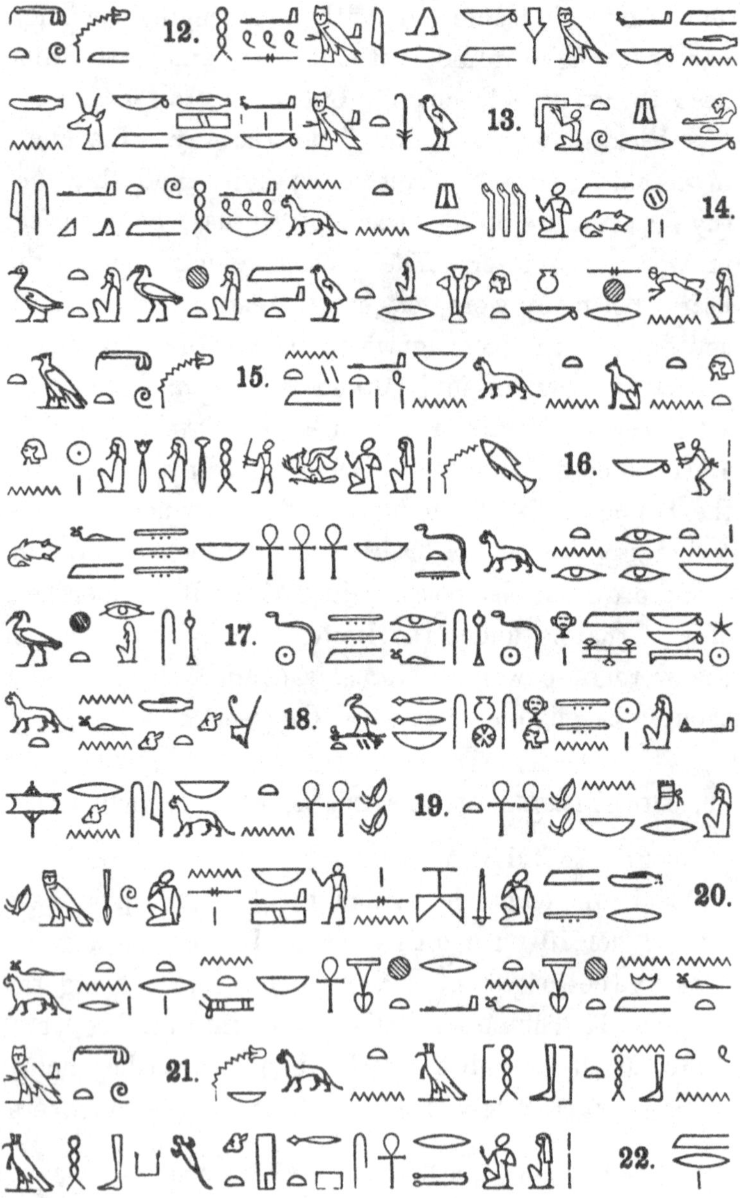
12.
13.
14.
15.
16.
17.
18.
19.
20.
21.
22.

"**12**. Come then with thy strength, with thy fierce "attack, and with thy red powers, and force it **13** to be "hidden before thee. Behold, the poison hath entered "into all the members of this Cat which is under my "fingers. Be not afraid, be not afraid, **14** my daughter, "my splendour, [for] I have set myself near (or, behind) "thee. I have overthrown the poison **15** which is in "all the limbs of this Cat. O thou Cat, thy head is "the head of Rā, the Lord of the Two Lands, the smiter "of the rebellious peoples. **16**. Thy[1] fear is in all "lands, O Lord of the living, Lord of eternity. O thou "Cat, thy two eyes are the Eye of the Lord of the Khut "uraeus, who illumineth **17** the Two Lands with his "Eye, and illumineth the face on the path of darkness. "O thou Cat, thy nose is the nose of **18** Thoth, the "Twice Great, Lord of Khemenu (Hermopolis), the "Chief of the Two Lands of Rā, who putteth breath "into the nostrils of every person. O thou Cat, thine "ears **19** are the ears of Nebertcher, who hearkeneth "unto the voice of all persons when they appeal to "him, and weigheth words (i.e., judgeth) in all the "earth. **20**. O thou Cat, thy mouth is the mouth of "Tem, the Lord of life, the uniter (?) of creation, who "hath caused the union (?) of creation; he shall deliver "thee from every **21** poison. O thou Cat, thy neck "(*neḥebt*) is the neck of Neḥeb-ka, President of the "Great House, vivifier of men and women by **22** means

[1] Literally, "his."

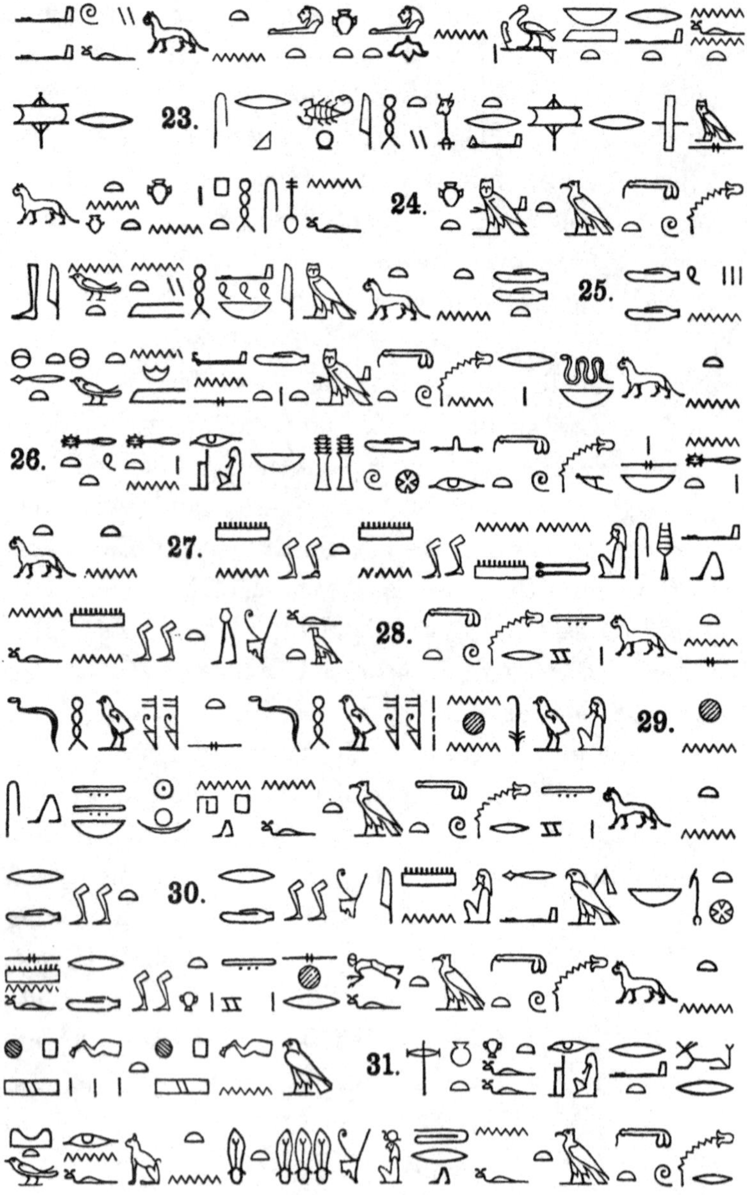

23.
24.
25.
26.
27.
28.
29.
30.
31.

"of the mouth of his two arms. O thou Cat, thy breast "is the breast of Thoth, the Lord of Truth, who hath "given to thee breath to **23** refresh (?) thy throat, and "hath given breath to that which is therein. O thou "Cat, thy heart is the heart of the god Ptaḥ, who "healeth **24** thy heart of the evil poison which is in all "thy limbs. O thou Cat, thy hands **25** are the hands "of the Great Company of the gods and the Little "Company of the gods, and they shall deliver thy hand "from the poison from the mouth of every serpent. O "thou Cat, **26** thy belly is the belly of Osiris, Lord of "Busiris, the poison shall not work any of its wishes in "thy belly. O thou Cat, **27** thy thighs are the thighs "of the god Menthu, who shall make thy thighs to "stand up, and shall bring the **28** poison to the ground. "O thou Cat, thy leg-bones are the leg-bones of "Khensu,[1] **29** who travelleth over all the Two Lands "by day and by night, and shall lead the poison to the "ground. O thou Cat, thy legs (or, feet) **30** are the "legs of Ȧmen the Great, Horus, Lord of Thebes, who "shall stablish thy feet on the earth, and shall over-"throw the poison. O thou Cat, thy haunches are the "haunches of Horus, **31** the avenger (or, advocate) of his "father Osiris, and they shall place Set in the evil which "he hath wrought. O thou Cat, thy soles are the soles "of Rā, who shall make the poison to return to the earth.

[1] He was the messenger of the gods, and travelled across the sky under the form of the Moon; he sometimes appears as a form of Thoth.

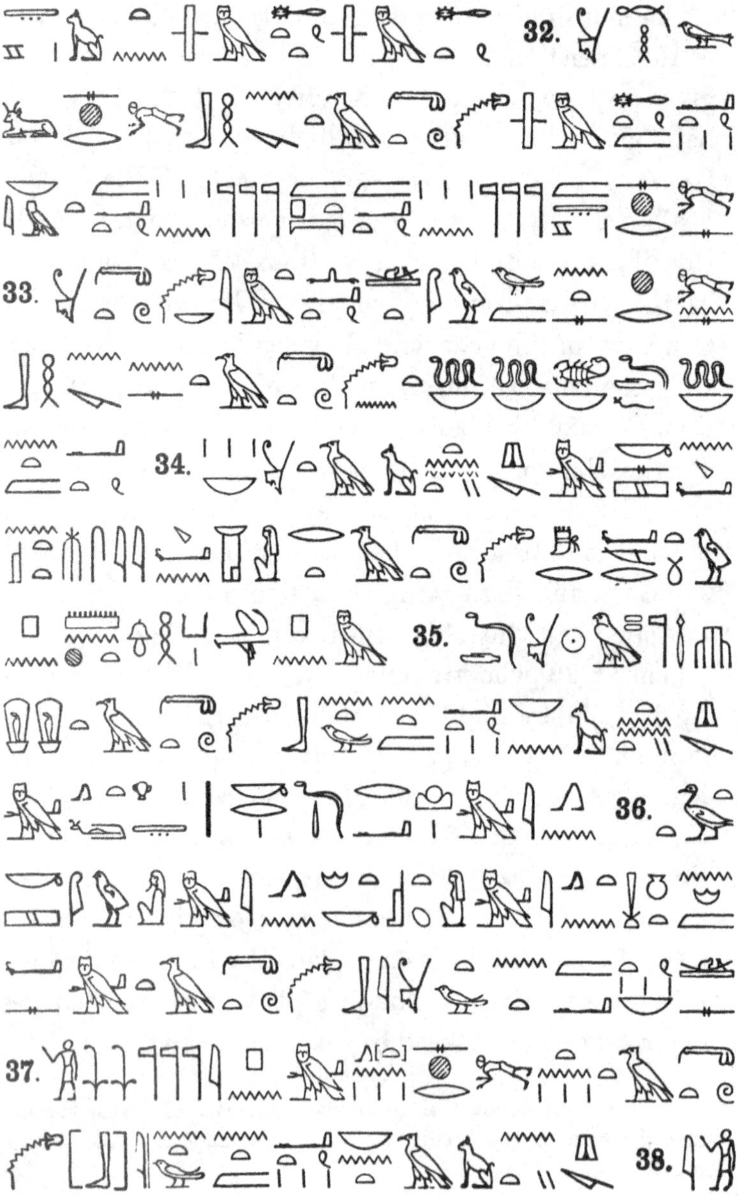
32.
33.
34.
35.
36.
37.
38.

"O thou Cat, thy bowels are the bowels of **32** the "Cow-goddess Meḥ-urt, who shall overthrow and cut "in pieces the poison which is in thy belly and in all "the members in thee, and in [all] the members of the "gods in heaven, and in [all] the members of the gods "on earth, and shall overthrow **33** every poison in thee. "There is no member in thee without the goddess who "shall overthrow and cut in pieces the poison of every "male serpent, and every female serpent, and every "scorpion, and every reptile, which may be in any "member **34** of this Cat which is under the knife. "Verily Isis weaveth and Nephthys spinneth against "the poison. This woven garment strengtheneth this "[being, i.e., Horus], who is perfect in words of power, "through **35** the speech of Rā Ḥeru-khuti, the great "god, President of the South and North: 'O evil poison "which is in any member of this Cat which is under "the knife, come, issue forth upon the earth.'"

ANOTHER CHAPTER.

Say the [following] words:—

"O Rā-[Khuti], come to **36** thy daughter. O Shu, "come to thy wife. O Isis, come to thy sister, and "deliver her from the evil poison which is in all her "members. **37**. Hail, O ye gods, come ye and overthrow "ye the evil poison which is in all the members of the "Cat which is under the knife.

"**38**. Hail, O aged one, who renewest thy youth in

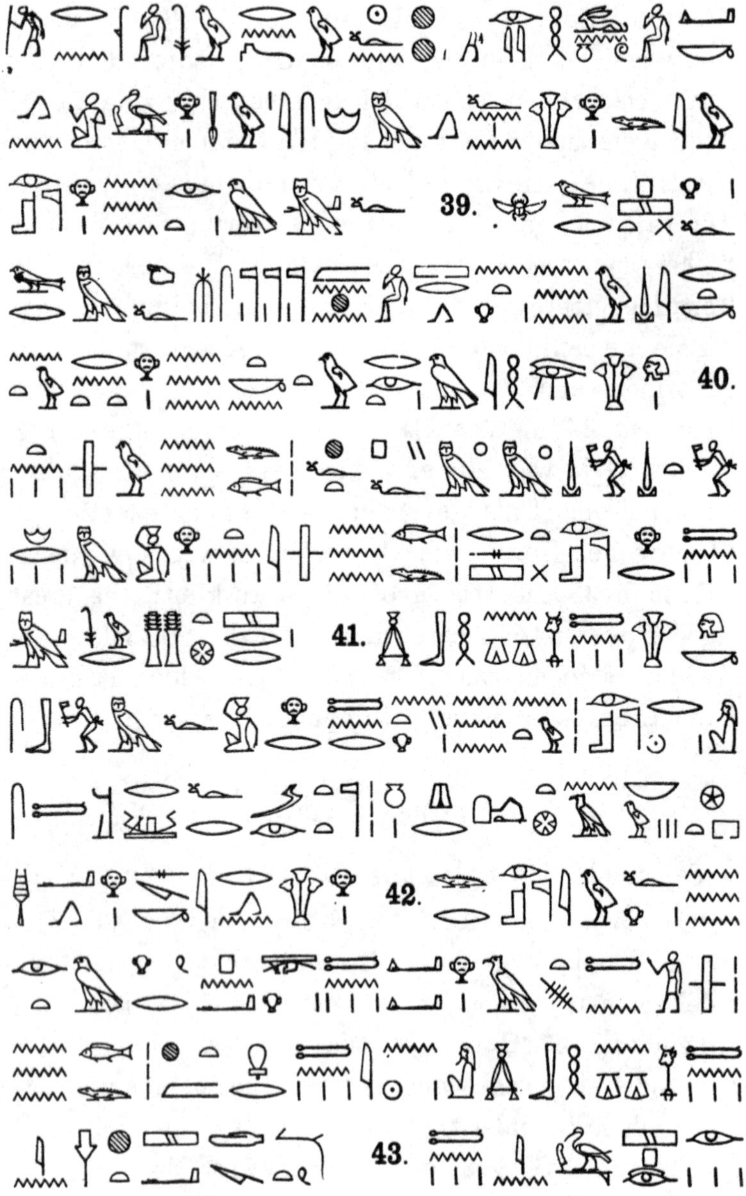
39.
40.
41.
42.
43.

"thy season, thou old man who makest thyself to be a "boy, grant thou that Thoth may come to me at [the "sound of] my voice, and behold, let him turn back "from me Neḥa-ḥer. Osiris is on the water, the Eye "of Horus is with him. **39**. A great Beetle spreadeth "himself over him, great by reason of his grasp, pro- "duced by the gods from a child. He who is over the "water appeareth in a healthy form. If he who is over "the water shall be approached (or, attacked), the Eye "of Horus, which weepeth, shall be approached.

"Get ye back, **40** O ye who dwell in the water, "crocodiles, fish, that Enemy, male dead person and "female dead person, male fiend and female fiend, of "every kind whatsoever, lift not up your faces, O ye "who dwell in the waters, ye crocodiles and fish. "When Osiris journeyeth over you, permit ye him to "go to Busiris. Let your nostrils [be closed], **41** your "throats stopped up.

"Get ye back, Sebȧ fiends! Lift ye not up your "faces against him that is on the water. . . . . Osiris- "Rā riseth up in his Boat to look at the gods of Kher- "āḥat, and the Lords of the Ṭuat stand up to slay thee "when [thou] comest, O Neḥa-ḥer, **42** against Osiris. "[When] he is on the water the Eye of Horus is over "him to turn your faces upside down and to set you on "your backs.

"Hail, ye who dwell in the water, crocodiles and "fish, Rā shutteth up your mouths, Sekhet stoppeth up "your throats, Thoth cutteth out your **43** tongues, and

44.
45.
46.
47.
48.

"Ḥeka blindeth your eyes. These are the four great "gods who protect Osiris by their magical power, and "they effect the protection of him that is on the water, "of men and women of every kind, and of beasts and "animals of every kind which are on the water **44** by "day. Protected are those who dwell in the waters, "protected is the sky wherein is Rā, protected is the "great god who is in the sarcophagus, protected is he "who is on the water.

"A voice [which] crieth loudly is in the House of "Net (Neith), a loud voice is in the Great House, **45** a "great outcry from the mouth of the Cat. The gods "and the goddesses say, 'What is it? What is it?' "[It] concerneth the Åbṭu Fish which is born. Make "to retreat from me thy footsteps, O Sebåu fiend. I "am Khnemu, the Lord of Ḥer-urt. Guard thyself "**46** again from the attack which is repeated, besides "this which thou hast done in the presence of the Great "Company of the gods. Get thee back, retreat thou "from me. I am the god. Oh, Oh, O [Rā], hast thou "not heard the **47** voice which cried out loudly until "the evening on the bank of Neṭit, the voice of all the "gods and goddesses which cried out loudly, the outcry "concerning the wickedness which thou hast done, O "wicked Sebåu fiend? Verily **48** the lord Rā thundered "and growled thereat, and he ordered thy slaughter "to be carried out. Get thee back, Sebå fiend! Hail! "Hail!"

II.—The Narrative of Isis.

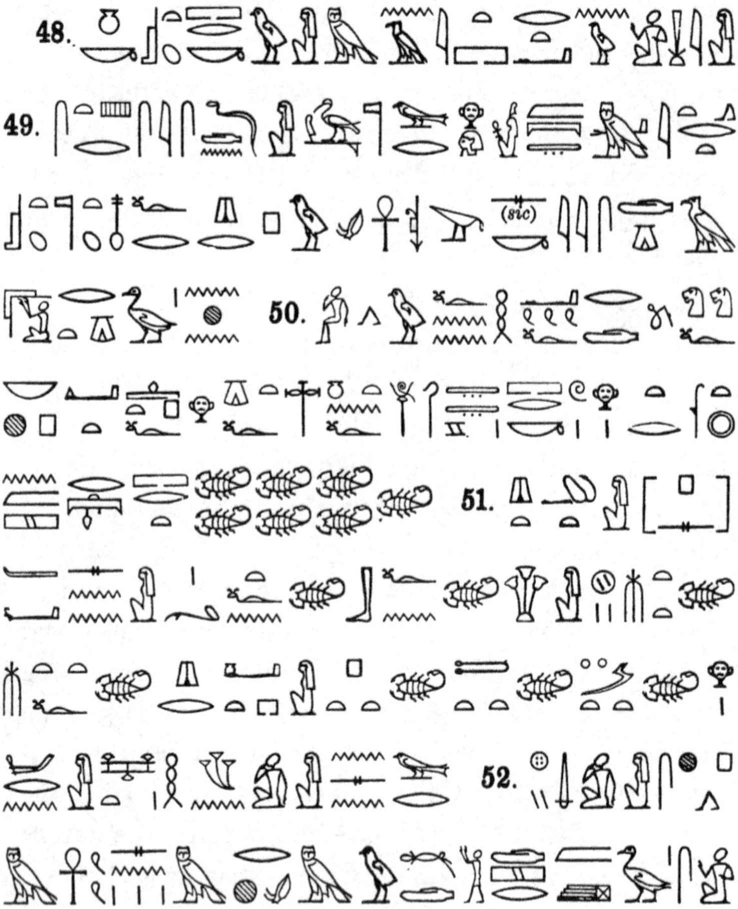

[1] I.e., Law, or Truth. [2] Or, obey.

[3] I.e., flourish.

[4] He avenged his father Osiris by vanquishing Set.

[5] I.e., tribal chief.

[6] I.e., Upper and Lower Egypt.

II.—The Narrative of Isis.

48. I am Isis, [and] I have come forth from the dwelling (or, prison) wherein my brother Set placed me. **49**. Behold the god Thoth, the great god, the Chief of Maāt[1] [both] in heaven and on the earth, said unto me, "Come now, O Isis, thou goddess, moreover it "is a good thing to hearken,[2] [for there is] life to one "who shall be guided [by the advice] of another. Hide "thou thyself with [thy] son the child, **50** and there "shall come unto him these things. His members "shall grow,[3] and two-fold strength of every kind shall "spring up [in him]. [And he] shall be made to take "his seat upon the throne of his father, [whom] he "shall avenge,[4] [and he shall take possession of] the "exalted position of Ḥeq[5] of the Two Lands."[6]

I came forth [from the dwelling] at the time of evening, and there came forth the Seven Scorpions **51** which were to accompany me and to strike (?) for me with [their] stings. Two scorpions, Tefen and Befen, were behind me, two scorpions, Mestet and Mestetef, were by my side, and three scorpions, Petet, Thetet, and Maatet (or, Martet), were for preparing the road for me. I charged them very strictly (or, in a loud voice), **52** and my words penetrated into their ears: "Have no knowledge of [any], make no cry to the "Ṭesheru beings, and pay no attention to the 'son of a "man' (i.e., anyone) who belongeth to a man of no "account," [and I said,] "Let your faces be turned

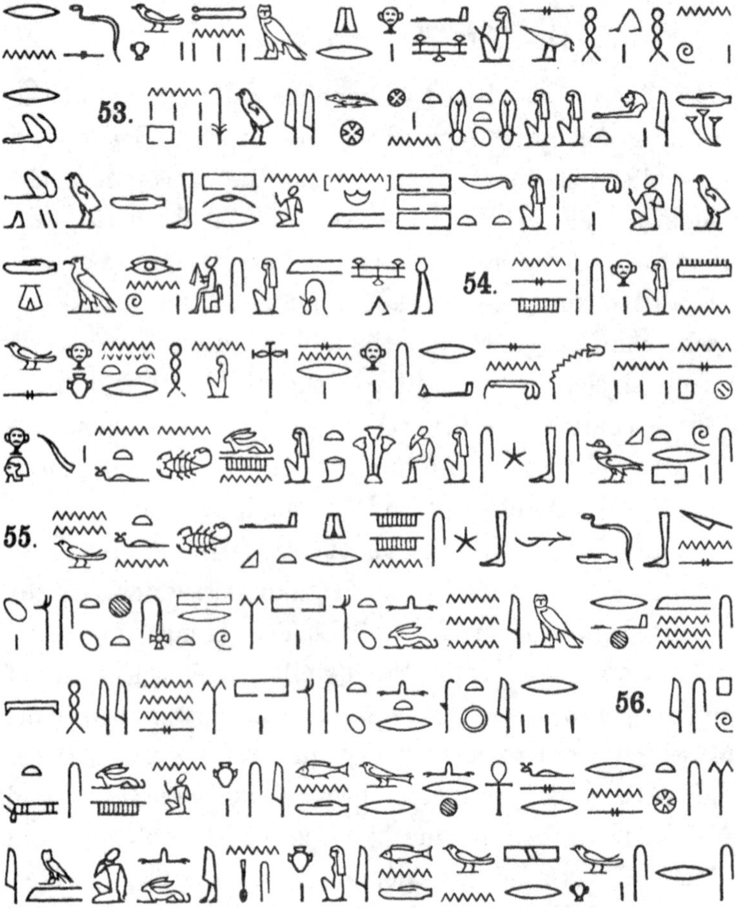

[1] "The House of the Crocodile," perhaps the same town as Pa-Sebekt, a district in the VIIth nome of Lower Egypt (Metelites).

[2] Perhaps , a district in the Metelite nome.

[3] In Egyptian *Ṭeb*, which may be the Ṭebut in the Metelite nome.

[4] *Taḥa* may be the name of a woman, or goddess, or the word may mean a "dweller in the swamps," as Golénischeff thinks.

[5] I.e., it was not the season of the inundation.

"towards the ground [that ye may show me] the way." So the guardian of the company brought me to the boundaries of the city of **53** Pa-Sui,[1] the city of the goddesses of the Divine Sandals, [which was situated] in front of the Papyrus Swamps.[2]

When I had arrived at the place where the people lived,[3] I came to the houses wherein dwelt the wives [and] husbands. And a certain woman of quality spied me as I was journeying along the road, and she shut **54** her doors on me. Now she was sick at heart by reason of those [scorpions] which were with me. Then [the Seven Scorpions] took counsel concerning her, and they all at one time shot out their venom on the tail of the scorpion Tefen; as for me, the woman Taḥa[4] opened her door, and I entered into the house of the miserable lady.

55. Then the scorpion Tefen entered in under the leaves of the door and smote (i.e., stung) the son of Usert, and a fire broke out in the house of Usert, and there was no water there to extinguish it; [but] the sky rained upon the house of Usert, though it was not the season for rain.[5]

56. Behold, the heart of her who had not opened her door to me was grievously sad, for she knew not whether he (i.e., her son) would live [or not], and although she went round about through her town uttering cries [for help], there was none who came at [the sound of] her voice. Now mine own heart was grievously sad for the sake of the child, and [I wished]

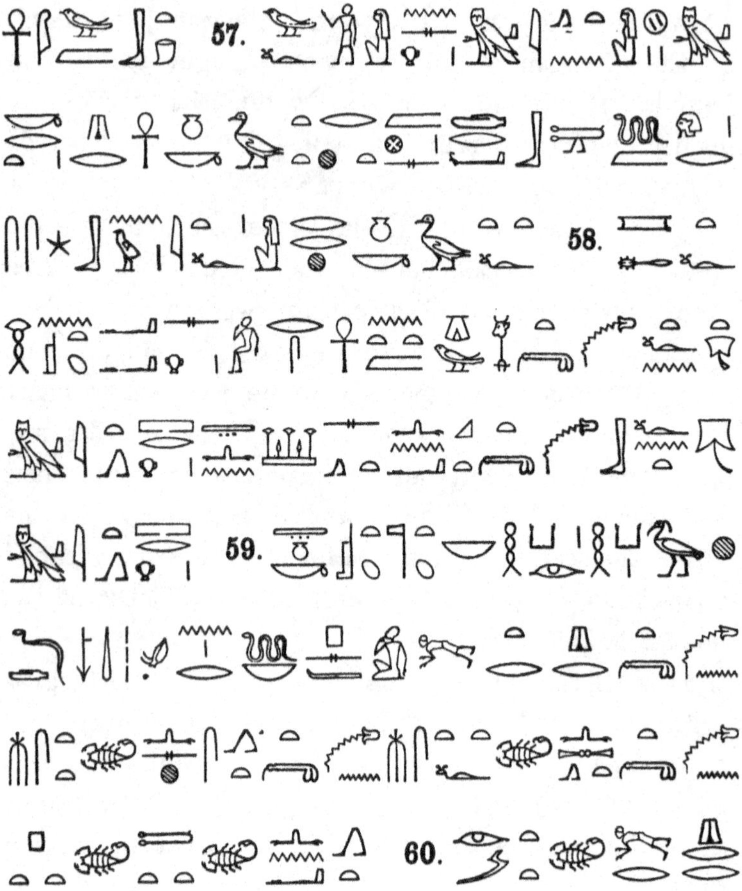

[1] By uttering spells Isis restored life to her husband Osiris for a season, and so became with child by him. She made a magical figure of a reptile, and having endowed it with life, it stung Rā as he passed through the sky, and the great god almost died. In Greek times it was believed that she discovered a medicine which would raise the dead, and she was reputed to be a great expert in the art of healing men's sicknesses. As a goddess she appeared to the sick, and cured them.

to make to live [again] him that was free from fault. **57**. [Thereupon] I cried out to the noble lady, "Come "to me. Come to me. Verily my mouth (?) possesseth "life. I am a daughter [well] known in her town, "[and I] can destroy the demon of death by the spell "(or, utterance) which my father taught me to know. "I am his daughter, **58** the beloved [offspring] of his "body."

Then Isis placed her two hands on the child in order to make to live him whose throat was stopped, [and she said],

"O poison of the scorpion Tefent, come forth and "appear on the ground! Thou shalt neither enter nor "penetrate [further into the body of the child]. O poison "of the scorpion Befent, come forth and appear on the "ground! **59**. I am Isis, the goddess, the lady (or, "mistress) of words of power, and I am the maker of "words of power (i.e., spells), and I know how to utter "words with magical effect.[1] Hearken ye unto me, O "every reptile which possesseth the power to bite (i.e., "to sting), and fall headlong to the ground! O poison "of the scorpion Mestet, make no advance [into his "body]. O poison of the scorpion Mestetef, rise not "up [in his body]. O poison of the scorpions Petet "and Thetet, penetrate not [into his body]. [O **60** "poison of] the scorpion Maatet (or, Martet), fall down "on the ground."

[Here follows the] "Chapter of the stinging [of scorpions]."

[1] Read 

[2]  or , the island of Chemmis of classical writers.

And Isis, the goddess, the great mistress of spells (or, words of power), she who is at the head of the gods, unto whom the god Ḳeb gave his own **61** magical spells for the driving away of poison at noon-day (?), and for making poison to go back, and retreat, and withdraw, and go backward, spake, saying, "Ascend not "into heaven, through the command **62** of the beloved "one of Rā, the egg of the Smen goose which cometh "forth from the sycamore. Verily my words are made "to command the uttermost limit **63** of the night. I "speak unto you, [O scorpions,] I am alone and in "sorrow because our names will suffer disgrace through-"out the nomes. **64**. Do not make love, do not cry "out to the Ṭesheru fiends, and cast no glances upon "the noble ladies in their houses. Turn your faces "towards the earth and [find out] the road, **65** so that "we may arrive at the hidden places in the town of "Khebt.[2] Oh the child shall live and the poison die! "Rā liveth and the poison dieth! Verily Horus shall "be in good case (or, healthy) **66** for his mother Isis. "Verily he who is stricken shall be in good case "likewise."

And the fire [which was in the house of Usert] was extinguished, and heaven was satisfied **67** with the utterance of Isis, the goddess.

Then the lady Usert came, and she brought unto me her possessions, and she filled the house of the woman Taḥ (?), for the Ka of Taḥ (?), **68** because [she] had opened to me her door. Now the lady Usert suffered

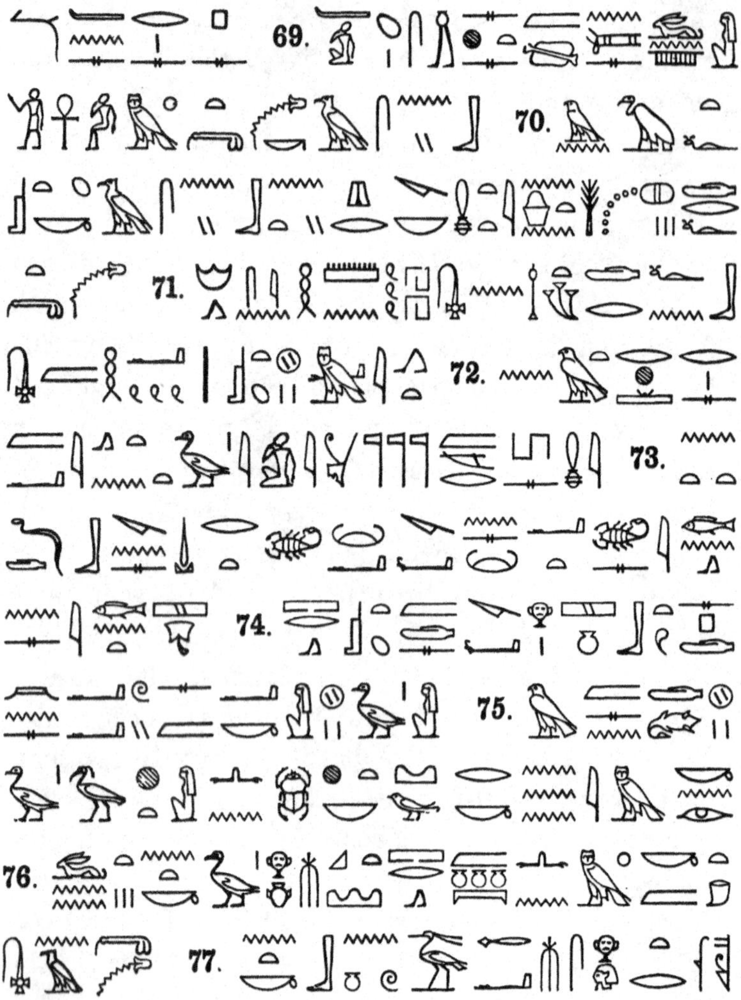

[1] Mesqet was originally the name of the bull's skin in which the deceased was wrapped in order to secure for him the new life; later the name was applied to the Other World generally. See *Book of the Dead*, Chap. xvii. 121.

[2] The Bennu who kept the book of destiny. See *Book of the Dead*, Chap. xvii. 25.

pain and anguish the whole night, and her mouth tasted (i.e., felt) the sting **69** [which] her son [had suffered]. And she brought her possessions as the penalty for not having opened the door to me. Oh the child shall live and the poison die! Verily Horus shall be in good case **70** for his mother Isis. Verily everyone who is stricken shall be in good case likewise.

Lo, a bread-cake [made] of barley meal shall drive out (or, destroy) the poison, **71** and natron shall make it to withdraw, and the fire [made] of *ḥetchet*-plant shall drive out (or, destroy) fever-heat from the limbs.

"O Isis, O Isis, come thou to thy **72** Horus, O thou "woman of the wise mouth! Come to thy son"—thus cried the gods who dwelt in her quarter of the town—"for he is as one **73** whom a scorpion hath stung, and "like one whom the scorpion Uḥāt, which the animal "Ȧntesh drove away, hath wounded."

74. [Then] Isis ran out like one who had a knife [stuck] in her body, and she opened her arms wide, [saying,] "Behold me, behold me, my son **75** Horus, "have no fear, have no fear, O son my glory! No evil "thing of any kind whatsoever shall happen unto thee, "[for] there is in thee the essence (or, fluid) which "made the things which exist. **76**. Thou art the son "from the country of Mesqet,[1] [thou hast] come forth "from the celestial waters Nu, and thou shalt not die "by the heat of the poison. **77**. Thou wast the Great "Bennu,[2] who art born (or, produced) on the top of the

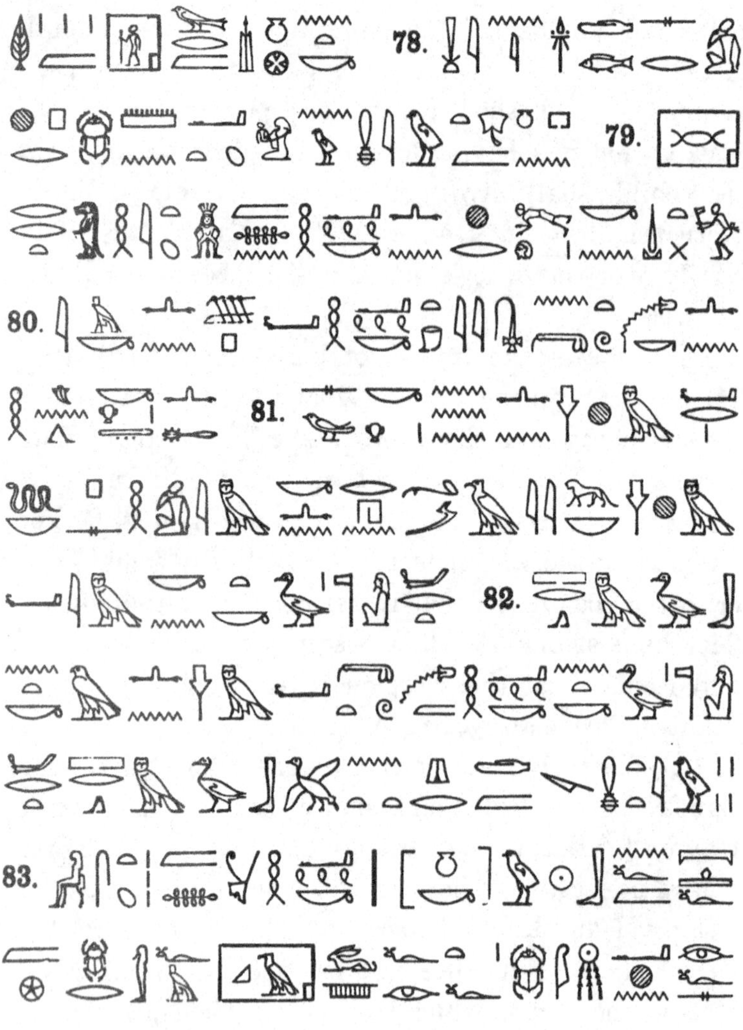

[2] The Ȧbṭu and Ȧnt Fishes swam before the Boat of Rā and guided it.

[3] This is the Cat who lived by the Persea tree in Heliopolis. See *Book of the Dead*, Chap. xvii. 18.

[4] A hippopotamus goddess.

"balsam-trees[1] which are in the House of the Aged "One in Ȧnu (Heliopolis). Thou **78** art the brother of "the Ȧbṭu Fish,[2] who orderest what is to be, and art "the nursling of the Cat[3] who dwelleth in **79** the "House of Neith. The goddess Reret,[4] the goddess "Ḥȧt, and the god Bes protect thy members. Thy "head shall not fall to the Tchat fiend **80** that attacketh "thee. Thy members shall not receive the fire of that "which is thy poison. Thou shalt not go backwards "on the land, and thou shalt not be brought low **81** on "the water. No reptile which biteth (or, stingeth) "shall gain the mastery over thee, and no lion shall "subdue thee or have dominion over thee. Thou art "the son of the sublime god **82** who proceeded from "Ḳeb. Thou art Horus, and the poison shall not gain "the mastery over thy members. Thou art the son of "the sublime god who proceeded from Ḳeb, and thus "likewise shall it be with those who are under the "knife. And the four **83** august goddesses shall pro- "tect thy members."

[Here the narrative is interrupted by the following texts:]

[I am] he who rolleth up into the sky, and who goeth down (i.e., setteth) in the Ṭuat, whose form is in the House of height, through whom when he openeth his Eye the light cometh into being, and when he closeth

[1] These are the balsam-trees for which Heliopolis has been always famous. They are described by Wansleben, *L'Histoire de l'Église*, pp. 88-93, and by 'Abd al-Laṭîf (ed. de Sacy), p. 88.

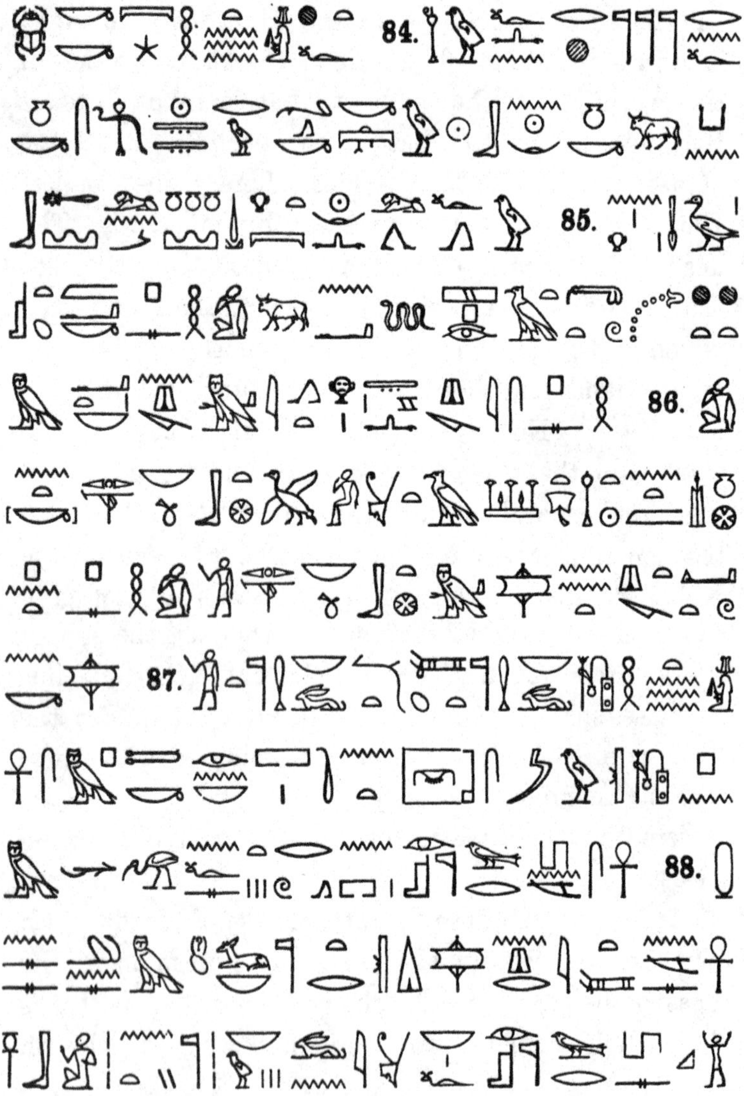

[3] The land of the sunset, the West.

[4] Perhaps an animal of the Lynx class.

his Eye it becometh night. [I am] the Water-god Ḥet when he giveth **84** commands, whose name is unknown to the gods. I illumine the Two Lands, night betaketh itself to flight, and I shine by day and by night.[1] I am the Bull of Bakha,[2] and the Lion of Manu.[3] I am he who traverseth the heavens by day and by night without being repulsed. I have come **85** by reason of the voice (or, cry) of the son of Isis. Verily the blind serpent Nā hath bitten the Bull. O thou poison which floweth through every member of him that is under the knife, come forth, I charge thee, upon the ground. Behold, he that is under the knife shall not be bitten. **86**. Thou art Menu, the Lord of Coptos, the child of the White Shat[4] which is in Ȧnu (Heliopolis), which was bitten [by a reptile]. O Menu, Lord of Coptos, give thou air unto him that is under the knife; and air shall be given to thee. **87**. Hail, divine father and minister of the god Nebun, [called] Mer-Tem, son of the divine father and minister of the god Nebun, scribe of the Water-god Ḥet, [called] Ānkh-Semptek (*sic*), son of the lady of the house Tent-Ḥet-nub! He restored this inscription after he had found it in a ruined state in the Temple of Osiris-Mnevis, because he wished to make to live **88** her name . . . . and to give air unto him that is under [the knife], and to give life unto the ancestors of all the gods. And his Lord Osiris-Mnevis shall make long his life with happiness

[1] I.e., always.

[2] The land of the sunrise, the East.

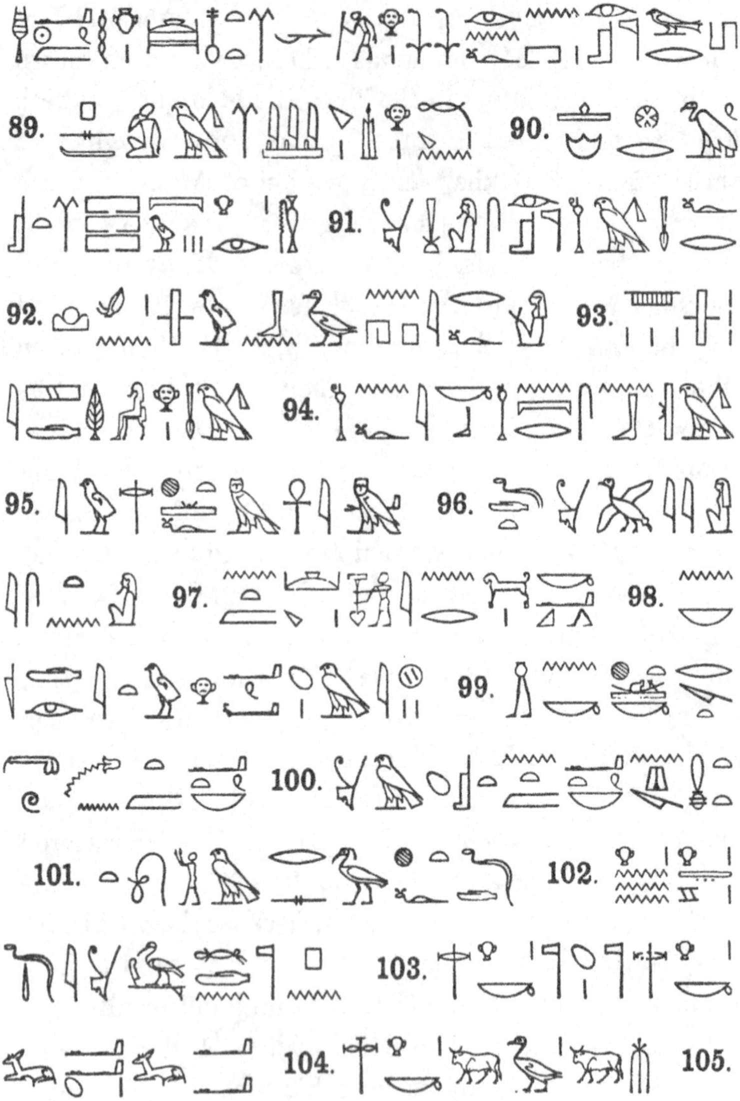

[1] The text appears to be corrupt in this passage.

of heart, [and shall give him] a beautiful burial after [attaining to] an old age, because of what he hath done for the Temple of Osiris-Mnevis.

89. Horus was bitten (i.e., stung) in Sekhet-Ån, to the north of **90** Ḥetep-ḥemt, whilst his mother Isis was in the celestial houses making a libation **91** for her brother Osiris. And Horus sent forth his cry into **92** the horizon, and it was heard by those who were in . . . . . . Thereupon the keepers of the doors **93** who were in the [temple of] the holy Acacia Tree started up at the voice of Horus. **94**. And one sent forth a cry of lamentation, and Heaven gave the order that Horus was to be healed. **95**. And [the gods] took counsel [together] concerning the life [of Horus, saying,] **96** "O goddess Pai (?), O god Åsten, **97** who dwellest "in Åat-Khus (?) . . . . . .[1] thy . . . . . . enter in "**98** . . . . . lord of sleep . . . . . . the child Horus. "Oh, Oh, **99** bring thou the things which are thine "to cut off the poison which is in every member "**100** of Horus, the son of Isis, and which is in "every member of him that is under the knife "likewise."

101. A HYMN OF PRAISE TO HORUS TO GLORIFY HIM, WHICH IS TO BE SAID **102** OVER THE WATERS AND OVER THE LAND. Thoth speaketh and this god reciteth [the following]:—

"**103**. Homage to thee, god, son of a god. Homage "to thee, heir, son of an heir. **104**. Homage to thee, "bull, son of a bull, who wast brought **105** forth by a

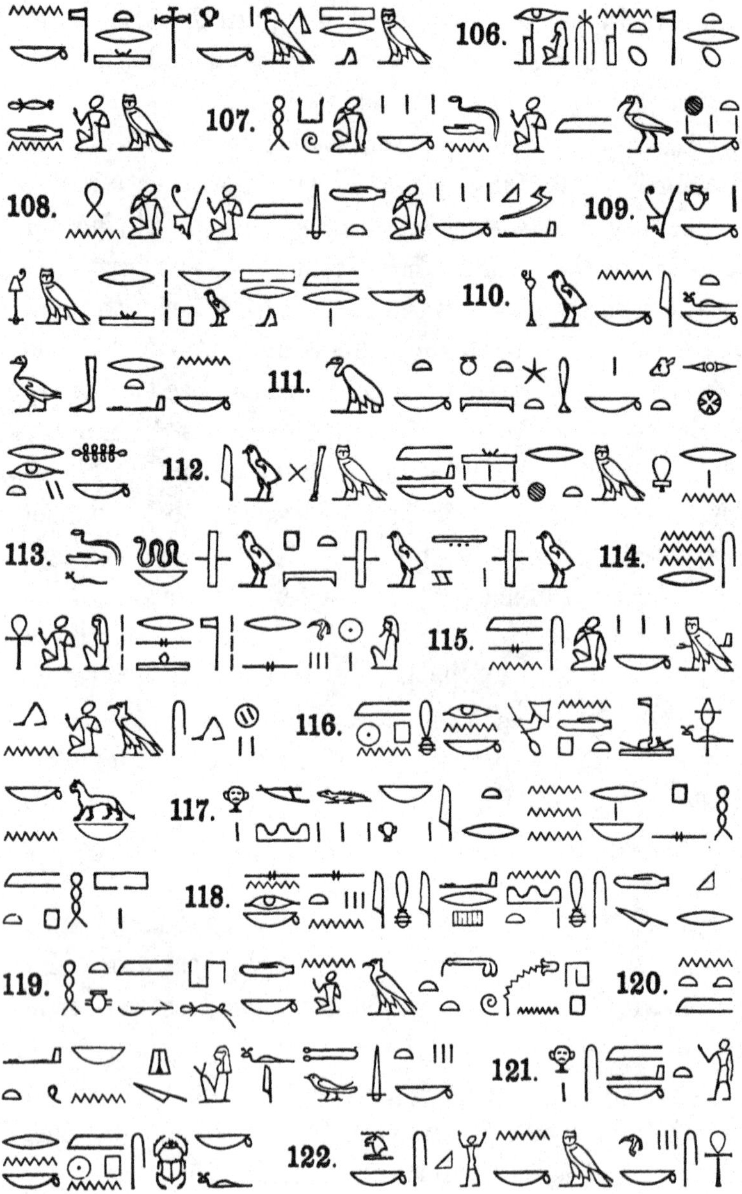
106.
107.
108.
109.
110.
111.
112.
113.
114.
115.
116.
117.
118.
119.
120.
121.
122.

"holy goddess. Homage to thee, Horus, who comest "forth from **106** Osiris, and wast brought forth by the "goddess Isis. I recite thy **107** words of power, I "speak with thy magical utterance. **108**. I pronounce "a spell in thine own words, which **109** thy heart hath "created, and all the spells and incantations which "have come forth from thy mouth, **110** which thy "father Ḳeb commanded thee [to recite], and thy "mother **111** Nut gave to thee, and the majesty of the "Governor of Sekhem taught thee to make use of for "thy protection, **112** in order to double (or, repeat) thy "protective formulae, to shut the mouth of **113** every "reptile which is in heaven, and on the earth, and in "**114** the waters, to make men and women to live, to "make the gods to be at peace [with thee], and to "make Rā to employ his magical spells **115** through "thy chants of praise. Come to me this day, quickly, "quickly, **116** as thou workest the paddle of the Boat of "the god. Drive thou away from me every lion **117** on the "plain, and every crocodile in the waters, and all mouths "which bite (or, sting) in their holes. **118**. Make thou "them before me like the stone of the mountain, like a "broken pot **119** lying about in a quarter of the town. "Dig thou out from me the poison which riseth and "**120** is in every member of him that is under the knife. "Keep thou watch over him . . . . . . **121** by means "of thy words. Verily let thy name be invoked this "day. Let thy power (*qefau*) come into being **122** in "him. Exalt thou thy magical powers. Make me to

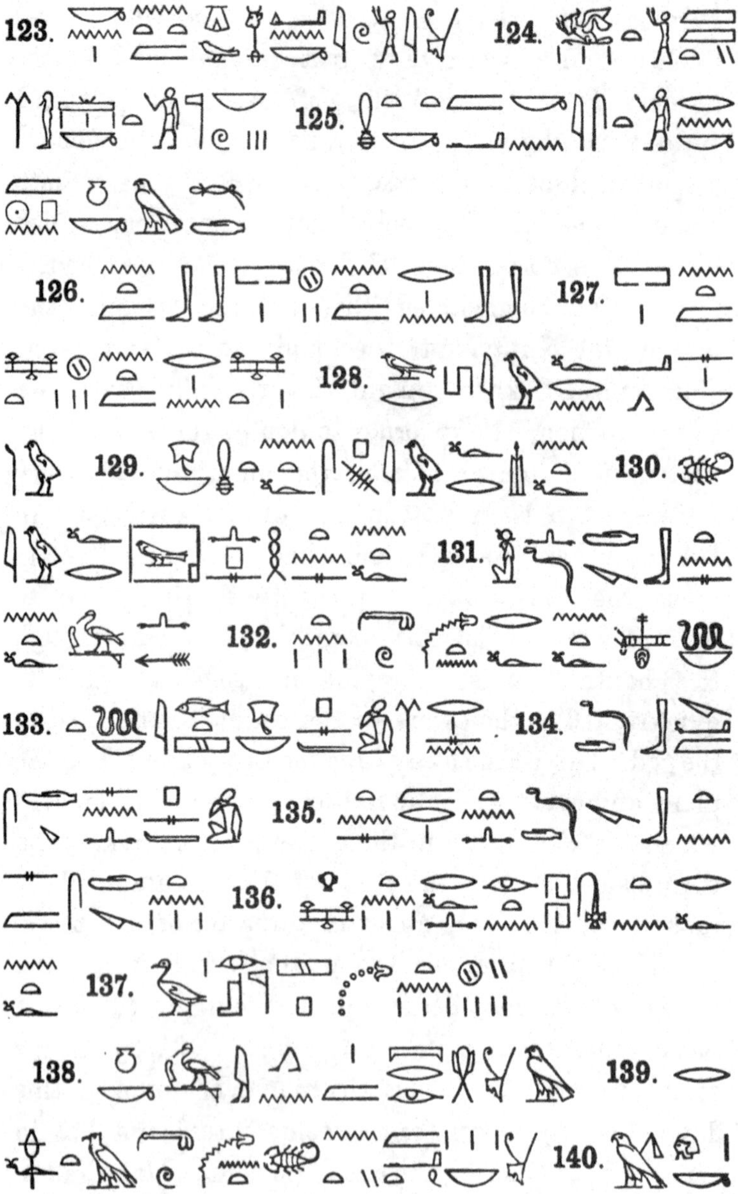
123.
124.
125.
126.
127.
128.
129.
130.
131.
132.
133.
134.
135.
136.
137.
138.
139.
140.

"live **123** and him whose throat is closed up. Then shall "mankind give thee praise, **124** and the righteous (?) "shall give thanks unto thy forms. And all the gods "likewise shall invoke thee, **125** and in truth thy "name shall be invoked this day. I am Horus [of] "Sheṭ[enu] (?).

"**126**. O thou who art in the cavern,[1] O thou who art "in the cavern. O thou who art at the mouth of the "cavern. **127**. O thou who art on the way, O thou "who art on the way. O thou who art at the "mouth of the way. **128**. He is Urmer (Mnevis) who "approacheth every man **129** and every beast. He is "like the god Sep who is in Ȧnu (Heliopolis). **130**. He "is the Scorpion-[god] who is in the Great House "(Ḥet-ur). Bite him not, for he is **131** Rā. Sting "him not, for he is Thoth. Shoot ye not **132** your "poison over him, for he is Nefer-Tem. O every male "serpent, **133** O every female serpent, O every *ȧntesh* "(scorpion ?) which bite with your mouths, **134** and "sting with your tails, bite **135** ye him not with your "mouths, and sting ye him not with your tails. "**136**. Get ye afar off from him, make ye not your fire "to be against him, for he is the son of Osiris. "**137**. Vomit ye." [Say] four times:—

"**138**. I am Thoth, I have come from heaven to make "protection of Horus, **139** and to drive away the poison "of the scorpion which is in every member of Horus. "**140**. Thy head is to thee, Horus; it shall be stable

[1] Or, den or hole.

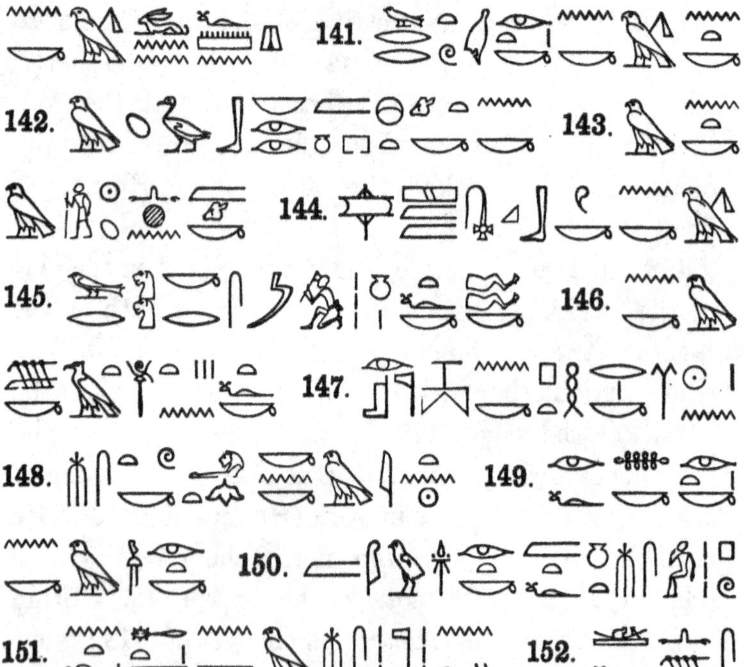

[1] We ought, perhaps, to translate  by "forearms."

"under **141** the Urert Crown. Thine eye is to thee, "Horus, [for] thou art **142** Horus, the son of Ḳeb, the "Lord of the Two Eyes, in the midst of the Company "[of the gods]. Thy nose is to thee, **143** Horus, [for] "thou art Horus the Elder, the son of Rā, and thou "shalt not inhale **144** the fiery wind. Thine arm is to "thee, Horus, **145** great is thy strength to slaughter the "enemies of thy father. Thy two thighs[1] **146** are to "thee, Horus. Receive thou the rank and dignity of "thy father **147** Osiris. Ptaḥ hath balanced for thee "thy mouth on the day of **148** thy birth. Thy heart "(or, breast) is to thee, Horus, and the Disk **149** maketh "thy protection. Thine eye is to thee, Horus; thy "right eye **150** is like Shu, and thy left eye like Tefnut, "who are the children **151** of Rā. Thy belly is to thee, "Horus, and the Children are the gods who are therein, "**152** and they shall not receive the essence (or, fluid) "of the scorpion. Thy strength is to thee, Horus, "**153** and the strength of Set shall not exist against "thee. Thy phallus is to thee, **154** Horus, and thou art "Kamutef, the protector **155** of his father, who maketh "an answer for his children **156** in the course of every "day. Thy thighs are to thee, Horus, and thy **157** "strength shall slaughter the enemies of thy father. "**158**. Thy calves are to thee, Horus; the god Khnemu "hath builded [them], **159** and the goddess Isis hath "covered them with flesh. The soles of thy feet are "to thee, Horus, **160** and the nations who fight "with the bow (Peti) fall under thy feet. Thou rulest

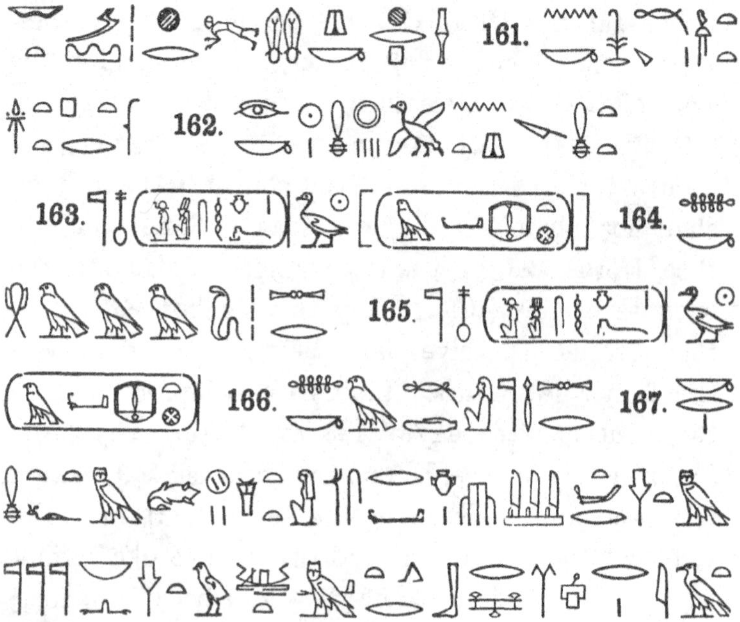

[1] Or, Àteḥ, the papyrus swamp.

[2] I.e., Set.

"**161** the South, North, West, and East, and thou seest "**162** like Rā. [Say] four times. And likewise him "that is under the knife."

163. Beautiful god, Senetchem-ȧb-Rā-setep-[en]-Ȧmen, son of Rā, Nekht-Ḥeru-Ḥebit, **164** thou art protected, and the gods and goddesses are protected, and conversely. **165**. Beautiful god, Senetchem-ȧb-Rā-setep-[en]-Rā, son of Rā, Nekht-Ḥeru-Ḥebit, **166** thou art protected, and Ḥeru-Sheṭ[enu], the great god, is protected, and conversely.

167. ANOTHER CHAPTER LIKE UNTO IT. "Fear not, "fear not, O Bast, the strong of heart, at the head of "the holy field, the mighty one among all the gods, "nothing shall gain the mastery over thee. Come "thou outside, following my speech (or, mouth), O evil "**168** poison which is in all the members of the lion "(or, cat) which is under the knife."

[The narrative of the stinging of Horus by a scorpion is continued thus]:

"I am Isis, who conceived a child by her husband, "and she became heavy with Horus, the divine [child]. "I gave birth to Horus, the son of Osiris, in a nest of "papyrus plants.[1] I rejoiced exceedingly over this, "because **169** I saw [in him one] who would make "answer for his father. I hid him, and I concealed "him through fear of that [fiend (?)].[2] I went away to "the city of Ȧm, [where] the people gave thanks [for "me] through [their] fear of my making trouble [for "them]. I passed the day in seeking to provide food

[1] I.e., to be my advocate.

[2] Literally "his thing."

[3] Ṭuat is a very ancient name of the Other World, which was situated either parallel with Egypt or across the celestial ocean which surrounded the world.

[4] The "perfect place," i.e., the Other World.

"for the child, [and] on returning to take Horus into "my arms I found him, Horus, the beautiful one **170** "of gold, the boy, the child, without [life]. He had "bedewed the ground with the water of his eye, and "with foam from his lips. His body was motionless, "his heart was powerless to move, and the sinews "(or, muscles) of his members were [helpless]. I sent "forth a cry, [saying]:

"'I, even I, **171** lack a son to make answer [for me].[1] "[My] two breasts are full to overflowing, [but] my "body is empty. [My] mouth wished for that which "concerned him.[2] A cistern of water and a stream of "the inundation was I. The child was the desire of "my heart, and I longed to protect him (?). I carried "him in my womb, I gave birth to him, **172** I endured "the agony of the birth pangs, I was all alone, and the "great ones were afraid of disaster and to come out at "the sound of my **173** voice. My father is in the "Ṭuat,[3] my mother is in Åqert,[4] and my elder brother "**174** is in the sarcophagus. Think of the enemy and "of how prolonged was the wrath of his heart **175** "against me, [when] I, the great lady, was in his house.'

"I cried then, [saying,] 'Who **176** among the people "will indeed let their hearts come round to me?' I "cried then **177** to those who dwelt in the papyrus "swamps (or, Aṭeḥ), and they inclined to me straight-"way. **178**. And the people came forth to me from "their houses, and they thronged about me **179** at "[the sound of] my voice, and they loudly bewailed

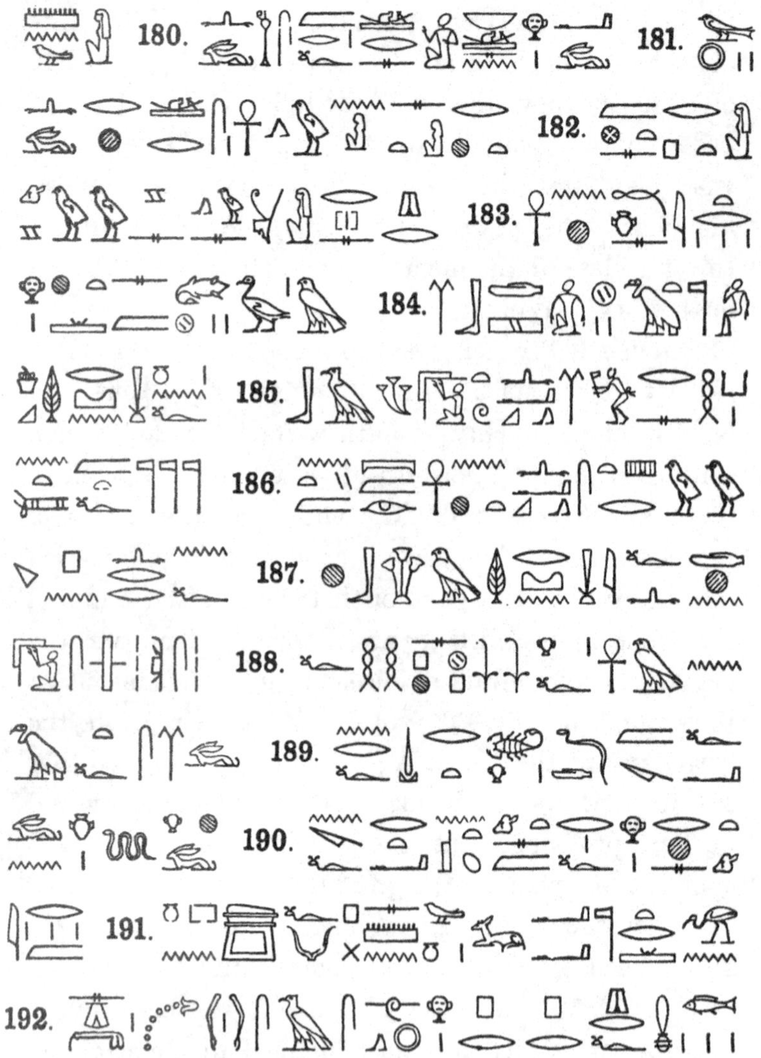

[1] Or perhaps, "a lady who was at the head of her district."

[2] I.e., the mouth of Horus.

[3] Literally, "pain" or "disease."

"with me the greatness of my affliction. **180**. There "was no man there who set restraint (?) on his mouth, "every person among them lamented **181** with great "lamentation. There was none there who knew how "to make [my child] to live.

"And there came forth unto me a woman who was "[well] known **182** in her city, a lady who was mistress "of her [own] estate.[1] She came forth to me. Her "mouth possessed **183** life, and her heart was filled "with the matter which was therein, [and she said,] "'Fear not, fear not, O son Horus! **184**. Be not cast "down, be not cast down, O mother of the god. The "child of the Olive-tree is by the mountain of his "brother, **185** the bush is hidden, and no enemy shall "enter therein. The word of power of Tem, the Father "of the gods, **186** who is in heaven, maketh to live. "Set shall not enter into this region, he shall not go "round about it. **187**. The marsh of Horus of the "Olive-tree is by the mountain of his brother; those "who are in his following shall not at any time ...... "it. **188**. This shall happen to him: Horus shall live "for his mother, and shall salute (?) [her] **189** with his "mouth. A scorpion hath smitten (i.e., stung) him, "and the reptile Āun-åb hath wounded him.'" **190**.

Then Isis placed her nose in his mouth[2] so that she might know whether he who was in **191** his coffin breathed, and she examined the wound[3] of the heir of the god, and she found that there was poison **192** in it. She threw her arms round him, and then quickly she

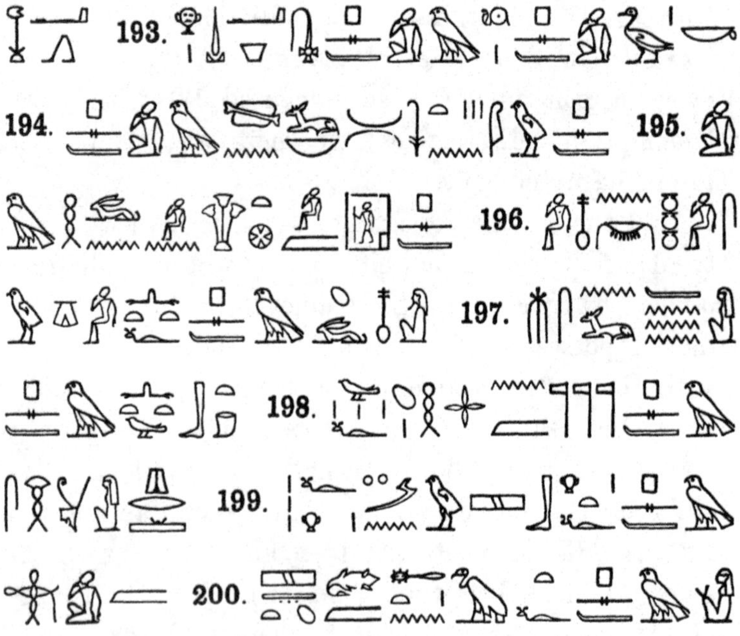

[1] He is nothing, i.e., he is dead.

[2] I.e., become an advocate for.

leaped about with him like fish when they are laid **193** upon the hot coals, [saying]:

"Horus is bitten, O Rā. Thy son is bitten, [O "Osiris]. **194**. Horus is bitten, the flesh and blood of "the Heir, the Lord of the diadems (?) of the kingdoms "of Shu. **195**. Horus is bitten, the Boy of the marsh "city of Åteḥ, the Child in the House of the Prince. "**196**. The beautiful Child of gold is bitten, the Babe "hath suffered pain and is not.[1] Horus is bitten, he "the son of Un-Nefer, **197** who was born of Åuḥ-mu (?). "Horus is bitten, he in whom there was nothing "abominable, **198** the son, the youth among the gods. "Horus is bitten, he for whose wants I prepared in "abundance, **199** for I saw that he would make answer[2] "for his father. Horus is bitten, he for whom [I] had "care **200** [when he was] in the hidden woman [and "for whom I was afraid when he was] in the womb of "his mother. Horus is bitten, he whom I guarded **201** "to look upon. I have wished for the life of his heart. "Calamity hath befallen the child **202** on the water, "and the child hath perished."

Then came Nephthys **203** shedding tears and uttering cries of lamentation, and going round about through the papyrus swamps. And Serq [came also and they said]: **204** "Behold, behold, what hath happened to Horus, son "of Isis, and who [hath done it]? Pray then to heaven, "**205** and let the mariners of Rā cease their labours for "a space, for the Boat of Rā cannot travel onwards "[whilst] son Horus **206** [lieth dead] on his place."

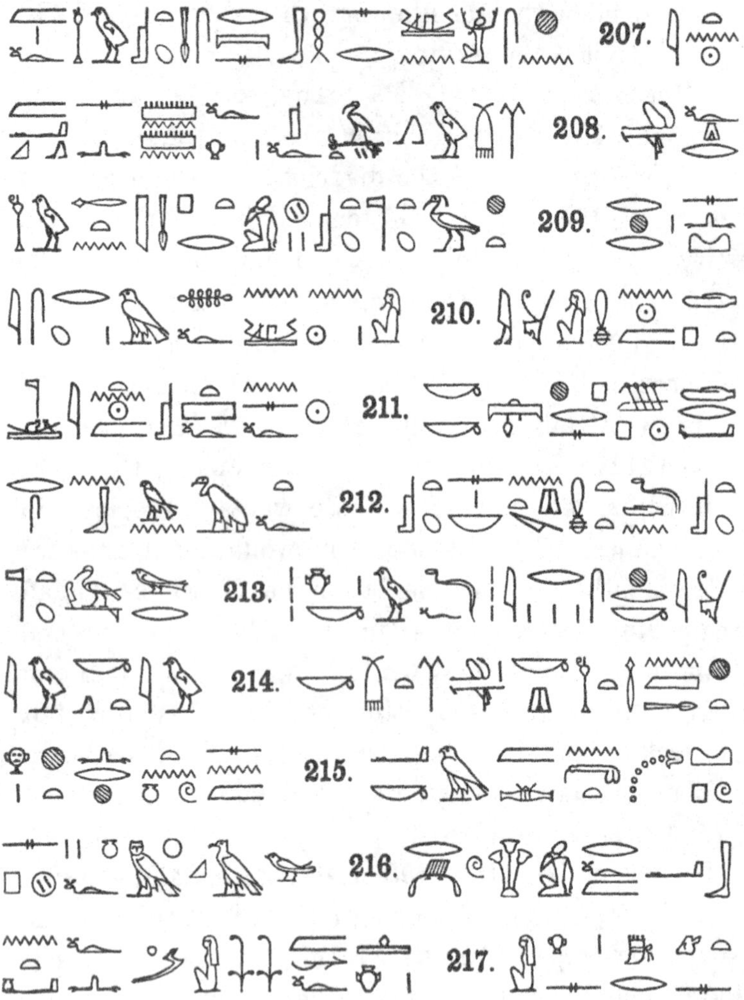

[1] Literally, "alighted."

[2] When a god or a man was declared to be *maā-kheru*, "true of voice," or "true of word," his power became illimitable. It gave him rule and authority, and every command uttered by him was immediately followed by the effect required.

And Isis sent forth her voice into heaven, and made supplication to the Boat of Millions of Years, and the **207** Disk stopped[1] in its journeying, and moved not from the place whereon it rested. Then came forth Thoth, who is equipped **208** with his spells (or, words of power), and possesseth the great word of command of *maā-kheru*,[2] [and said:] "What [aileth thee], what "[aileth thee], O Isis, thou goddess who hast magical "spells, **209** whose mouth hath understanding? As-"suredly no evil thing hath befallen [thy] son Horus, "[for] the Boat of Rā hath him under its protection. "**210**. I have come this day in the Divine Boat of the "Disk from the place where it was yesterday, **211**—"now darkness came and the light was destroyed—in "order to heal Horus for his mother **212** Isis and every "person who is under the knife likewise."

And Isis, the goddess, said: "O Thoth, great things "**213** [are in] thy heart, [but] delay belongeth to thy "plan. Hast thou come **214** equipped with thy spells "and incantations, and having the great formula of "*maā-kheru*, and one [spell] after the other, the num-"bers whereof are not known? **215**. Verily Horus is in "the cradle (?) of the poison. Evil, evil is his case, "death, [and] misery **216** to the fullest [extent]. The "cry of his mouth is towards his mother (?). I cannot "[bear] to see these things in his train. My heart "[hath not] rested because of them **217** since the be-"ginning (?) [when] I made haste to make answer [for] "Horus-Rā (?), placing [myself] on the earth, [and]

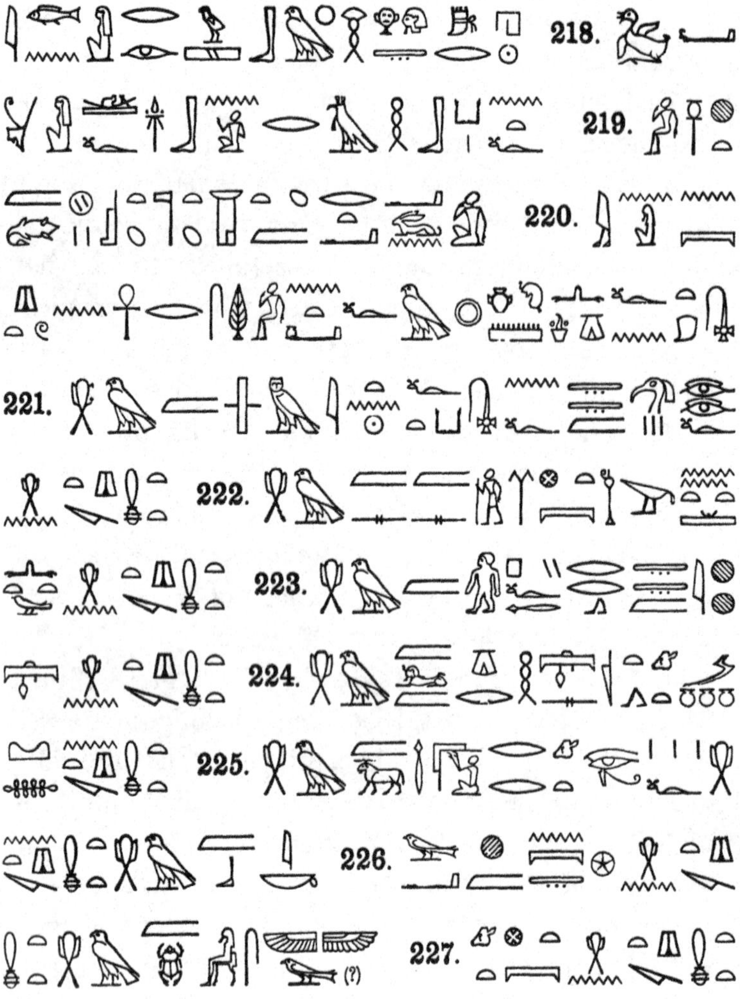

[1] I.e., "Be of good courage."

[2] The Sun-god.

[3] The Sun and Moon.

[4] Osiris (?).

[5] Bes (?).

[6] Probably the Ram, Lord of Ṭaṭṭu, or the Ram of Mendes.

[7] Ḥeru-Beḥuṭet.

"since the day [when] **218** I was taken possession of "by him. I desired Neḥeb-ka . . . . **219**"

[And Thoth said:] "Fear not, fear not, O goddess "Isis, fear not, fear not, O Nephthys, and let not "anxiety [be to you]. **220**. I have come from heaven "having life to heal (?) the child for his mother, Horus "is . . . Let thy heart be firm;[1] he shall not sink "under the flame. **221**. Horus is protected as the "Dweller in his Disk,[2] who lighteth up the Two Lands "by the splendour of his two Eyes;[3] and he who is "under the knife is likewise protected. **222**. Horus is "protected as the First-born son in heaven,[4] who is "ordained to be the guide of the things which exist and "of the things which are not yet created; and he who "is under the knife is likewise protected. **223**. Horus "is protected as that great Dwarf (*nemu*)[5] who goeth "round about the Two Lands in the darkness; and he "who is under the knife is protected likewise. **224**. "Horus is protected as the Lord (?) in the night, who "revolveth at the head of the Land of the Sunset "(Manu); and he who is under the knife is protected "likewise. **225**. Horus is protected as the Mighty "Ram[6] who is hidden, and who goeth round about in "front of his Eyes; and he who is under the knife is "protected likewise. Horus is protected as the Great "Hawk[7] **226** which flieth through heaven, earth, and the "Other World (Ṭuat); and he who is under the knife "is protected likewise. Horus is protected as the Holy "Beetle, the mighty (?) wings of which **227** are at the

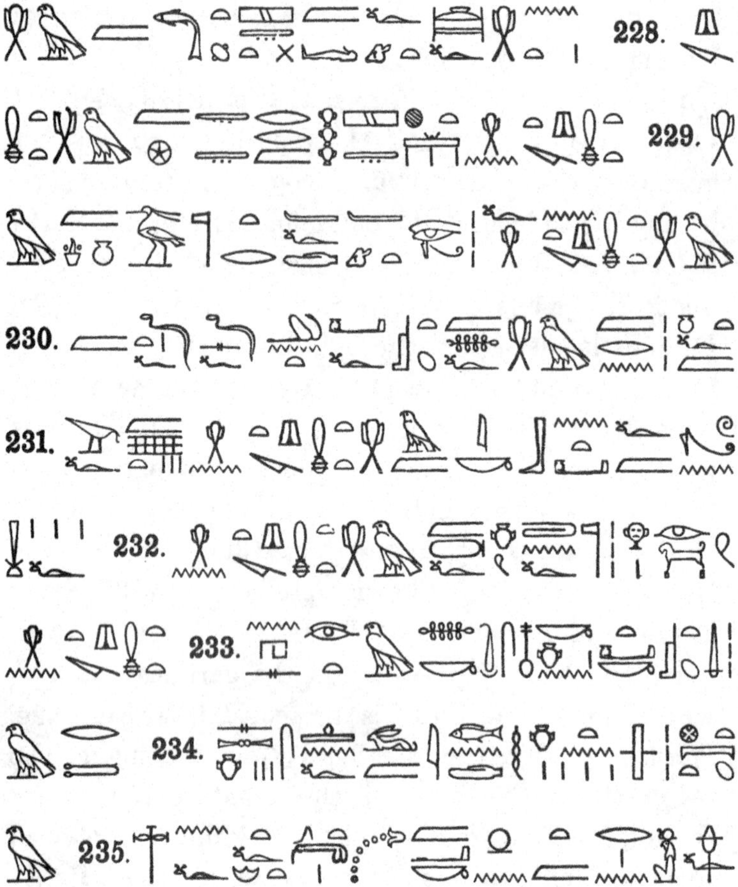

[1] The beetle of Kheperâ, a form of the Sun-god when he is about to rise on this earth.

[2] The Hidden Body is Osiris, who lay in his sarcophagus, with Isis and Nephthys weeping over it.

[3] The Bennu was the soul of Rā and the incarnation of Osiris.

[4] See the names of Osiris and his sanctuaries in Chapter CXLII. of the Book of the Dead.

"head of the sky;[1] and he who is under the knife is "protected likewise. Horus is protected as the Hidden "Body,[2] and as he whose mummy is in his sarcophagus; "and he who is under the knife is protected likewise. "**228**. Horus is protected [as the Dweller] in the Other "World [and in the] Two Lands, who goeth round "about 'Those who are over Hidden Things'; and he "who is under the knife is protected likewise. **229**. "Horus is protected as the Divine Bennu[3] who alighteth "in front of his two Eyes; and he who is under the "knife is protected likewise. Horus is protected **230** "in his own body, and the spells which his mother Isis "hath woven protect him. Horus is protected by the "names of his father [Osiris] in **231** his forms in the "nomes;[4] and he who is under the knife is protected "likewise. Horus is protected by the weeping of his "mother, and by the cries of grief of his brethren; and "he **232** who is under the knife is protected likewise. "Horus is protected by his own name and heart, and "the gods go round about him to make his funeral bed; "and he who is under the knife is protected likewise."

[And Thoth said:]

"**233**. Wake up, Horus! Thy protection is estab- "lished. Make thou happy the heart of thy mother "Isis. The words of Horus shall bind **234** up hearts, "he shall cause to be at peace him who is in affliction. "Let your hearts be happy, O ye who dwell in the "heavens (Nut). Horus, he **235** who hath avenged "(or, protected) his father shall cause the poison to

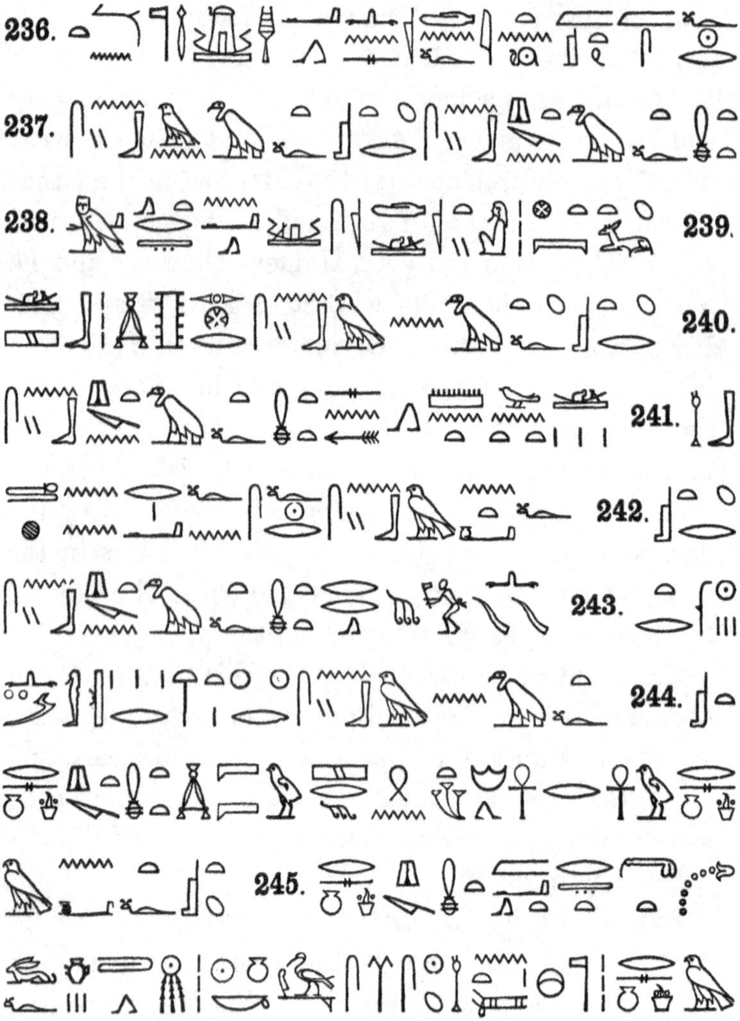

[1] We should probably strike out the words "of his mother."

[2] The city in the Delta called by the Greeks Letopolis.

[3] Thoth stood by during the fight between Horus and Set, and healed the wounds which they inflicted on each other.

"retreat. Verily that which is in the mouth of Rā "shall go round about (i.e., circulate), and the **236** "tongue of the Great God shall repulse [opposition]. "The Boat [of Rā] standeth still, and travelleth not "onwards. The Disk is in the [same] place where it "was yesterday to heal **237** Horus for his mother Isis, "and to heal him that is under the knife of his mother[1] "likewise. **238**. Come to the earth, draw nigh, O Boat "of Rā, make the boat to travel, O mariners of heaven, "**239** transport provisions (?) of . . . . . . Sekhem[2] to "heal Horus for his mother Isis, and to heal **240** him "that is under the knife of his mother likewise. Hasten "away, O pain which is in the **241** region round about, "and let it (i.e., the Boat) descend upon the place "where it was yesterday to heal Horus for his mother "Isis, **242** and to heal him that is under the knife of "his mother likewise. Get thee round and round, O "bald (?) fiend, without horns **243** at the seasons (?), "not seeing the forms through the shadow of the two "Eyes, to heal Horus for his mother **244** Isis, and to "heal him that is under the knife likewise. Be filled, "O two halves of heaven, be empty, O papyrus roll, "return, O life, into the living to heal Horus for his "mother Isis, **245** and to heal him that is under the "knife likewise. Come thou to earth, O poison. Let "hearts be glad, and let radiance (or, light) go round "about.

"I am Thoth,[3] the firstborn son, the son of Rā, and "Tem and the Company of the gods have commanded

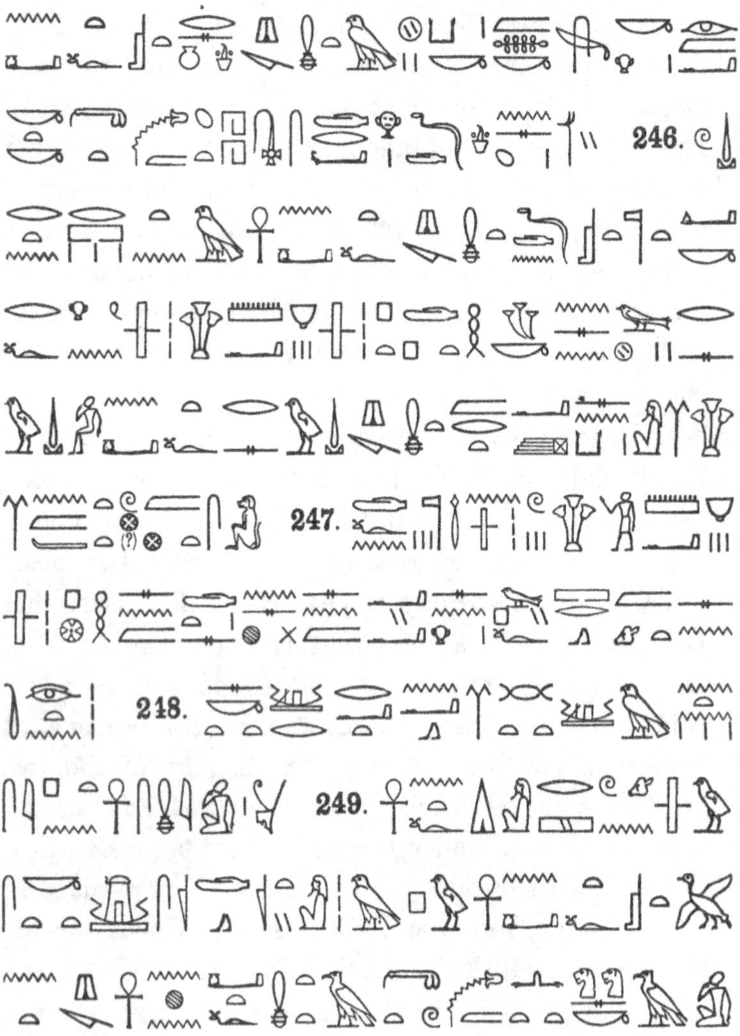

[1] The boat in which Rā travelled from noon to sunset, or perhaps until midnight.

[2] The boat in which Rā travelled from dawn, or perhaps from midnight, to noon.

"me to heal Horus for his mother Isis, and to heal him "that is under the knife likewise. O Horus, O Horus, "thy KA protecteth thee, and thy Image worketh pro- "tection for thee. The poison is as the daughter of its "[own] flame; [it is] destroyed [because] it smote the "strong son. **246**. Your temples are in good condition "for you, [for] Horus liveth for his mother, and he who "is under the knife likewise."

And the goddess Isis said:

"Set thou his face towards those who dwell in the "North Land (Ateḥ), the nurses who dwell in the city "Pe-Ṭept (Buto), for they have offered very large "offerings in order to cause the child to be made "strong for his mother, and to make strong him that is "under the knife likewise. Do not allow them to "recognize the divine KA in the Swamp Land, in the "city (?) of Nemḥettu (?) [and] in her city."

247. Then spake Thoth unto the great gods who dwell in the Swamp-Land [saying]: "O ye nurses "who dwell in the city of Pe, who smite [fiends] with "your hands, and overthrow [them] with your arms on "behalf of that Great One who appeareth in front of "you . . . . . . **248** [in] the Sektet Boat,[1] let the Mātet[2] "(Māntchet) Boat travel on. Horus is to you, he is "counted up for life, and he is declared for **249** the life "of his father [Osiris]. I have given gladness unto "those who are in the Sektet Boat, and the mariners "[of Rā] make it to journey on. Horus liveth for his "mother Isis, and he who is under the knife liveth for

250.
251.

"his mother likewise. As for the poison, the strength "thereof has been made powerless. Verily I am a "favoured one, and I will join myself **250** to his hour[1] "to hurl back the report of evil to him that sent it "forth. The heart of Rā-Ḥeru-Khuti rejoiceth. Thy "son Horus is counted up for life [which is] on this "child to make him to smite, and to retreat (?) from "those who are above, and to turn back the paths of the "Sebȧu fiends from him, so that he may take possession "of the throne of the Two Lands. Rā is in heaven to "make answer on **251** behalf of him and his father. "The words of power of his mother have lifted up his "face, and they protect him and enable him to go "round about wheresoever he pleaseth, and to set the "terror of him in celestial beings. I have made haste "......"

[1] I.e., I will be with him at the moment of his need.

THE HISTORY OF ISIS AND OSIRIS,

WITH EXPLANATIONS OF THE SAME, COLLECTED BY PLUTARCH, AND SUPPLEMENTED BY HIS OWN VIEWS.

I. Though it be the wise man's duty, O CLEA,[1] to apply to the gods for every good thing which he hopes to enjoy, yet ought he more especially to pray to them for their assistance in his search after that knowledge which more immediately regards themselves, as far as such knowledge may be attained, inasmuch as there is nothing which they can bestow more truly beneficial to mankind, or more worthy themselves, than truth. For whatever other good things are indulged to the wants of men, they have all, properly speaking, no relation to, and are of a nature quite different from, that of their divine donors. For 'tis not the abundance of their gold and silver, nor the command of the thunder, but wisdom and knowledge which constitute the power and happiness of those heavenly beings. It is therefore well observed by Homer (*Iliad*, xiii. 354), and indeed with more propriety than he usually talks of the gods, when, speaking of Zeus and Poseidon, he

[1] She is said to have been a priestess of Isis and of Apollo Delphicus.

tells us that "both were descended from the same "parents, and born in the same region, but that Zeus "was the elder and knew most"; plainly intimating thereby that the empire of the former was more august and honourable than that of his brother, as by means of his age he was his superior, and more advanced in wisdom and science. Nay, 'tis my opinion, I own, that even the blessedness of that eternity which is the portion of the Deity himself consists in that universal knowledge of all nature which accompanies it; for setting this aside, eternity might be more properly styled an endless duration than an enjoyment of existence.

II. To desire, therefore, and covet after truth, those truths more especially which concern the divine nature, is to aspire to be partakers of that nature itself, and to profess that all our studies and inquiries are devoted to the acquisition of holiness. This occupation is surely more truly religious than any external purifications or mere service of the temple can be. But more especially must such a disposition of mind be highly acceptable to that goddess to whose service you are dedicated, for her especial characteristics are wisdom and foresight, and her very name seems to express the peculiar relation which she bears to knowledge. For "Isis"[1] is a Greek word, and means "knowledge," and

[1] The Egyptian form of the name is Ȧs-t, , or 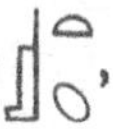, or . Plutarch wishes to derive the name from some form of *οἶδα*.

"Typhon,"[1] the name of her professed adversary, is also a Greek word, and means "pride and insolence." This latter name is well adapted to one who, full of ignorance and error, tears in pieces and conceals that holy doctrine which the goddess collects, compiles, and delivers to those who aspire after the most perfect participation in the divine nature. This doctrine inculcates a steady perseverance in one uniform and temperate course of life, and an abstinence from particular kinds of foods, as well as from all indulgence of the carnal appetite, and it restrains the intemperate and voluptuous part within due bounds, and at the same time habituates her votaries to undergo those austere and rigid ceremonies which their religion obliges them to observe. The end and aim of all these toils and labours is the attainment of the knowledge of the First and Chief Being, who alone is the object of the understanding of the mind; and this knowledge the goddess invites us to seek after, as being near and dwelling continually with her. And this also is what the very name of her temple promiseth to us, that is to say, the knowledge and understanding of the eternal and self-existent Being (τοῦ ὄντας)—now, it is called "Iseion," which suggests that if we approach the temple of the goddess rightly, and with purity, we shall obtain the knowledge of that eternal and self-existent Being (τὸ ὂν).

III. The goddess Isis is said by some authors to be

[1] In Egyptian, Tebh, 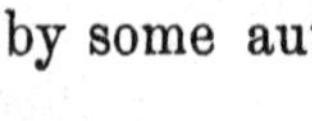.

the daughter[1] of Hermes,[2] and by others of Prometheus, both of them famous for their philosophic turn of mind. The latter is supposed to have first taught mankind wisdom and foresight, as the former is reputed to have invented letters and music.

They likewise call the former of the two Muses at Hermopolis[3] Isis as well as Dikaiosune,[4] she being none other, it is said, than Wisdom pointing out the knowledge of divine truths to her votaries, the true Hierophori and Hierostoli. Now, by the former of these are meant such who carry about them locked up in their souls, as in a chest, the sacred doctrine concerning the gods, purified from all such superfluities as superstition may have added thereto. And the holy apparel with which the Hierostoli adorn the statues of these deities, which is partly of a dark and gloomy and partly of a more bright and shining colour, seems aptly

[1] According to the Egyptian Heliopolitan doctrine, Isis was the daughter of Ḳeb, the Earth-god, and Nut, the Sky-goddess; she was the wife of Osiris, mother of Horus, and sister of Set and Nephthys.

[2] The Egyptian ṬEḤUTI, or Thoth, , who invented letters, mathematics, &c. He was the "heart of Rā," the scribe of the gods, and he uttered the words which created the world; he composed the "words of power," or magical formulae which were beneficial for the dead, and the religious works which were used by souls in their journey from this world to the next.

[3] The Hermopolis here referred to is the city of Khemenu in Upper Egypt, wherein was the great sanctuary of Thoth.

[4] I.e., Righteousness, or Justice. The goddess referred to is probably Maāt, .

enough to represent the notions which this doctrine teaches us to entertain of the divine nature itself, partly clear and partly obscure. And inasmuch as the devotees of Isis after their decease are wrapped up in these sacred vestments, is not this intended to signify that this holy doctrine still abides with them, and that this alone accompanies them in another life? For as 'tis not the length of the beard or the coarseness of the habit which makes a philosopher, so neither will these frequent shavings, or the mere wearing of a linen vestment, constitute a votary of Isis. He alone is a true servant or follower of this goddess who, after he has heard, and has been made acquainted in a proper manner with the history of the actions of these gods, searches into the hidden truths which lie concealed under them, and examines the whole by the dictates of reason and philosophy.

IV. Nor, indeed, ought such an examination to be looked on as unnecessary whilst there are so many ignorant of the true reason even of the most ordinary rites observed by the Egyptian priests, such as their shavings[1] and wearing linen garments. Some, indeed, there are who never trouble themselves to think at all about these matters, whilst others rest satisfied with the most superficial accounts of them: "They pay a

[1] A rubric in the papyrus of Nes-Menu in the British Museum orders the priestesses of Isis and Nephthys to have "the hair of their bodies shaved off" (No. 10,188, col. 1), but they are also ordered to wear fillets of rams' wool, , on their heads.

peculiar veneration to the sheep,[1] therefore they think it their duty not only to abstain from eating its flesh, but likewise from wearing its wool. They are continually mourning for their gods, therefore they shave themselves. The light azure blossom of the flax resembles the clear and bloomy colour of the ethereal sky, therefore they wear linen"; whereas the true reason of the institution and observation of these rites is but one, and that common to all of them, namely, the extraordinary notions which they entertain of cleanliness, persuaded as they are, according to the saying of Plato, "none but the pure ought to approach the pure." Now, no superfluity of our food, and no excrementitious substance, is looked upon by them as pure and clean; such, however, are all kinds of wool and down, our hair and our nails. It would be the highest absurdity, therefore, for those who, whilst they are in a course of purification, are at so much pains to take off the hair from every part of their own bodies, at the same time to clothe themselves with that of other animals. So when we are told by Hesiod "not to pare our nails whilst we are present at the festivals of the gods," [2] we ought to understand that he intended hereby to inculcate that purity wherewith we ought to

[1] Probably the ram of Amen. Animal sacrifices were invariably bulls and cows.

[2] This saying is by Pythagoras—Παρὰ θυσίαν μὴ ὀνυχίζου. The saying of Hesiod (*Works and Days*, 740) is rendered by Goodwin:—

"Not at a feast of Gods from five-branched tree,
With sharp-edged steel to part the green from dry."

come prepared before we enter upon any religious duty, that we have not to make ourselves clean whilst we ought to be occupied in attending to the solemnity itself. Now, with regard to flax, this springs out of the immortal earth itself; and not only produces a fruit fit for food, but moreover furnishes a light and neat sort of clothing, extremely agreeable to the wearer, adapted to all the seasons of the year, and not in the least subject, as is said, to produce or nourish vermin; but more of this in another place.

V. Now, the priests are so scrupulous in endeavouring to avoid everything which may tend to the increase of the above-mentioned excrementitious substances, that, on this account, they abstain not only from most sorts of pulse, and from the flesh of sheep and swine, but likewise, in their more solemn purifications, they even exclude salt from their meals. This they do for many reasons, but chiefly because it whets their appetites, and incites them to eat more than they otherwise would. Now, as to salt being accounted impure because, as Aristagoras tells us, many little insects are caught in it whilst it is hardening, and are thereby killed therein—this view is wholly trifling and absurd. From these same motives also they give the Apis Bull his water from a well specially set apart for the purpose,[1] and they prevent him altogether from

[1] It is quite possible that Apis drank from a special well, but the water in it certainly came from the Nile by infiltration. In all the old wells at Memphis the water sinks as the Nile sinks, and rises as it rises.

drinking of the Nile, not indeed that they regard the river as impure, and polluted because of the crocodiles which are in it, as some pretend, for there is nothing which the Egyptians hold in greater veneration than the Nile, but because its waters are observed to be particularly nourishing[1] and fattening. And they strive to prevent fatness in Apis as well as in themselves, for they are anxious that their bodies should sit as light and easy about their souls as possible, and that their mortal part should not oppress and weigh down the divine and immortal.

VI. The priests of the Sun at Heliopolis[2] never carry wine into their temples, for they regard it as indecent for those who are devoted to the service of any god to indulge in the drinking of wine whilst they are under the immediate inspection of their Lord and King.[3] The priests of the other deities are not so scrupulous in this respect, for they use it, though sparingly. During their more solemn purifications they abstain from wine wholly, and they give themselves up entirely to study and meditation, and to the hearing and teaching of those divine truths which treat of the divine nature. Even the kings, who are likewise

[1] On account of the large amount of animal matter contained in it.

[2] Called Ȧnu, , in the Egyptian texts; it was the centre of the great solar cult of Egypt. It is the "On" of the Bible.

[3] The Sun-god was called Rā, .

priests, only partake of wine in the measure which is prescribed for them in the sacred books, as we are told by Hecataeus. This custom was only introduced during the reign of Psammetichus, and before that time they drank no wine at all. If they used it at any time in pouring out libations to the gods, it was not because they looked upon it as being acceptable to them for its own sake, but they poured it out over their altars as the blood of their enemies who had in times past fought against them. For they believe the vine to have first sprung out of the earth after it was fattened by the bodies of those who fell in the wars against the gods. And this, they say, is the reason why drinking its juice in great quantities makes men mad and beside themselves, filling them, as it were, with the blood of their own ancestors. These things are thus related by Eudoxus in the second book of his *Travels*, as he had them from the priests themselves.

VII. As to sea-fish, the Egyptians in general do not abstain from all kinds of them, but some from one sort and some from another. Thus, for example, the inhabitants of Oxyrhynchus[1] will not touch any that have been taken with an angle; for as they pay especial reverence to the Oxyrhynchus Fish,[2] from whence they derive their name, they are afraid lest perhaps the hook may be defiled by having been at

[1] The Per-Mātchet, .

[2] Probably the pike, or "fighting fish."

some time or other employed in catching their favourite fish. The people of Syene[1] in like manner abstain from the Phagrus Fish[2]; for as this fish is observed by them to make his first appearance upon their coasts just as the Nile begins to overflow, they pay special regard to these voluntary messengers as it were of that most joyful news. The priests, indeed, entirely abstain from all sorts in general.[3] Therefore, upon the ninth day of the first month, when all the rest of the Egyptians are obliged by their religion to eat a fried fish before the door of their houses, they only burn them, not tasting them at all. For this custom they give two reasons: the first and most curious, as falling in with the sacred philosophy of Osiris and Typhon, will be more properly explained in another place. The second, that which is most obvious and manifest, is that fish is neither a dainty nor even a necessary kind of food, a fact which seems to be abundantly confirmed by the writings of Homer, who never makes either the delicate Pheacians or the Ithacans (though both peoples were islanders) to feed upon fish, nor even the companions of Ulysses during their long and most

[1] In Egyptian, SUNU, 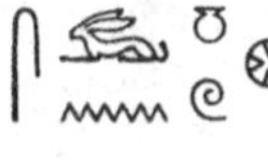, the Sewêneh of the Bible, and the modern Aswân.

[2] A kind of bream, the *ȧn*, 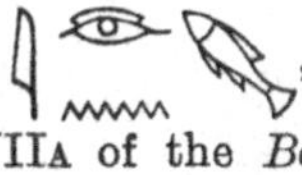, of the Egyptian texts.

[3] Compare Chap. CXXXVIIA of the *Book of the Dead.* "And "behold, these things shall be performed by a man who is clean, "and is ceremonially pure, one who hath eaten neither meat nor "fish, and who hath not had intercourse with women" (ll. 52, 53).

tedious voyage, till they were reduced thereto by extreme necessity. In short, they consider the sea to have been forced out of the earth by the power of fire, and therefore to lie out of nature's confines; and they regard it not as a part of the world, or one of the elements, but as a preternatural and corrupt and morbid excrement.

VIII. This much may be depended upon: the religious rites and ceremonies of the Egyptians were never instituted upon irrational grounds, never built upon mere fable and superstition, but founded with a view to promote the morality and happiness of those who were to observe them, or at least to preserve the memory of some valuable piece of history, or to represent to us some of the phenomena of nature. As concerning the abhorrence which is expressed for onions, it is wholly improbable that this detestation is owing to the loss of Diktys, who, whilst he was under the guardianship of Isis, is supposed to have fallen into the river and to have been drowned as he was reaching after a bunch of them. No, the true reason of their abstinence from onions is because they are observed to flourish most and to be in the greatest vigour at the wane of the moon, and also because they are entirely useless to them either in their feasts[1] or in their times of abstinence and purification, for in the former

[1] Bunches of onions were offered to the dead at all periods of Egyptian history, and they were regarded as typical of the "white teeth" of Horus. The onion was largely used in medicine.

case they make tears come from those who use them, and in the latter they create thirst. For much the same reason they likewise look upon the pig as an impure animal, and to be avoided, observing it to be most apt to engender upon the decrease of the moon, and they think that those who drink its milk are more subject to leprosy and such-like cutaneous diseases than others. The custom of abstaining from the flesh of the pig[1] is not always observed, for those who sacrifice a sow to Typhon once a year, at the full moon, afterwards eat its flesh. The reason they give for this practice is this: Typhon being in pursuit of this animal at that season of the moon, accidentally found the wooden chest wherein was deposited the body of Osiris, which he immediately pulled to pieces. This story, however, is not generally admitted, there being some who look upon it, as they do many other relations of the same kind, as founded upon some mistake or misrepresentation. All agree, however, in saying that so great was the abhorrence which the ancient Egyptians expressed for whatever tended to promote luxury, expense, and voluptuousness, that in order to expose it as much as possible they erected a column in one of the temples of Thebes, full of curses against their king Meinis, who first drew them off from their

[1] The pig was associated with Set, or Typhon, and the black variety was specially abominated because it was a black pig which struck Horus in the eye, and damaged it severely. See *Book of the Dead*, Chap. CXII.

former frugal and parsimonious course of life. The immediate cause for the erection of the pillar is thus given: Technatis,[1] the father of Bocchoris, leading an army against the Arabians, and his baggage and provisions not coming up to him as soon as he expected, was therefore obliged to eat some of the very poor food which was obtainable, and having eaten, he lay down on the bare ground and slept very soundly. This gave him a great affection for a mean and frugal diet, and induced him to curse the memory of Meinis, and with the permission of the priests he made these curses public by cutting them upon a pillar.[2]

IX. Now, the kings of Egypt were always chosen either out of the soldiery or priesthood, the former order being honoured and respected for its valour, and the latter for its wisdom. If the choice fell upon a soldier, he was immediately initiated into the order of priests, and by them instructed in their abstruse and hidden philosophy, a philosophy for the most part involved in fable and allegory, and exhibiting only dark hints and obscure resemblances of the truth. This the priesthood hints to us in many instances, particularly by the sphinxes, which they seem to have placed designedly before their temples as types of the enigmatical nature of their theology. To this purpose,

[1] In Egyptian, TAFNEKHT, 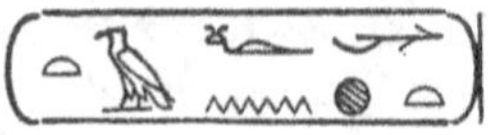, the first king of the XXIVth Dynasty.

[2] An unlikely story, for Tafnekht had no authority at Thebes.

likewise, is that inscription which they have engraved upon the base of the statue of Athene[1] at Saïs, whom they identify with Isis: "I am everything that has "been, that is, and that shall be: and my veil no man "hath raised." In like manner the word "Amoun," or as it is expressed in the Greek language, "Ammôn," which is generally looked upon as the proper name of the Egyptian Zeus, is interpreted by Manetho[2] the Sebennite[3] to signify "concealment" or "something which is hidden."[4] Hecataeus of Abdera indeed tells us that the Egyptians make use of this term when they call out to one another. If this be so, then their invoking Amoun is the same thing as calling upon the supreme being, whom they believe to be "hidden" and "concealed" in the universal nature, to appear and manifest itself to them. So cautious and reserved was

[1] The Egyptian goddess Net,  or , in Greek Νηιθ, the great goddess of Saïs, in the Western Delta. She was self-existent, and produced her son, the Sun-god, without union with a god. In an address to her, quoted by Mallet (*Culte de Neit*, p. 140), are found the words, "thy garment hath not been unloosed," 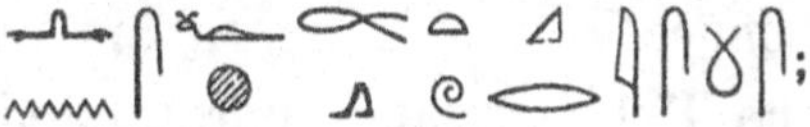; thus Plutarch's quotation is correct.

[2] He compiled a History of Egypt for Ptolemy II., and flourished about B.C. 270; only the King-List from this work is preserved.

[3] He was a native of the town of Sebennytus, 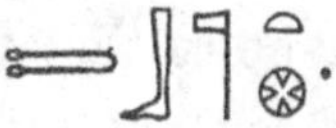.

[4] *Ȧmen*, 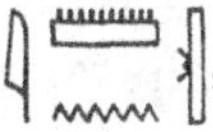, means "hidden," and ȦMEN, 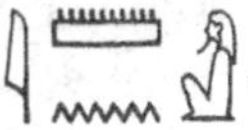, is the "hidden god."

the Egyptian wisdom in those things which appertained to religion.

X. And this is still farther evinced from those voyages which have been made into Egypt by the wisest men among the Greeks, namely, by Solo, Thales, Plato, Eudoxus, Pythagoras, and, as some say, even by Lycurgus himself, on purpose to converse with the priests. And we are also told that Eudoxus was a disciple of Chnouphis the Memphite, Solo of Sonchis the Saïte, and Pythagoras of Oinuphis the Heliopolite. But none of these philosophers seems either to have been more admired and in greater favour with the priests, or to have paid a more especial regard to their method of philosophising, than this last named, who has particularly imitated their mysterious and symbolical manner in his own writings, and like them conveyed his doctrines to the world in a kind of riddle. For many of the precepts of Pythagoras come nothing short of the hieroglyphical representations themselves, such as, "eat not in a chariot," "sit not on a measure (choenix)," "plant not a palm-tree," and "stir not the fire with a sword in the house." And I myself am of the opinion that, when the Pythagoreans appropriated the names of several of the gods to particular numbers, as that of Apollo to the unit, of Artemis to the duad, of Athene to the seven, and of Poseidon to the first cube, in this they allude to something which the founder of their sect saw in the Egyptian temples, or to some ceremonies performed in them, or to some symbols there exhibited. Thus their great king and lord Osiris is represented by the hieroglyphics for an eye and a sceptre,[1] the name itself signifying "many-eyed," as we are told by some[2] who would derive it from the words *os*,[3] "many," and *iri*,[4] an "eye," which have this meaning in the Egyptian language. Similarly, because the heavens are eternal and are never consumed or wax old, they represent them by a heart with a censer placed under it. Much in the same way are those statues of the Judges at Thebes without hands, and their chief, or president, is represented with his eyes turned downwards, which signifies that justice ought not to be obtainable by bribes, nor guided by favour or affection. Of a like nature is the Beetle which we see engraven upon the seals of the soldiers, for there is no such thing as a female beetle of this species; for they are all males, and they propagate their kind by casting their seed into round balls of dirt, which afford not only a proper place wherein the young may be hatched, but also nourishment for them as soon as they are born.

[1] The oldest form of the name is ÅS-ÅR, 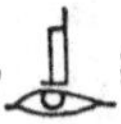 ; the first sign, 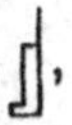, is a throne, and the second, , is an eye, but the exact meaning represented by the two signs is not known. In late times a sceptre, 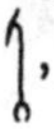, took the place of the throne, but only because of its phonetic value *as* or *us*. Thus we have the forms 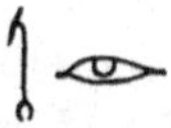 and .

[2] This is a mistake. [3] In Egyptian,  *āsh*, "many."

[4] In Egyptian, 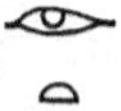 *årt*, Coptic ϵιⲁⲧ, "eye."

XI. When you hear, therefore, the mythological tales which the Egyptians tell of their gods, their wanderings, their mutilations, and many other disasters which befell them, remember what has just been said, and be assured that nothing of what is thus told you is really true, or ever happened in fact. For can it be imagined that it is the dog[1] itself which is reverenced by them under the name of Hermes[2]? It is the qualities of this animal, his constant vigilance, and his acumen in distinguishing his friends from his foes, which have rendered him, as Plato says, a meet emblem of that god who is the chief patron of intelligence. Nor can we imagine that they think that the sun, like a newly born babe, springs up every day out of a lily. It is quite true that they represent the rising sun in this manner,[3] but the reason is because they wish to indicate thereby that it is moisture to which we owe the first kindling of this luminary. In like manner, the cruel and bloody king of Persia, Ochus, who not only put to death great numbers of the people, but even slew the Apis Bull himself, and afterwards served him up in a banquet to his friends, is represented by them by a

[1] The animal here referred to must be the dog-headed ape, , which we see in pictures of the Judgment assisting Thoth to weigh the heart of the dead. This dog-headed ape is a wonderfully intelligent creature, and its weird cleverness is astonishing.

[2] The Egyptian Ṭeḥuti, or Thoth.

[3] .

sword, and by this name he is still to be found in the catalogue of their kings. This name, therefore, does not represent his person, but indicates his base and cruel qualities, which were best suggested by the picture of an instrument of destruction. If, therefore, O Clea, you will hear and entertain the story of these gods from those who know how to explain it consistently with religion and philosophy, if you will steadily persist in the observance of all these holy rites which the laws require of you, and are moreover fully persuaded that to form true notions of the divine nature is more acceptable to them than any sacrifice or mere external act of worship can be, you will by this means be entirely exempt from any danger of falling into superstition, an evil no less to be avoided than atheism itself.

XII. Now, the story of Isis and Osiris, its most insignificant and superfluous parts being omitted, runs thus:—

The goddess Rhea,[1] they say, having accompanied with Kronos[2] by stealth, was discovered by Helios,[3] who straightway cursed her, and declared that she should not be delivered in any month or year. Hermes, however, being also in love with the same goddess, in return for the favours which he had

[1] I.e., Nut, 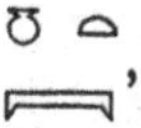, the Sky-goddess.

[2] I.e., Ḳeb, , the Earth-god.

[3] I.e., Rā, .

received from her, went and played at dice with Selene,[1] and won from her the seventieth part of each day. These parts he joined together and made from them five complete days, and he added them to the three hundred and sixty days of which the year formerly consisted. These five days are to this day called the "Epagomenae,"[2] that is, the superadded, and they are observed by them as the birthdays of their gods.[3] On the first of these, they say, Osiris was born, and as he came into the world a voice was heard saying, "The Lord of All[4] is born." Some relate the matter in a different way, and say that a certain person named Pamyles, as he was fetching water from the temple of Dios at Thebes, heard a voice commanding

[1] I.e., ÀĀḤ, 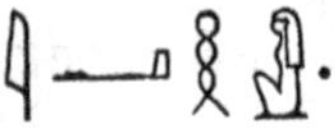.

[2] In Egyptian, "the five days over the year," 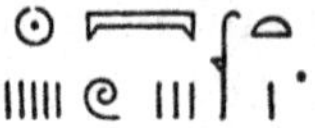.

[3] In Egyptian thus:—

I. Birthday of Osiris, .

II. " Horus, .

III. " Set, .

IV. " Isis, 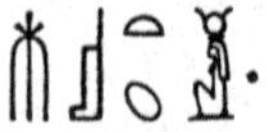.

V. " Nephthys, .

[4] One of the chief titles of Osiris was *Neb er tcher*, , i.e., "lord to the uttermost limit of everything."

him to proclaim aloud that the good and great king Osiris was then born, and that for this reason Kronos committed the education of the child to him, and that in memory of this event the Pamylia were afterwards instituted, which closely resemble the Phallephoria or Priapeia of the Greeks. Upon the second of these days was born Aroueris,[1] whom some call Apollo, and others the Elder Horus. Upon the third day Typhon was born, who came into the world neither at the proper time nor by the right way, but he forced a passage through a wound which he made in his mother's side. Upon the fourth day Isis was born, in the marshes of Egypt,[2] and upon the fifth day Nephthys, whom some call Teleute, or Aphrodite, or Nike, was born. As regards the fathers of these children, the first two are said to have been begotten by Helios, Isis by Hermes, and Typhon and Nephthys by Kronos. Therefore, since the third of the superadded days was the birthday of Typhon, the kings considered it to be unlucky,[3] and in consequence they neither transacted any business in it, nor even suffered themselves to take any refreshment until the evening. They further add that Typhon married Nephthys,[4] and that Isis and Osiris, having a

[1] I.e., Ḥeru-ur, 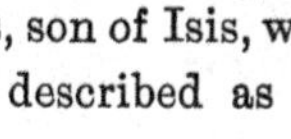. "Horus the Elder."

[2] It was Horus, son of Isis, who was born in the marshes of Egypt.

[3] This day is described as unlucky, 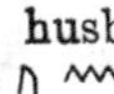, in the hieroglyphic texts.

[4] Set and Nephthys are regarded as husband and wife in the texts; their offspring was Anubis, Ȧnpu, 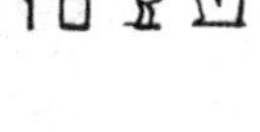.

mutual affection, enjoyed each other in their mother's womb before they were born, and that from this commerce sprang Aroueris, whom the Egyptians likewise call Horus the Elder, and the Greeks Apollo.

XIII. Osiris having become king of Egypt, applied himself to civilizing his countrymen by turning them from their former indigent and barbarous course of life. He taught them how to cultivate and improve the fruits of the earth, and he gave them a body of laws whereby to regulate their conduct, and instructed them in the reverence and worship which they were to pay to the gods. With the same good disposition he afterwards travelled over the rest of the world, inducing the people everywhere to submit to his discipline, not indeed compelling them by force of arms, but persuading them to yield to the strength of his reasons, which were conveyed to them in the most agreeable manner, in hymns and songs, accompanied with instruments of music. From this last circumstance the Greeks identified him with their Dionysos, or Bacchus. During the absence of Osiris from his kingdom, Typhon had no opportunity of making any innovations in the state, Isis being extremely vigilant in the government, and always upon her guard. After his return, however, having first persuaded seventy-two other people to join with him in the conspiracy, together with a certain queen of Ethiopia called Aso, who chanced to be in Egypt at that time, he formed a crafty plot against him. For having privily taken the measure of the body of Osiris, he caused a chest to be made of exactly the same size, and it was very beautiful and highly decorated. This chest he brought into a certain banqueting room, where it was greatly admired by all who were present, and Typhon, as if in jest, promised to give it to that man whose body when tried would be found to fit it. Thereupon the whole company, one after the other, went into it, but it did not fit any of them; last of all Osiris himself lay down in it. Thereupon all the conspirators ran to the chest, and clapped the cover upon it, and then they fastened it down with nails on the outside, and poured melted lead over it. They next took the chest to the river, which carried it to the sea through the Tanaïtic mouth of the Nile; and for this reason this mouth of the Nile is still held in the utmost abomination by the Egyptians, and is never mentioned by them except with marks of detestation. These things, some say, took place on the seventeenth day of the month of Hathor, when the sun was in Scorpio, in the twenty-eighth year of the reign of Osiris, though others tell us that this was the year of his life and not of his reign.

XIV. The first who had knowledge of the accident which had befallen their king were the Pans and Satyrs, who inhabited the country round about Chemmis,[1] and they having informed the people about

[1] In Egyptian, KHEBT, , in the VIIIth nome of Lower Egypt.

it, gave the first occasion to the name of Panic Terrors, which has ever since been made use of to signify any sudden fright or amazement of a multitude. As soon as the report reached Isis, she immediately cut off one of the locks of her hair, and put on mourning apparel in that very place where she happened to be; for this reason the place has ever since been called "Koptos," or the "city of mourning," though some are of opinion that this word rather signifies "deprivation." After this she wandered round about through the country, being full of disquietude and perplexity, searching for the chest, and she inquired of every person she met, including some children whom she saw, whether they knew what was become of it. Now, it so happened that these children had seen what Typhon's accomplices had done with the body, and they accordingly told her by what mouth of the Nile it had been conveyed to the sea. For this reason the Egyptians look upon children as endued with a kind of faculty of divining, and in consequence of this notion are very curious in observing the accidental prattle which they have with one another whilst they are at play, especially if it be in a sacred place, forming omens and presages from it. Isis meanwhile having been informed that Osiris, deceived by her sister Nephthys, who was in love with him, had unwittingly enjoyed her instead of herself, as she concluded from the melilot-garland which he had left with her, made it her business likewise to search out the child, the fruit of this unlawful commerce (for her sister, dreading the anger of her husband Typhon, had exposed it as soon as it was born). Accordingly, after much pains and difficulty, by means of some dogs that conducted her to the place where it was, she found it and bred it up; and in process of time it became her constant guard and attendant, and obtained the name of Anubis, and it is thought that it watches and guards the gods as dogs do men.

XV. At length Isis received more particular news that the chest had been carried by the waves of the sea to the coast of Byblos, and there gently lodged in the branches of a bush of tamarisk, which in a short time had grown up into a large and beautiful tree, and had grown round the chest and enclosed it on every side so completely that it was not to be seen. Moreover, the king of the country, amazed at its unusual size, had cut the tree down, and made that part of the trunk wherein the chest was concealed into a pillar to support the roof of his house. These things, they say, having been made known to Isis in an extraordinary manner by the report of demons, she immediately went to Byblos, where, setting herself down by the side of a fountain, she refused to speak to anybody except the queen's women who chanced to be there. These, however, she saluted and caressed in the kindest manner possible, plaiting their hair for them, and transmitting into them part of that wonderful odour which issued from her own body. This raised a great desire in the queen their mistress to see the stranger who had this admirable faculty of transfusing so fragrant a smell from herself into the hair and skin of other people. She therefore sent for her to court, and, after a further acquaintance with her, made her nurse to one of her sons. Now, the name of the king who reigned at this time at Byblos was Melkander (Melkarth ?), and that of his wife was Astarte, or, according to others, Saôsis, though some call her Nemanoun, which answers to the Greek name Athenais.

XVI. Isis nursed the child by giving it her finger to suck instead of the breast. She likewise put him each night into the fire in order to consume his mortal part, whilst, having transformed herself into a swallow, she circled round the pillar and bemoaned her sad fate. This she continued to do for some time, till the queen, who stood watching her, observing the child to be all of a flame, cried out, and thereby deprived him of some of that immortality which would otherwise have been conferred upon him. The goddess then made herself known, and asked that the pillar which supported the roof might be given to her. Having taken the pillar down, she cut it open easily, and having taken out what she wanted, she wrapped up the remainder of the trunk in fine linen, and having poured perfumed oil over it, she delivered it again into the hands of the king and queen. Now, this piece of wood is to this day preserved in the temple, and worshipped by the people of Byblos. When this was done, Isis threw herself upon the chest, and made at the same time such loud and terrible cries of lamentation over it, that the younger of the king's sons who heard her was frightened out of his life. But the elder of them she took with her, and set sail with the chest for Egypt. Now, it being morning the river Phaedrus sent forth a keen and chill air, and becoming angry she dried up its current.

XVII. At the first place where she stopped, and when she believed that she was alone, she opened the chest, and laying her face upon that of her dead husband, she embraced him and wept bitterly. Then, seeing that the little boy had silently stolen up behind her, and had found out the reason of her grief, she turned upon him suddenly, and, in her anger, gave him so fierce and terrible a look that he died of fright immediately. Others say that his death did not happen in this manner, but, as already hinted, that he fell into the sea. Afterwards he received the greatest honour on account of the goddess, for this Maneros, whom the Egyptians so frequently call upon at their banquets, is none other than he. This story is contradicted by those who tell us that the true name of this child was Palaestinus, or Pelusius, and that the city of this name was built by the goddess in memory of him. And they further add that this Maneros is thus honoured by the Egyptians at their feasts because he was the first who invented music. Others again state that Maneros is not the name of any particular person, but a mere customary form of complimentary greeting which the Egyptians use towards each other at their more solemn feasts and banquets, meaning no more by it than to wish "that what they were then about might "prove fortunate and happy to them." This is the true import of the word. In like manner they say that the human skeleton which is carried about in a box on festal occasions, and shown to the guests, is not designed, as some imagine, to represent the particular misfortunes of Osiris, but rather to remind them of their mortality, and thereby to excite them freely to make use of and to enjoy the good things which are set before them, seeing that they must quickly become such as they there saw. This is the true reason for introducing the skeleton at their banquets. But to proceed with the narrative.

XVIII. When Isis had come to her son Horus, who was being reared at Buto,[1] she deposited the chest in a remote and unfrequented place. One night, however, when Typhon was hunting by the light of the moon, he came upon it by chance, and recognizing the body which was enclosed in it, he tore it into several pieces, fourteen[2] in all, and scattered them in different places

[1] In Egyptian, the double city Pe-Ṭep, 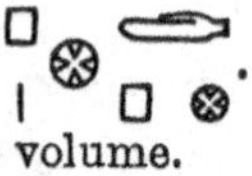. See the texts from the Metternich Stele printed in this volume.

[2] The fourteen members are: head, feet, bones, arms, heart, interior, tongue, eyes, fists, fingers, back, ears, loins, and body. Some of the lists in Egyptian add the face of a ram and the hair. The cities in which Isis buried the portions of his body are: Koptos, Philae in Elephantine, Herakleopolis Magna, Kusae, Heliopolis, Diospolis of Lower Egypt, Letopolis, Saïs, Hermopolis

up and down the country. When Isis knew what had been done, she set out in search of the scattered portions of her husband's body; and in order to pass more easily through the lower, marshy parts of the country, she made use of a boat made of the papyrus plant. For this reason, they say, either fearing the anger of the goddess, or else venerating the papyrus, the crocodile never injures anyone who travels in this sort of vessel.[1] And this, they say, hath given rise to the report that there are very many different sepulchres of Osiris in Egypt, for wherever Isis found one of the scattered portions of her husband's body, there she buried it. Others, however, contradict this story, and tell us that the variety of sepulchres of Osiris was due rather to the policy of the queen, who, instead of the real body, as she pretended, presented to these cities only an image of her husband. This she did in order to increase the honours which would by these means be paid to his memory, and also to defeat Typhon, who, if he were victorious in his fight against Horus in which he was about to engage, would search for the body of Osiris, and being distracted by the number of sepulchres would despair of ever being able to find the true one. We are told, moreover, that notwithstanding all her efforts, Isis was never able to discover the phallus of

of Lower Egypt, Athribis, Āq (Schedia), Āb in the Libyan nome, Netert, Apis.

[1] Moses was laid in an ark of bulrushes, i.e., papyrus, and was found uninjured.

Osiris, which, having been thrown into the Nile immediately upon its separation from the rest of the body,[1] had been devoured by the Lepidotus, the Phagrus, and the Oxyrhynchus, fish which above all others, for this reason, the Egyptians have in more especial avoidance. In order, however, to make some amends for the loss, Isis consecrated the phallus made in imitation of it, and instituted a solemn festival to its memory, which is even to this day observed by the Egyptians.

XIX. After these things Osiris returned from the other world, and appeared to his son Horus, and encouraged him to fight, and at the same time instructed him in the exercise of arms. He then asked him what he thought was the most glorious action a man could perform, to which Horus replied, "To revenge the "injuries offered to his father[2] and mother." Osiris then asked him what animal he thought most serviceable to a soldier, and Horus replied, "A horse." On this Osiris

[1] We meet with a similar statement in the *Tale of the Two Brothers*, where we are told that the younger brother, having declared his innocence to the elder brother, cut off his phallus and threw it into the river, where it was devoured by the *nāru* fish.

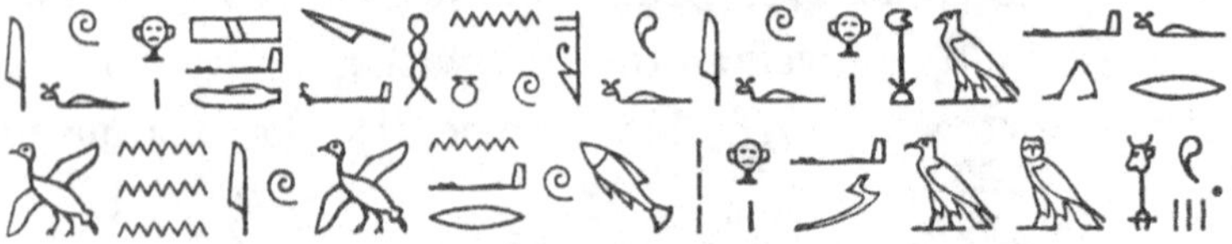

[2] The texts give as a very common title of Horus, 

, "Horus, the avenger of his father."

wondered, and he questioned him further, asking him why he preferred a horse to a lion, and Horus replied, "Though the lion is the more serviceable creature to "one who stands in need of help, yet is the horse more "useful in overtaking and cutting off a flying enemy."[1] These replies caused Osiris to rejoice greatly, for they showed him that his son was sufficiently prepared for his enemy. We are, moreover, told that amongst the great numbers who were continually deserting from Typhon's party was his concubine Thoueris,[2] and that a serpent which pursued her as she was coming over to Horus was slain by his soldiers. The memory of this action is, they say, still preserved in that cord which is thrown into the midst of their assemblies, and then chopped in pieces. Afterwards a battle took place between Horus and Typhon, which lasted many days, but Horus was at length victorious, and Typhon was taken prisoner. He was delivered over into the custody of Isis, who, instead of putting him to death, loosed his fetters and set him free. This action of his mother incensed Horus to such a degree that he seized her, and pulled the royal crown off her head; but Hermes came forward, and set upon her head the head of an ox

[1] There is no evidence that the Egyptians employed the horse in war before the XVIIIth Dynasty, a fact which proves that the dialogue here given is an invention of a much later date than the original legend of Osiris.

[2] In Egyptian, TA-URT, , or  the hippopotamus goddess.

instead of a helmet.[1] After this Typhon accused Horus of illegitimacy, but, by the assistance of Hermes, his legitimacy was fully established by a decree of the gods themselves.[2] After this two other battles were fought between Horus and Typhon, and in both Typhon was defeated. Moreover, Isis is said to have had union with Osiris after his death,[3] and she brought forth Harpokrates,[4] who came into the world before his time, and was lame in his lower limbs.

XX. Such then are the principal circumstances of

[1] According to the legend given in the Fourth Sallier Papyrus, the fight between Horus and Set began on the 26th day of the month of Thoth, and lasted three days and three nights. It was fought in or near the hall of the lords of Kher-āḥa, i.e., near Heliopolis, and in the presence of Isis, who seems to have tried to spare both her brother Set and her son Horus. For some reason Horus became enraged with his mother, and attacking her like a "leopard of the south," he cut off the head of Isis, 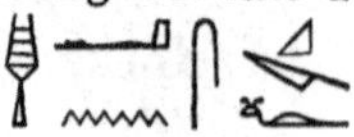 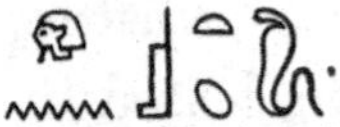. Thereupon Thoth came forward, and using words of power, created a substitute in the form of a cow's head, and placed it on her body (Sallier, iv., p. 2; see *Select Papyri*, pl. cxlv.).

[2] Horus inherited the throne by his father's will, a fact which is so often emphasized in the texts that it seems there may be some ground for Plutarch's view.

[3] This view is confirmed by the words in the hymn to Osiris,  , "she moved the inactivity of the Still-Heart "(Osiris), she drew from him his essence, she made an heir."

[4] In Egyptian, ḤERU-PA-KHARṬ, , i.e., "Horus the Child."

this famous story, the more harsh and shocking parts of it, such as the cutting up of Horus and the beheading of Isis, being omitted. Now, if such could be supposed to be the real sentiments of the Egyptians concerning those divine Beings whose most distinguishing characteristics are happiness and immortality, or could it be imagined that they actually believed what they thus tell us ever to have actually taken place, I should not need to warn you, O Clea, you who are already sufficiently averse to such impious and absurd notions of the God, I should not, I say, have need to caution you, to testify your abhorrence of them, and, as Aeschylus expresses it, "to spit and wash your mouth" after the recital of them. In the present case, however, it is not so. And I doubt not that you yourself are conscious of the difference between this history and those light and idle fictions which the poets and other writers of fables, like spiders, weave and spin out of their own imaginations, without having any substantial ground or firm foundation to work upon. There must have been some real distress, some actual calamity, at the bottom as the ground-work of the narration; for, as mathematicians assure us, the rainbow is nothing else but a variegated image of the sun, thrown upon the sight by the reflection of his beams from the clouds; and thus ought we to look upon the present story as the representation, or rather reflection, of something real as its true cause. And this notion is still farther suggested to us as well by that solemn air of grief and sadness which appears in their sacrifices, as by the very form and arrangement of their temples, which extend into long avenues and open aisles in some portions,[1] and in others retreating into dark and gloomy chapels which resembled the underground vaults which are allotted to the dead. That the history has a substantial foundation is proved by the opinion which obtains generally concerning the sepulchres of Osiris. There are many places wherein his body is said to have been deposited, and among these are Abydos and Memphis, both of which are said to contain his body. It is for this reason, they say, that the richer and more prosperous citizens wish to be buried in the former of these cities, being ambitious of lying, as it were, in the grave with Osiris.[2] The title of Memphis to be regarded

[1] Plutarch refers to the long colonnaded courts which extend in a straight line to the sanctuary, which often contains more than one shrine, and to the chambers wherein temple properties, vestments, &c., were kept.

[2] In what city the cult of Osiris originated is not known, but it is quite certain that before the end of the VIth Dynasty Abydos became the centre of his worship, and that he dispossessed the local god Ȧn-Ḥer in the affections of the people. Tradition affirmed that the head of Osiris was preserved at Abydos in a box, and a picture of it, 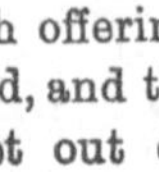, became the symbol of the city. At Abydos a sort of miracle play, in which all the sufferings and resurrection of Osiris were commemorated, was performed annually, and the raising up of a model of his body, and the placing of his head upon it, were the culminating ceremonies. At Abydos was the famous shaft into which offerings were cast for transmission to the dead in the Other World, and through the Gap in the hills close by souls were believed to set out on their journey thither. One tradition places the

as the grave of Osiris seems to rest upon the fact that the Apis Bull, who is considered to be the image of the soul of Osiris, is kept in that city for the express purpose that it may be as near his body as possible.[1] Others again tell us that the interpretation of the name Memphis[2] is "the haven of good men," and that the true sepulchre of Osiris lies in that little island which the Nile makes at Philae.[3] This island is, they say, inaccessible, and neither bird can alight on it, nor fish swim near it, except at the times when the priests go over to it from the mainland to solemnize their customary rites to the dead, and to crown his tomb with flowers, which, they say, is overshadowed by the branches of a tamarisk-tree, the size of which exceeds that of an olive-tree.

XXI. Eudoxus indeed asserts that, although there

Elysian Fields in the neighbourhood of Abydos. A fine stone bier, a restoration probably of the XXVIth Dynasty, which represented the original bier of Osiris, was discovered there by M. Amélineau. It is now in the Egyptian Museum at Cairo.

[1] Apis is called the "life of Osiris," , and on the death of the Bull, its soul went to heaven and joined itself to that of Osiris, and it formed with him the dual-god Ȧsȧr-Ḥep, i.e., Osiris-Apis, or Sarapis. The famous Serapeum at Memphis was called 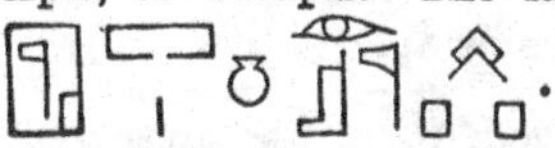.

[2] In Egyptian, MEN-NEFER, 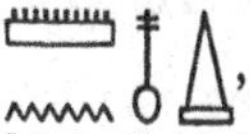, i.e., "fair haven."

[3] Osiris and Isis were worshipped at Philae until the reign of Justinian, when his general, Narses, closed the temple and carried off the statues of the gods to Constantinople, where they were probably melted down.

are many pretended sepulchres of Osiris in Egypt, the place where his body actually lies is Busiris,[1] where likewise he was born.[2] As to Taphosiris, there is no need to mention it particularly, for its very name indicates its claim to be the tomb of Osiris. There are likewise other circumstances in the Egyptian ritual which hint to us the reality upon which this history is grounded, such as their cleaving the trunk of a tree, their wrapping it up in linen which they tear in pieces for that purpose, and the libations of oil which they afterwards pour upon it; but these I do not insist on, because they are intermixed with such of their mysteries as may not be revealed.

[FIRST EXPLANATION OF THE STORY.]

XXII. Now as to those who, from many things of this kind, some of which are proclaimed openly, and others are darkly hinted at in their religious institutions, would conclude that the whole story is no other than a mere commemoration of the various actions of

[1] In Egyptian, Pa-Àsår-neb-Ṭeṭu, 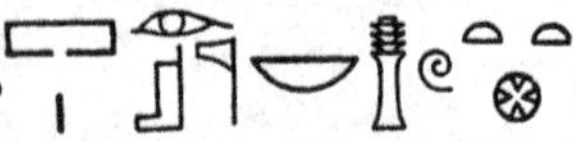, "the house of Osiris, the lord of Ṭeṭu." In the temple of Neb-Seḳert, 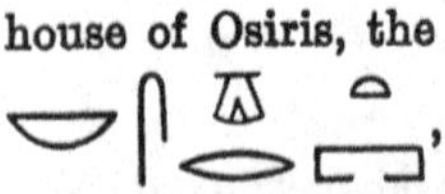, the backbone of the god, , was preserved, according to one text, but another says it was his jaws (?) and interior, .

[2] This view represents a late tradition, or at all events one which sprang up after the decay of Abydos.

their kings and other great men, who, by reason of their excellent virtue and the mightiness of their power, added to their other titles the honour of divinity, though they afterwards fell into many and grievous calamities, those, I say, who would in this manner account for the various scenes above-mentioned, must be owned indeed to make use of a very plausible method of eluding such difficulties as may arise about this subject, and ingeniously enough to transfer the most shocking parts of it from the divine to the human nature. Moreover, it must be admitted that such a solution is not entirely destitute of any appearance of historical evidence for its support. For when the Egyptians themselves tell us that Hermes had one hand shorter than another, that Typhon was of red complexion, Horus fair, and Osiris black, does not this show that they were of the human species, and subject to the same accidents as all other men?[1] Nay, they go farther, and even declare the particular work in which each was engaged whilst alive. Thus they say that Osiris was a general, that Canopus, from whom the star took its name, was a pilot, and that the ship which the Greeks call Argo, being made in imitation of the ship of Osiris, was, in honour of him, turned into a constellation and placed near Orion and the Dog-star, the former being sacred to Horus and the latter to Isis.

[1] Red is the colour attributed to all fiends in the Egyptian texts. One of the forms of Horus is described as being "blue-eyed," and the colour of the face of Osiris is often green, and sometimes black.

XXIII. But I am much afraid that to give in to this explanation of the story will be to move things which ought not to be moved; and not only, as Simonides says, "to declare war against all antiquity," but likewise against whole families and nations who are fully possessed with the belief in the divinity of these beings. And it would be no less than dispossessing those great names of their heaven, and bringing them down to the earth. It would be to shake and loosen a worship and faith which have been firmly settled in nearly all mankind from their infancy. It would be to open a wide door for atheism to enter in at, and to encourage the attempts of those who would humanize the divine nature. More particularly it would give a clear sanction and authority to the impostures of Euhemerus the Messenian, who from mere imagination, and without the least appearance of truth to support it, has invented a new mythology of his own, asserting that "all those in general who are called and declared to be "gods are none other than so many ancient generals "and sea-captains and kings." Now, he says that he found this statement written in the Panchaean dialect in letters of gold, though in what part of the globe his Panchaeans dwell, any more than the Tryphillians, whom he mentions at the same time with them, he does not inform us. Nor can I learn that any other person, whether Greek or Barbarian, except himself, has ever yet been so fortunate as to meet with these imaginary countries.

[In § XXIV. Plutarch goes on to say that the Assyrians commemorate Semiramis, the Egyptians Sesostris, the Phrygians Manis or Masdis, the Persians Cyrus, and the Macedonians Alexander, yet these heroes are not regarded as gods by their peoples. The kings who have accepted the title of gods have afterwards had to suffer the reproach of vanity and presumption, and impiety and injustice.]

[SECOND EXPLANATION OF THE STORY.]

XXV. There is another and a better method which some employ in explaining this story. They assert that what is related of Typhon, Osiris, and Isis is not to be regarded as the afflictions of gods, or of mere mortals, but rather as the adventures of certain great Daemons. These beings, they say, are supposed by some of the wisest of the Greek philosophers, that is to say, Plato, Pythagoras, Xenocrates, and Chrysippus, in accordance with what they had learned from ancient theologians, to be stronger and more powerful than men, and of a nature superior to them. They are, at the same time, inferior to the pure and unmixed nature of the gods, as partaking of the sensations of the body, as well as of the perceptions of the soul, and consequently liable to pain as well as pleasure, and to such other appetites and affections as flow from their various combinations. Such affections, however, have a greater power and influence over some of them than over others, just as there are different degrees of virtue and vice found in these Daemons as well as in mankind. In like manner, the wars of the Giants and the Titans which are so much spoken of by the Greeks, the detestable actions of Kronos, the combats between Apollo and the Python, the flights of Dionysos, and the wanderings of Demeter, are exactly of the same nature as the adventures of Osiris and Typhon. Therefore, they all are to be accounted for in the same manner, and every treatise of mythology will readily furnish us with an abundance of other similar instances. The same thing may also be affirmed of those other things which are so carefully concealed under the cover of mysteries and imitations.

[In § XXVI. Plutarch points out that Homer calls great and good men "god-like" and "God's compeers," but the word Daemon is applied to the good and bad indifferently (see *Odyssey*, vi. 12; *Iliad*, xiii. 810, v. 438, iv. 31, &c.). Plato assigns to the Olympian Gods good things and the odd numbers, and the opposite to the Daemons. Xenocrates believed in the existence of a series of strong and powerful beings which take pleasure in scourgings and fastings, &c. Hesiod speaks of "holy daemons" (*Works and Days*, 126) and "guardians of mankind," and "bestowers of wealth," and these are regarded by Plato as a "middle order of beings between "the gods and men, interpreters of the wills of the "gods to men, and ministering to their wants, carrying "the prayers and supplications of mortals to heaven, "and bringing down thence in return oracles and all "other blessings of life." Empedocles thought that the Daemons underwent punishment, and that when chastened and purified they were restored to their original state.]

[§ XXVII. To this class belonged Typhon, who was punished by Isis. In memory of all she had done and suffered, she established certain rites and mysteries which were to be types and images of her deeds, and intended these to incite people to piety, and to afford them consolation. Isis and Osiris were translated from good Daemons into gods, and the honours due to them are rightly of a mixed kind, being those due to gods and Daemons. Osiris is none other than Pluto, and Isis is not different from Proserpine.]

[§ XXX. Typhon is held by the Egyptians in the greatest contempt, and they do all they can to vilify him. The colour red being associated with him, they treat with contumely all those who have a ruddy complexion; the ass[1] being usually of a reddish colour, the men of Koptos are in the habit of sacrificing asses by casting them down precipices. The inhabitants of Busiris and Lycopolis never use trumpets, because their sounds resemble the braying of an ass. The

[1] The ass is associated with Set, or Typhon, in the texts, but on account of his virility he also typifies a form of the Sun-god. In a hymn the deceased prays, "May I smite the Ass, may I crush the serpent-fiend Sebâu," but the XLth Chapter of the Book of the Dead is entitled, "Chapter of driving back the Eater of the Ass." The vignette shows us the deceased in the act of spearing a monster serpent which has fastened its jaws in the back of an ass. In Chapter CXXV. there is a dialogue between the Cat and the Ass.

cakes which are offered at the festivals during Paoni and Paopi are stamped with the figure of a fettered ass. The Pythagoreans regarded Typhon as a daemon, and according to them he was produced in the even number fifty-six; and Eudoxus says that a figure of fifty-six angles typifies the nature of Typhon.]

[§ XXXI. The Egyptians only sacrifice red-coloured bulls, and a single black or white hair in the animal's head disqualifies it for sacrifice. They sacrifice creatures wherein the souls of the wicked have been confined, and through this view arose the custom of cursing the animal to be sacrificed, and cutting off its head and throwing it into the Nile. No bullock is sacrificed which has not on it the seal of the priests who were called "Sealers." The impression from this seal represents a man upon his knees, with his hands tied behind him, and a sword pointed at his throat. The ass is identified with Typhon not only because of his colour, but also because of his stupidity and the sensuality of his disposition. The Persian king Ochus was nicknamed the "Ass," which made him to say, "This ass shall dine upon your ox," and accordingly he slew Apis. Typhon is said to have escaped from Horus by a flight of seven days on an ass.]

[Third Explanation of the Story.]

XXXII. Such then are the arguments of those who endeavour to account for the above-mentioned history of Isis and Osiris upon a supposition that they were of the order of Daemons; but there are others who pretend to explain it upon other principles, and in more philosophical manner. To begin, then, with those whose reasoning is the most simple and obvious. As the Greeks allegorize their Kronos into Time, and their Hera into Air, and tell us that the birth of Hephaistos is no other but the change of air into fire, so these philosophers say that by Osiris the Egyptians mean the Nile, by Isis that part of the country which Osiris, or the Nile, overflows, and by Typhon the sea, which, by receiving the Nile as it runs into it, does, as it were, tear it into many pieces, and indeed entirely destroys it, excepting only so much of it as is admitted into the bosom of the earth in its passage over it, which is thereby rendered fertile. The truth of this explanation is confirmed, they say, by that sacred dirge which they make over Osiris when they bewail "him who was "born on the right side of the world and who perished "on the left."[1] For it must be observed that the Egyptians look upon the east as the front or face of the world,[2] upon the north as its right side,[3] and upon

[1] Plutarch here refers to Osiris as the Moon, which rises in the West.

[2] According to the texts the front of the world was the south, *khent*, 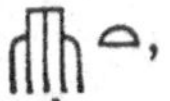, and from this word is formed the verb  , "to sail to the south."

[3] In the texts the west is the right side, *unemi*, , in Coptic, ΟΥΝΑΜ.

the south as its left.[1] As, therefore, the Nile rises in the south, and running directly northwards is at last swallowed up by the sea, it may rightly enough be said to be born on the right and to perish on the left side, This conclusion, they say, is still farther strengthened from that abhorrence which the priests express towards the sea, as well as salt, which they call "Typhon's foam." And amongst their prohibitions is one which forbids salt being laid on their tables. And do they not also carefully avoid speaking to pilots, because this class of men have much to do with the sea and get their living by it? And this is not the least of their reasons for the great dislike which they have for fish, and they even make the fish a symbol of "hatred," as is proved by the pictures which are to be seen on the porch of the temple of Neith at Saïs. The first of these is a child, the second is an old man, the third is a hawk, and then follow a fish and a hippopotamus. The meaning of all these is evidently, "O you who are "coming into the world, and you who are going out of "it (i.e., both young and old), God hateth impudence." For by the child is indicated "all those who are coming into life"; by the old man, "those who are going out of it"; by the hawk, "God"; by the fish, "hatred," on account of the sea, as has been before stated; and by the hippopotamus, "impudence," this creature being said first to slay his sire, and afterwards to force his

[1] In the texts the east is the left side, *àbti*, 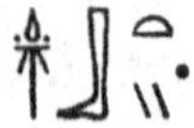.

dam.[1] The Pythagoreans likewise may be thought perhaps by some to have looked upon the sea as impure, and quite different from all the rest of nature, and that thus much is intended by them when they call it the "tears of Kronos."

[§§ XXXIII., XXXIV. Some of the more philosophical priests assert that Osiris does not symbolize the Nile only, nor Typhon the sea only, but that Osiris represents the principle and power of moisture in general, and that Typhon represents everything which is scorching, burning, and fiery, and whatever destroys moisture. Osiris they believe to have been of a black colour, because water gives a black[2] tinge to everything with which it is mixed. The Mnevis Bull[3] kept at Heliopolis is, like Osiris, black in colour, "and even Egypt[4] itself, by reason of the

[1] Each of these signs, , except the last, does mean what Plutarch says it means, but his method of reading them together is wrong, and it proves that he did not understand that hieroglyphics were used alphabetically as well as ideographically.

[2] Experiments recently conducted by Lord Rayleigh indicate that the true colour of water is blue.

[3] In Egyptian, , Nem-ur, or Men-ur, and he was called the "life of Rā."

[4] The commonest name of Egypt is KEMT, , the "black land," as opposed to the reddish-yellow sandy deserts on each side of the "valley of black mud." The word for "black" is *kam*, , in Coptic, ⲕⲁⲙⲉ, ⲕⲁⲙⲏ, ⲕⲏⲙ, ϫⲁⲙⲉ, or ϫⲁⲙⲏ.

"extreme blackness of the soil, is called by them "'Chemia,' the very name which is given to the black "part or pupil of the eye.[1] It is, moreover, represented "by them under the figure of a human heart." The Sun and Moon are not represented as being drawn about in chariots, but as sailing round the world in ships, which shows that they owe their motion, support, and nourishment to the power of humidity.[2] Homer and Thales both learned from Egypt that "water was "the first principle of all things, and the cause of "generation."[3]]

[§ XXXVI. The Nile and all kinds of moisture are called the "efflux of Osiris." Therefore a water-pitcher[4] is always carried first in his processions, and the leaf of a fig-tree represents both Osiris and Egypt.[5] Osiris is

[1] Plutarch seems to have erred here. The early texts call the pupil of the eye , "the child in the eye," as did the Semitic peoples (see my *Liturgy of Funerary Offerings*, p. 136). The Copts spoke of the "black of the eye," **ⲔⲀⲔⲈ Ⲛ̄ ⲂⲀⲖ**, the **ⲔⲀⲔⲈ** being derived from the hieroglyphic 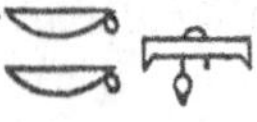, "darkness," "blackness."

[2] There is no support for this view in the texts.

[3] It was a very common belief in Egypt that all things arose from the great celestial ocean called Nu, 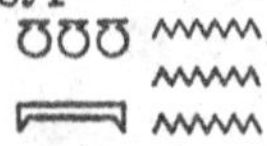, whence came the Nile.

[4] Plutarch refers to the vessel of water, , with which the priest sprinkles the ground to purify it.

[5] He seems to refer here to the *olive*-tree: Beqet, 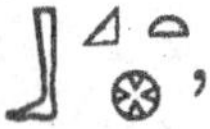, "olive land," was one of the names of Egypt.

the great principle of fecundity, which is proved by the Pamylia festivals, in which a statue of the god with a triple phallus is carried about.[1] The three-fold phallus merely signifies any great and indefinite number.]

[§ XXXVIII. The Sun is consecrated to Osiris, and the lion is worshipped, and temples are ornamented with figures of this animal, because the Nile rises when the sun is in the constellation of the Lion. Horus, the offspring of Osiris, the Nile, and Isis, the Earth, was born in the marshes of Buto, because the vapour of damp land destroys drought. Nephthys, or Teleute, represents the extreme limits of the country and the sea-shore, that is, barren land. Osiris (i.e., the Nile) overflowed this barren land, and Anubis[2] was the result.[3]]

[§ XXXIX. In the first part of this chapter Plutarch continues his identification of Typhon with drought, and his ally Aso, Queen of Ethiopia, he considers to be the Etesian or north winds, which blow for a long period when the Nile is falling. He goes on to say:—]

As to what they relate of the shutting up of Osiris in a box, this appears to mean the withdrawal of the

[1] Plutarch seems to be confounding Osiris with Menu, the god of generation, who is generally represented in an ithyphallic form. The festival of the phallus survived in Egypt until quite recently.

[2] The Egyptian Ȧnpu, . The texts make one form of him to be the son of Set and Nephthys.

[3] Plutarch's explanations in this chapter are unsupported by the texts.

Nile to its own bed. This is the more probable as this misfortune is said to have happened to Osiris in the month of Hathor, precisely at that season of the year when, upon the cessation of the Etesian or north winds, the Nile returns to its own bed, and leaves the country everywhere bare and naked. At this time also the length of the nights increases, darkness prevails, whilst light is diminished and overcome. At this time the priests celebrate doleful rites, and they exhibit as a suitable representation of the grief of Isis a gilded ox covered with a fine black linen cloth. Now, the ox is regarded as the living image of Osiris. This ceremony is performed on the seventeenth and three following days,[1] and they mourn: 1. The falling of the Nile; 2. The cessation of the north winds; 3. The decrease in the length of the days; 4. The desolate condition of the land. On the nineteenth of the month Pachons they march in procession to the sea, whither the priests and other officials carry the sacred chest, wherein is enclosed a small boat of gold; into this they first pour some water, and then all present cry out with a loud voice, "Osiris is found." This done, they throw some earth, scent, and spices into the water, and mix it well

[1] The 17th day is very unlucky, 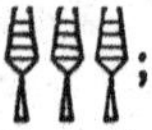; the 18th is very lucky; the 19th and 20th are very unlucky. On the 17th day Isis and Nephthys made great lamentation for their brother Un-nefer, , at Saïs; on the 19th no man should leave the house; and the man born on the 20th would die of the plague.

together, and work it up into the image of a crescent, which they afterwards dress in clothes. This shows that they regard the gods as the essence and power of water and earth.

[§ XL. Though Typhon was conquered by Horus, Isis would not allow him to be destroyed. Typhon was once master of all Egypt, i.e., Egypt was once covered by the sea, which is proved by the sea-shells which are dug out of the mines, and are found on the tops of the hills. The Nile year by year creates new land, and thus drives away the sea further and further, i.e., Osiris triumphs over Typhon.]

[Fourth Explanation of the Story.]

[§ XLI. Osiris is the Moon, and Typhon is the Sun; Typhon is therefore called Seth,[1] a word meaning "violence," "force," &c. Herakles accompanies the Sun, and Hermes the Moon. In § XLII. Plutarch connects the death-day of Osiris, the seventeenth of Hathor, with the seventeenth day of the Moon's revolution, when she begins to wane. The age of Osiris, twenty-eight years, suggests the comparison with the twenty-eight days of the Moon's revolution. The tree-trunk which is made into the shape of a crescent at the funeral of Osiris refers to the crescent moon when she

[1] In Egyptian, , or , which Plutarch seems to connect with *seṭ*, 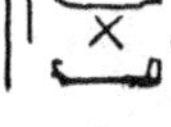.

wanes. The fourteen pieces into which Osiris was broken refer to the fourteen days in which the moon wanes.]

[§ XLIII. The height of the Nile in flood at Elephantine is twenty-eight cubits, at Mendes and Xoïs low Nile is seven cubits, and at Memphis middle Nile is fourteen cubits; these figures are to be compared with the twenty-eight days of the Moon's revolution, the seven-day phase of the Moon, and the fourteen days' Moon, or full moon. Apis was begotten by a ray of light from the Moon, and on the fourteenth day of the month Phamenoth[1] Osiris entered the Moon. Osiris is the power of the Moon, Isis the productive faculty in it.]

[FIFTH EXPLANATION OF THE STORY.]

[§ XLIV. The philosophers say that the story is nothing but an enigmatical description of the phenomena of Eclipses. In § XLV. Plutarch discusses the five explanations which he has described, and begins to state his own views about them. It must be concluded, he says, that none of these explanations taken by itself contains the true explanation of the foregoing history, though all of them together do. Typhon means every phase of Nature which is hurtful and destructive, not only drought, darkness, the sea, &c. It is impossible

[1] Marked in the papyrus Sallier IV. as a particularly unlucky day,
.

that any one cause, be it bad or even good, should be the common principle of all things. There must be two opposite and quite different and distinct Principles. In § XLVI. Plutarch compares this view with the Magian belief in Ormazd and Ahriman, the former springing from light (§ XLVII.), and the latter from darkness. Ormazd made six good gods, and Ahriman six of a quite contrary nature. Ormazd increased his own bulk three times, and adorned the heaven with stars, making the Sun to be the guard of the other stars. He then created twenty-four other gods, and placed them in an egg, and Ahriman also created twenty-four gods; the latter bored a hole in the shell of the egg, and effected an entrance into it, and thus good and evil became mixed together. In § XLVIII. Plutarch quotes Empedocles, Anaxagoras, Aristotle, and Plato in support of his hypothesis of the Two Principles, and refers to Plato's Third Principle. § XLIX. Osiris represents the good qualities of the universal Soul, and Typhon the bad; Bebo[1] is a malignant being like Typhon, with whom Manetho identifies him. § L. The ass, crocodile, and hippopotamus are all associated with Typhon; in the form of a crocodile Typhon escaped from Horus.[2]

[1] In Egyptian, Bebi, , or , Baba,  , or Babai, ; he was the first-born son of Osiris.

[2] See the *Legend of Ḥeru-Beḥuṭet*, p. 67.

The cakes offered on the seventh day of the month Tybi have a hippopotamus stamped on them. § LI. Osiris symbolizes wisdom and power, and Typhon all that is malignant and bad.]

The remaining sections contain a long series of fanciful statements by Plutarch concerning the religion and manners and customs of the Egyptians, of which the Egyptian texts now available give no proofs.

COMPLETE SONNETS, William Shakespeare. Over 150 exquisite poems deal with love, friendship, the tyranny of time, beauty's evanescence, death, and other themes in language of remarkable power, precision, and beauty. Glossary of archaic terms. Includes a selection from the Common Core State Standards Initiative. 80pp. 0-486-26686-9

THE COUNT OF MONTE CRISTO: Abridged Edition, Alexandre Dumas. Falsely accused of treason, Edmond Dantès is imprisoned in the bleak Chateau d'If. After a hair-raising escape, he launches an elaborate plot to extract a bitter revenge against those who betrayed him. 448pp. 0-486-45643-9

CRAFTSMAN BUNGALOWS: 59 Homes from "The Craftsman," Edited by Gustav Stickley. Best and most attractive designs from the Arts and Crafts Movement publication from 1903 to 1916 includes sketches, photographs of homes, floor plans, and descriptive text. 128pp. 0-486-25829-7

CRIME AND PUNISHMENT, Fyodor Dostoyevsky. Translated by Constance Garnett. Supreme masterpiece tells the story of Raskolnikov, a student tormented by his own thoughts after he murders an old woman. Overwhelmed by guilt and terror, he confesses and goes to prison. A selection of the Common Core State Standards Initiative. 448pp. 0-486-41587-2

CYRANO DE BERGERAC, Edmond Rostand. A quarrelsome, hot-tempered, and unattractive swordsman falls hopelessly in love with a beautiful woman and woos her for a handsome but slow-witted suitor. A witty and eloquent drama. 144pp. 0-486-41119-2

DANIEL BOONE'S OWN STORY & THE ADVENTURES OF DANIEL BOONE, Daniel Boone and Francis Lister Hawks. This two-part tale features reminiscences in the legendary frontiersman's own words and a profile of his entire life, with exciting accounts of blazing the Wilderness Road and serving as a militiaman during the Revolutionary War. 128pp. 0-486-47690-1

THE DECLARATION OF INDEPENDENCE AND OTHER GREAT DOCUMENTS OF AMERICAN HISTORY: 1775-1865, Edited by John Grafton. Thirteen compelling and influential documents: Henry's "Give Me Liberty or Give Me Death," Declaration of Independence, The Constitution, Washington's First Inaugural Address, The Monroe Doctrine, The Emancipation Proclamation, Gettysburg Address, more. Includes 3 selections from the Common Core State Standards Initiative. 64pp. 0-486-41124-9

A DOLL'S HOUSE, Henrik Ibsen. Ibsen's best-known play displays his genius for realistic prose drama. An expression of women's rights, the play climaxes when the central character, Nora, rejects a smothering marriage and life in "a doll's house." A selection of the Common Core State Standards Initiative. 80pp. 0-486-27062-9

DOOMED SHIPS: Great Ocean Liner Disasters, William H. Miller, Jr. Nearly 200 photographs, many from private collections, highlight tales of some of the vessels whose pleasure cruises ended in catastrophe: the *Morro Castle, Normandie, Andrea Doria, Europa,* and many others. 128pp. 0-486-45366-9

THE DORÉ BIBLE ILLUSTRATIONS, Gustave Doré. Detailed plates from the Bible: the Creation scenes, Adam and Eve, horrifying visions of the Flood, the battle sequences with their monumental crowds, depictions of the life of Jesus, 241 plates in all. 241pp. 0-486-23004-X

DUBLINERS, James Joyce. A fine and accessible introduction to the work of one of the 20th century's most influential writers, this collection features 15 tales, including a masterpiece of the short-story genre, "The Dead." 160pp. 0-486-26870-5

THE EARLY SCIENCE FICTION OF PHILIP K. DICK, Philip K. Dick. This anthology presents short stories and novellas that originally appeared in pulp magazines of the early 1950s, including "The Variable Man," "Second Variety," "Beyond the Door," "The Defenders," and more. 272pp. 0-486-49733-X

JULIUS CAESAR, William Shakespeare. Great tragedy based on Plutarch's account of the lives of Brutus, Julius Caesar, and Mark Antony. Evil plotting, ringing oratory, high tragedy with Shakespeare's incomparable insight, dramatic power. Explanatory footnotes. 96pp. 0-486-26876-4

THE JUNGLE, Upton Sinclair. 1906 bestseller shockingly reveals intolerable labor practices and working conditions in the Chicago stockyards as it tells the grim story of a Slavic family that emigrates to America full of optimism but soon faces despair. 304pp. 0-486-41923-1

JUST WHAT THE DOCTOR DISORDERED: Early Writings and Cartoons of Dr. Seuss, Dr. Seuss. Edited and with an Introduction by Rick Marschall. The Doctor's visual hilarity, nonsense language, and offbeat sense of humor illuminate this compilation of items from his early career, created for periodicals such as *Judge, Life, College Humor,* and *Liberty.* 144pp. 0-486-49846-8

KING LEAR, William Shakespeare. Powerful tragedy of an aging king, betrayed by his daughters, robbed of his kingdom, descending into madness. Perhaps the bleakest of Shakespeare's tragic dramas, complete with explanatory footnotes. 144pp. 0-486-28058-6

KNITTING FOR ANARCHISTS: The What, Why and How of Knitting, Anna Zilboorg. Every knitter takes a different approach, and this revolutionary guide encourages experimentation and self-expression. Suitable for active knitters and beginners alike, it offers illustrated patterns for sweaters, pullovers, and cardigans. 160pp. 0-486-79466-0

THE LADY OR THE TIGER?: and Other Logic Puzzles, Raymond M. Smullyan. Created by a renowned puzzle master, these whimsically themed challenges involve paradoxes about probability, time, and change; metapuzzles; and self-referentiality. Nineteen chapters advance in difficulty from relatively simple to highly complex. 1982 edition. 240pp. 0-486-47027-X

LEAVES OF GRASS: The Original 1855 Edition, Walt Whitman. Whitman's immortal collection includes some of the greatest poems of modern times, including his masterpiece, "Song of Myself." Shattering standard conventions, it stands as an unabashed celebration of body and nature. 128pp. 0-486-45676-5

LES MISÉRABLES, Victor Hugo. Translated by Charles E. Wilbour. Abridged by James K. Robinson. A convict's heroic struggle for justice and redemption plays out against a fiery backdrop of the Napoleonic wars. This edition features the excellent original translation and a sensitive abridgment. 304pp. 0-486-45789-3

LIGHT FOR THE ARTIST, Ted Seth Jacobs. Intermediate and advanced art students receive a broad vocabulary of effects with this in-depth study of light. Diagrams and paintings illustrate applications of principles to figure, still life, and landscape paintings. 144pp. 0-486-49304-0

LILITH: A Romance, George MacDonald. In this novel by the father of fantasy literature, a man travels through time to meet Adam and Eve and to explore humanity's fall from grace and ultimate redemption. 240pp. 0-486-46818-6

LINE: An Art Study, Edmund J. Sullivan. Written by a noted artist and teacher, this well-illustrated guide introduces the basics of line drawing. Topics include third and fourth dimensions, formal perspective, shade and shadow, figure drawing, and other essentials. 208pp. 0-486-79484-9

THE LODGER, Marie Belloc Lowndes. Acclaimed by *The New York Times* as "one of the best suspense novels ever written," this novel recounts an English couple's doubts about their boarder, whom they suspect of being a serial killer. 240pp. 0-486-78809-1

THE MONEY CHANGERS, Upton Sinclair. Originally published in 1908, this cautionary novel from the author of *The Jungle* explores corruption within the American system as a group of power brokers joins forces for personal gain, triggering a crash on Wall Street. 192pp. 0-486-46917-4

THE MOST POPULAR HOMES OF THE TWENTIES, William A. Radford. With a New Introduction by Daniel D. Reiff. Based on a rare 1925 catalog, this architectural showcase features floor plans, construction details, and photos of 26 homes, plus articles on entrances, porches, garages, and more. 250 illustrations, 21 color plates. 176pp. 0-486-47028-8

THE MYSTERIOUS MICKEY FINN, Elliot Paul. A multimillionaire's disappearance incites a maelstrom of kidnapping, murder, and a plot to restore the French monarchy. "One of the funniest books we've read in a long time." — *The New York Times.* 256pp. 0-486-24751-1

MYSTICISM: A Study in the Nature and Development of Spiritual Consciousness, Evelyn Underhill. Classic introduction to mysticism and mystical consciousness: awakening of the self, purification, voices and visions, ecstasy and rapture, dark night of the soul, much more. 544pp. 0-486-42238-0

NARRATIVE OF THE LIFE OF FREDERICK DOUGLASS, Frederick Douglass. The impassioned abolitionist and eloquent orator provides graphic descriptions of his childhood and horrifying experiences as a slave as well as a harrowing record of his dramatic escape to the North and eventual freedom. A selection of the Common Core State Standards Initiative. 96pp. 0-486-28499-9

NEW YORK'S FABULOUS LUXURY APARTMENTS: with Original Floor Plans from the Dakota, River House, Olympic Tower and Other Great Buildings, Andrew Alpern. Magnificently illustrated directory of 73 of Manhattan's most splendid addresses includes mini-histories of each building, noting the architect, builder, date of construction, and more. 221 photographs and drawings. 176pp. 0-486-25318-X

THE NIGHT OF THE LONG KNIVES, Fritz Leiber. Deathland's residents are consumed by the urge to murder each other, making partnership of any sort a lethal risk. Novel-length magazine story from the Cold War era by an influential science-fiction author. 112pp. 0-486-79801-1

NUTS & BOLTS: Industrial Jewelry in the Steampunk Style, Marthe Le Van. Use tubes, rods, metal sheets, and other industrial items to create chic jewelry. Detailed instructions for 24 projects feature illustrated step-by-step directions for assembling earrings, necklaces, pins, and other ornaments. 128pp. 0-486-79027-4

OBELISTS FLY HIGH, C. Daly King. Masterpiece of detective fiction portrays murder aboard a 1935 transcontinental flight. Combining an intricate plot and "locked room" scenario, the mystery was praised by *The New York Times* as "a very thrilling story." 288pp. 0-486-25036-9

THE ODYSSEY, Homer. Excellent prose translation of ancient epic recounts adventures of the homeward-bound Odysseus. Fantastic cast of gods, giants, cannibals, sirens, other supernatural creatures — true classic of Western literature. A selection of the Common Core State Standards Initiative. 256pp. 0-486-40654-7

OEDIPUS REX, Sophocles. Landmark of Western drama concerns the catastrophe that ensues when King Oedipus discovers he has inadvertently killed his father and married his mother. Masterly construction, dramatic irony. A selection of the Common Core State Standards Initiative. 64pp. 0-486-26877-2

ONE OF OURS, Willa Cather. The Pulitzer Prize–winning novel about a young Nebraskan looking for something to believe in. Alienated from his parents, rejected by his wife, he finds his destiny on the bloody battlefields of World War I. 352pp. 0-486-45599-8

VILLETTE, Charlotte Brontë. Acclaimed by Virginia Woolf as "Brontë's finest novel," this moving psychological study features a remarkably modern heroine who abandons her native England for a new life as a schoolteacher in Belgium. 480pp. 0-486-45557-2

VOYAGE OF THE BEAGLE, Charles Darwin. Classic of adventure travel and cornerstone in the development of evolutionary theory recounts Darwin's five-year sojourn in South America, where he made the observations that led to his concept of natural selection. 528pp. 0-486-42489-8

WALDEN; OR, LIFE IN THE WOODS, Henry David Thoreau. Accounts of Thoreau's daily life on the shores of Walden Pond outside Concord, Massachusetts, are interwoven with musings on the virtues of self-reliance and individual freedom, on society, government, and other topics. A selection of the Common Core State Standards Initiative. 224pp. 0-486-28495-6

WATERCOLOR, John Pike. From one of America's most popular artists comes information on everything from advice on choosing a brush to producing a variety of washes, brush strokes, and textures. 166 illustrations. 224pp. 0-486-44783-9

WHAT EINSTEIN DIDN'T KNOW: Scientific Answers to Everyday Questions, Robert L. Wolke. From simple (How do magnets work?) to complex (Where does uranium get its energy?), this volume offers intriguing insights into scientific facts. Definitive accounts of workings behind everyday phenomena include related do-it-yourself experiments. 240pp. 0-486-49289-3

WHERE NO MAN HAS GONE BEFORE: A History of NASA's Apollo Lunar Expeditions, William David Compton. Introduction by Paul Dickson. This official NASA history traces behind-the-scenes conflicts and cooperation between scientists and engineers. The first half concerns preparations for the Moon landings, and the second half documents the flights that followed *Apollo 11.* 1989 edition. 432pp. 0-486-47888-2

WORLD WAR II: THE ENCYCLOPEDIA OF THE WAR YEARS, 1941-1945, Norman Polmar and Thomas B. Allen. Authoritative and comprehensive, this reference surveys World War II from an American perspective. Over 2,400 entries cover battles, weapons, and participants as well as aspects of politics, culture, and everyday life. 85 illustrations. 960pp. 0-486-47962-5

WUTHERING HEIGHTS, Emily Brontë. Somber tale of consuming passions and vengeance — played out amid the lonely English moors — recounts the turbulent and tempestuous love story of Cathy and Heathcliff. Poignant and compelling. 256pp. 0-486-29256-8